SCHOOL
DISCIPLINE
AND SAFETY

DEBATING ISSUES
in American Education

SCHOOL DISCIPLINE
AND SAFETY

VOLUME EDITORS

SUZANNE E. ECKES
INDIANA UNIVERSITY, BLOOMINGTON

CHARLES J. RUSSO
UNIVERSITY OF DAYTON

5

VOLUME

DEBATING ISSUES
in American Education

SERIES
EDITORS

CHARLES J. RUSSO
ALLAN G. OSBORNE, JR.

⑤SAGE reference

Los Angeles | London | New Delhi
Singapore | Washington DC

Los Angeles | London | New Delhi
Singapore | Washington DC

FOR INFORMATION:

SAGE Publications, Inc.
2455 Teller Road
Thousand Oaks, California 91320
E-mail: order@sagepub.com

SAGE Publications Ltd.
1 Oliver's Yard
55 City Road
London EC1Y 1SP
United Kingdom

SAGE Publications India Pvt. Ltd.
B 1/I 1 Mohan Cooperative Industrial Area
Mathura Road, New Delhi 110 044
India

SAGE Publications Asia-Pacific Pte. Ltd.
3 Church Street
#10-04 Samsung Hub
Singapore 049483

Publisher: Rolf A. Janke
Acquisitions Editor: Jim Brace-Thompson
Assistant to the Publisher: Michele Thompson
Developmental Editors: Diana E. Axelsen, Carole Maurer
Production Editor: Tracy Buyan
Reference Systems Manager: Leticia Gutierrez
Reference Systems Coordinator: Laura Notton
Copy Editor: Sheree Van Vreede
Typesetter: C&M Digitals (P) Ltd.
Proofreader: Victoria Reed-Castro
Indexer: Mary Mortensen
Cover Designer: Janet Kiesel
Marketing Manager: Carmel Schrire

Printed in the United States of America.

Library of Congress Cataloging-in-Publication Data

School discipline and safety / volume editors, Suzanne E. Eckes, Charles J. Russo.

p. cm. – (Debating issues in American education ; v. 5)

Includes bibliographical references and index.

ISBN 978-1-4129-8756-1 (cloth : alk. paper)

1. School discipline. 2. Schools—Safety measures. I. Eckes, Suzanne. II. Russo, Charles J.

LB3012.S346 2012
371.5—dc23   2011027019

12 13 14 15 16 10 9 8 7 6 5 4 3 2 1

CONTENTS

ABOUT THE
EDITORS-IN-CHIEF

Charles J. Russo, JD, EdD, is the Joseph Panzer Chair in Education in the School of Education and Allied Professions and an adjunct professor in the School of Law at the University of Dayton. He was the 1998–1999 president of the Education Law Association and 2002 recipient of its McGhehey (Achievement) Award. He has authored or coauthored more than 200 articles in peer-reviewed journals; has authored, coauthored, edited, or coedited 40 books; and has in excess of 800 publications. Russo also speaks extensively on issues in education law in the United States and abroad.

Along with having spoken in 33 states and 25 nations on 6 continents, Russo has taught summer courses in England, Spain, and Thailand; he also has served as a visiting professor at Queensland University of Technology in Brisbane and the University of Newcastle, Australia; the University of Sarajevo, Bosnia and Herzegovina; South East European University, Macedonia; the Potchefstroom Campus of North-West University in Potchefstroom, South Africa; the University of Malaya in Kuala Lumpur, Malaysia; and the University of São Paulo, Brazil. He regularly serves as a visiting professor at the Potchefstroom Campus of North-West University.

Before joining the faculty at the University of Dayton as professor and chair of the Department of Educational Administration in July 1996, Russo taught at the University of Kentucky in Lexington from August 1992 to July 1996 and at Fordham University in his native New York City from September 1989 to July 1992. He taught high school for 8½ years before and after graduation from law school. He received a BA (classical civilization) in 1972, a JD in 1983, and an EdD (educational administration and supervision) in 1989 from St. John's University in New York City. He also received a master of divinity degree from the Seminary of the Immaculate Conception in Huntington, New York, in 1978, as well as a PhD Honoris Causa from the Potchefstroom Campus of North-West University, South Africa, in May 2004 for his contributions to the field of education law.

Russo and his wife, a preschool teacher who provides invaluable assistance proofreading and editing, travel regularly both nationally and internationally to Russo's many speaking and teaching engagements.

Allan G. Osborne, Jr. is the retired principal of the Snug Harbor Community School in Quincy, Massachusetts, a nationally recognized *Blue Ribbon School of Excellence.* During his 34 years in public education, he served as a special education teacher, director of special education, assistant principal, and principal. He also served as an adjunct professor of special education and education law at several colleges, including Bridgewater State University and American International University.

Osborne earned an EdD in educational leadership from Boston College and an MEd in special education from Fitchburg State College (now Fitchburg State University) in Massachusetts. He received a BA in psychology from the University of Massachusetts.

Osborne has authored or coauthored numerous peer-reviewed journal articles, book chapters, monographs, and textbooks on legal issues in education, along with textbooks on other aspects of education. Although he writes and presents in several areas of educational law, he specializes in legal and policy issues in special education. He is the coauthor, with Charles J. Russo, of five texts published by Corwin, a SAGE company.

A past president of the Education Law Association (ELA), Osborne has been an attendee and presenter at most ELA conferences since 1991. He has also written a chapter now titled "Students With Disabilities" for the *Yearbook of Education Law,* published by ELA, since 1990. He is on the editorial advisory committee of *West's Education Law Reporter* and is coeditor of the "Education Law Into Practice" section of that journal, which is sponsored by ELA. He is also on the editorial boards of several other education journals.

In recognition of his contributions to the field of education law, Osborne was presented with the McGhehey Award by ELA in 2008, the highest award given by the organization. He is also the recipient of the City of Quincy Human Rights Award, the Financial Executives Institute of Massachusetts Principals Award, the Junior Achievement of Massachusetts Principals Award, and several community service awards.

Osborne spends his time in retirement writing, editing, and working on his hobbies, genealogy and photography. He and his wife Debbie, a retired elementary school teacher, enjoy gardening, traveling, attending theater and musical performances, and volunteering at the Dana Farber Cancer Institute in Boston.

ABOUT THE
VOLUME EDITORS

Suzanne E. Eckes is an associate professor in the Educational Leadership and Policy Studies Department at Indiana University. She has published more than 70 articles and book chapters on school law, is an editor of the *Principal's Legal Handbook,* and is a member of the board of directors for the Education Law Association. She is the recipient of the Jack A. Culbertson Award for outstanding achievements in education from the University Council of Educational Administration. Prior to joining the faculty at Indiana University, Eckes was a high school French teacher and an attorney. She earned her master's degree in education from Harvard University and her law degree and PhD from the University of Wisconsin–Madison.

Charles J. Russo, JD, EdD, is the Joseph Panzer Chair in Education in the School of Education and Allied Professions and adjunct professor in the School of Law at the University of Dayton. He has authored or coauthored more than 200 articles in peer-reviewed journals; has authored, coauthored, edited, or coedited 40 books; and has more than 800 publications.

Before joining the faculty at the University of Dayton as professor and chair of the Department of Educational Administration in July 1996, Russo taught at the University of Kentucky in Lexington and at Fordham University in New York City. He earned a BA in classical civilization in 1972, a JD in 1983, and an EdD in educational administration and supervision in 1989, all from St. John's University in New York City. He also earned a master of divinity degree from the Seminary of the Immaculate Conception in Huntington, New York, in 1978.

ABOUT THE CONTRIBUTORS

M. David Alexander is a professor at Virginia Tech. He is the coauthor of five books, one of which, *American Public School Law*, in its eighth edition, with Kern Alexander, is widely used in graduate courses. Another book *The Law of Schools, Students and Teachers in a Nutshell* is a popular book with school practitioners. He has also written numerous research reports and articles.

Phillip Blackman received his JD from the UCLA School of Law and is a PhD candidate in Higher Education at Pennsylvania State University. His research is focused on the legal issues surrounding state funding for public institutions of higher education. Blackman is currently serving as the director of special projects at McDaniel College where he oversees focused fundraising efforts.

Susan C. Bon is an associate professor in the Education Leadership Program at George Mason University in Fairfax, Virginia. Previously, Bon worked as the ombudsman in the State Superintendent's Division of the Ohio Department of Education. She has published numerous school law articles and book chapters and is a member of the Board of Directors for the Education Law Association. Bon received her law degree and doctorate from The Ohio State University.

Mary C. Bradley is currently an assistant professor and program coordinator for the counselor education master's degree at Indiana University Southeast. She has been researching forms of school violence for nearly 10 years. She loves teaching and supervising graduate students and is grateful to those working to keep our schools safe.

Sarah B. Burke is a graduate of Indiana University, where she earned her EdS in school psychology and MS in educational psychology. She has worked as a school psychologist in Illinois and Wisconsin and is currently raising her 2-year-old son while focusing on research, writing, and editing.

Nathan Burroughs is a research associate at the Institute for Research on Mathematics and Science Education at Michigan State University, and recently of the Center for Evaluation and Education Policy at Indiana University. He received his PhD in political science from the University of Georgia.

Luke M. Cornelius is an associate professor of educational leadership at the University of North Florida. He teaches and researches in the areas of education law, school finance, educational policy and politics, and sports law.

Janet R. Decker is an assistant professor in the School of Education at the University of Cincinnati where she teaches education law courses. Her research and publications focus on legal and policy issues related to negligence, special education, charter schools, and technology.

Todd A. DeMitchell is a professor and chair of the Department of Education, and the Lamberton Professor in the Justice Studies Program at the University of New Hampshire. Most recently he was named Distinguished Professor. His research focuses on the legal mechanisms that impact schools and colleges. He has authored/coauthored five books and more than 145 publications.

Robin L. Fankhauser is an associate professor in the Educational Leadership Program and director of graduate studies at the Indiana University Southeast School of Education. Prior to teaching in the graduate program, she served as a public school educator for 28 years as an elementary teacher, elementary principal, Kentucky Distinguished Educator, budget director, and superintendent.

Allison S. Fetter-Harrott is an assistant professor of political science at Franklin College, in Franklin, Indiana. Her research interests include public school anti-harassment measures, free speech, and the interplay between public schools and the First Amendment's religion clauses.

Richard Fossey is a professor and Mike Moses Endowed Chair in Educational Leadership at the University of North Texas. He received his JD from the University of Texas School of Law and his EdD from Harvard University. He is editor of the *Journal of Cases in Education Leadership* and *Catholic Southwest.*

Aimee Vergon Gibbs is an attorney with the law firm of Dickinson Wright, PLLC, Detroit, Michigan, which has a long-standing tradition of providing superior legal services to schools, colleges, and universities throughout the Great Lakes region. Her practice focuses on school law. Gibbs has served as general counsel to both public and private educational entities and has advised clients regarding various student matters, including discipline, special education, and First Amendment issues.

Jesulon S. R. Gibbs is an assistant professor of educational leadership at the University of South Carolina in Columbia. Her research and teaching foci are public school law and educational policy analysis. She is also a contract attorney for Boykin & Davis, LLC, a school law firm. Dr. Gibbs's recent book is titled *Student Speech on the Internet: The Role of First Amendment Protections.*

Michelle Gough McKeown is the assistant director of legal affairs at the Indiana Department of Education. She is currently at the dissertation stage of her graduate coursework in education policy and leadership at Indiana University School of Education. She earned her JD from Indiana University–Bloomington Maurer School of Law in 2006 and her BA in English literature from DePauw University in 2003. She has practiced education law at the law firm of Deatherage, Myers & Lackey in Hopkinsville, Kentucky.

Stephen M. Harper received his JD from Indiana University–Bloomington Maurer School of Law. He currently is a legal fellow in the Indiana University General Counsel's Office.

Allison A. Howland is an assistant professor and program coordinator for special education at Indiana University–Purdue University Columbus and researcher at the Center for Adolescent and Family Studies at Indiana University–Bloomington. Her work focuses on how parent engagement policies support academic achievement and social-emotional competency in school-aged youth.

Ralph D. Mawdsley holds a JD from the University of Illinois and a PhD from the University of Minnesota. He has authored more than 500 publications on the subject of education law. Mawdsley was president of the Education Law Association in 2001 and was awarded that organization's Marion A. McChehey Award in 2004. He has received two Fulbright Awards, one to South Africa and one to Australia.

Stephanie D. McCall is a doctoral candidate in the Department of Curriculum and Teaching at Teachers College, Columbia University. Her research interests include curriculum theory, gender issues in education, single-gender education policies and practices, and qualitative research.

Peter L. Moran is a doctoral candidate in the Higher Education program at Pennsylvania State University. He earned a JD from Brooklyn Law School, and he researches the history of legal education and legal issues in higher education. Moran currently serves as an administrative fellow at Pennsylvania State University, Altoona College.

Theresa A. Ochoa is an associate professor at Indiana University. Her areas of research and interests include emotional and behavioral disorders, special education law, and teacher preparation.

Emily Richardson is a PhD candidate in education policy at Indiana University–Bloomington School of Education. She received her JD from Indiana University–Bloomington Maurer School of Law.

Diana Rogers-Adkinson is currently a professor and chair of the Department of Special Education at the University of Wisconsin–Whitewater.

Erin B. Snell is an experienced educator and provider of teacher professional development. She began her career as a teacher with Teach For America (TFA), has worked in various capacities for TFA, and recently returned to the classroom as a 5th grade teacher. Snell earned her PhD in educational leadership and policy studies from Indiana University

Amy Steketee is an attorney at Baker & Daniels in South Bend, Indiana where she practices school law as well as labor and employment law. Steketee has authored or coauthored numerous articles on school law topics. Prior to working as an attorney, Steketee was a high school teacher and guidance counselor. She earned her master's in education and her law degree from Indiana University.

Jennifer Sughrue earned her PhD in educational leadership and policy studies at Virginia Tech in 1997. Prior to that, Sughrue was in K–12 international education for nearly 20 years. She began her higher education career as an assistant professor of educational leadership and policy studies at Virginia Tech; then she joined the faculty in the Department of Educational Leadership at Florida Atlantic University in 2004 and became an associate professor. She is now an associate professor at Old Dominion University.

Dana N. Thompson Dorsey is an assistant professor in the Department of Educational Leadership and Policy at the University of North Carolina at Chapel Hill. Thompson Dorsey's research focuses on legal issues in education and policy as they relate to educational equity, race, poverty, and critical race theory in education.

Potheini Vaiouli is a PhD student in special education at Indiana University–Bloomington. She is a graduate of New York University with a master's in Music Therapy. As a music therapist in special education units, Vaiouli has developed a strong focus on the use of music and its role for the social, emotional, and/or educational growth of students with special needs.

Charles B. Vergon, an attorney, holds faculty appointments in educational leadership and public administration at Youngstown State University and the University of Michigan–Flint, respectively. He has worked extensively on issues of fair and effective discipline, carrying out federal court-mandated studies and providing technical assistance on behalf of the U.S. Department of Education to school districts and state education agencies.

Spencer C. Weiler is an assistant professor in educational leadership and policy studies at the University of Northern Colorado. His research focuses on equal access to knowledge for all children. Specifically, Weiler explores access issues from a school law, school finance, and leadership perspective.

INTRODUCTION

S tudent discipline and safety is one of the most complex issues confronting educators on a daily basis. With the creation of public schools in mid-19th-century America, there came a need for discipline policies designed to maintain control of schools while keeping students safe. From the outset, there was little debate about whether teachers had the right and responsibility to address discipline and school safety. Yet, disagreements remain regarding how best to address the need to ensure the safety of students and staff.

It is difficult to generalize about what occurs in public schools throughout the United States because individual state legislatures provide guidelines for student punishment. Typically, state statutes permit school officials to exclude students from instruction if their conduct disrupts school operations. However, because the power to suspend or expel students from school is statutory, the use of disciplinary punishments varies between jurisdictions. Also, although each state is free to set its own disciplinary statutes and regulations, some jurisdictions have created statutory obligations for state and local school boards to create student codes of conduct. Accordingly, local school boards have the discretion to institute more detailed discipline policies than those described by state law. When establishing discipline codes, educational officials should ensure that students and their parents clearly understand the rules for school behavior.

When dealing with school discipline, the United States has adopted the doctrine of in loco parentis (literally, "in the place of the parent") from English common law. Although it is still a matter of common law rather than statute in most states, in loco parentis affords nonparental caregivers of children, including teachers and school officials, specified rights and responsibilities. To this end, in loco parentis is often cited as the basis for school officials' authority to discipline students. Policies enacted pursuant to in loco parentis permit educators to exercise their custodial powers in a reasonable manner by intervening when students create dangerous situations that put themselves or others at risk of injury. At the same time, as highlighted in one of the debates in this volume, some contend that in loco parentis has gone too far and that school officials are playing too big a role in disciplining students. Some teachers voice concern about the role they must play in disciplining students for misbehavior. There are other concerns related to disciplinary issues undermining classroom learning and bringing down teacher morale. One study reports that many teachers consider quitting as a result of student discipline issues (see Billitteri, 2008).

Despite ongoing debate about the appropriate limits of school discipline, educational laws and policies permit teachers to exercise reasonable custodial powers by intervening to discipline students who violate school rules. In exercising these powers, teachers have relied on a variety of disciplinary measures. In early years, corporal punishment was the most prevalent form of intervention. In its only case to address the merits of this issue, the U.S. Supreme Court decided that corporal punishment in public schools is not considered to be cruel and unusual punishment in violation of the Eighth Amendment (*Ingraham v. Wright,* 1977). However, during the 1960s and 1970s, protections for students also broadened (see Billitteri, 2008). In the 1960s, the Supreme Court expanded students' speech rights (see *Tinker v. Des Moines Independent Community School District,* 1969) and afforded them additional due process rights when facing discipline in schools (see *Goss v. Lopez,* 1975).

The Supreme Court's ruling in *Ingraham* notwithstanding, approximately 30 states now ban corporal punishment. Of the states allowing corporal punishment, all but 6 leave the decision whether it can be imposed to the discretion of local school boards. This volume includes a debate over whether corporal punishment should be abolished in public schools.

As the United States began to see an increase in school violence in the 1980s, zero tolerance policies became more widely used in an attempt to protect students while ensuring that they obey reasonable school rules. The use of suspensions and expulsions has also increased as a means for disciplining students. When school board officials suspend or expel students, they must ensure that students' due process rights are protected. Generally, if discipline procedures applied by school officials satisfy the due process requirements of the Fourteenth Amendment, the courts uphold their actions as long as they are reasonable. Substantive due process prohibits state actions infringing on the fundamental liberties of individuals, while procedural due process usually requires officials to provide students with notice and hearing procedures before they can be deprived of rights such as liberty or property. In the context of school discipline, punishment does not conflict with substantive due process unless an action is "arbitrary, capricious, or wholly unrelated to the legitimate state goal of maintaining an atmosphere conducive to learning" (*Jefferson v. Yselta Independent School District,* 1987, pp. 305–306).

The courts have considered education to be a property right, thus triggering due process rights if public school officials attempt to deprive students of their education. In *Goss,* when nine public high school students were suspended for 10 days without a hearing, the Supreme Court reasoned that "a student's legitimate entitlement to a public education [is] a property interest which is protected by the Due Process Clause and may not be taken away ... without adherence to the minimum procedure required by the Clause" (*Goss v. Lopez,* 1975, p. 574).

Goss, then, set the standard for requiring minimal constitutional requirements when students are faced with short-term suspensions of 10 days or less. The Supreme Court held that when students face such short-term suspensions, officials must provide them with oral or written notice of the charges against them. If accused students deny the charges, officials must explain the evidence against them while affording them an opportunity to present their side of the story in an informal setting. Some courts have interpreted this to mean that school officials may informally discuss the alleged misconduct with students. As a result of *Goss,* when students are facing expulsion or suspension, they are entitled to some form of procedural due process. The due process requirements differ according to the length of the exclusion from school.

Unfortunately, *Goss* did not provide specific guidance for longer suspensions or expulsions. Instead, the Supreme Court ambiguously pointed out that more formal procedures are necessary when students are removed for longer periods of time. As a result, some school officials look to *Dixon v. Alabama State Board of Education* (1961), a case from the Fifth Circuit (now Eleventh Circuit as a result of a shift in the federal court system), for guidance regarding expulsion. In *Dixon,* students attending a state college were expelled without notice of the charges they faced and without a hearing after they participated in a lunch counter sit-in. The court found that students involved in expulsion hearings should be given the names of the witnesses against them and an oral or written report on the acts to which each witness testifies. Students should also be given the opportunity to present their own defense against the charges and to produce either oral testimony or written affidavits of witnesses (Skiba, Eckes, & Brown, 2009/2010).

In response to *Goss* and *Dixon,* the details of the required disciplinary procedures for students vary from one state to the next. The reason for this differentiation is that state legislators and school boards used different laws and regulations to define the procedures for due process. At the same time, procedural requirements may vary depending on the circumstances of a given situation. Once students are expelled, school boards generally are not required to provide education services to general education students unless such local board policy and/or state law require them to do so. However, students with disabilities who face disciplinary sanctions and/or expulsions have significantly greater rights to procedural due and cannot have their right to an education discontinued totally (Osborne & Russo, 2009).

In response to the perception that violence in schools has increased, zero tolerance policies mandating harsher consequences for both major and minor violations began to be implemented widely in schools and districts. Zero tolerance policies in schools are generally understood as being applicable to prescribed, mandatory sanctions, typically expulsions or suspensions for infractions, with little or no consideration of the circumstances or consequences of the offenses.

Congress has recognized the increase in school violence and as a result passed the Gun-Free Schools Act of 1990, which was subsequently rewritten after the Supreme Court invalidated it (Russo, 1995); it is now known as the Gun-Free Schools Act of 1995. The act requires each state receiving federal funds to expel, for at least one year, any student who possesses a firearm on school grounds. Pursuant to this act, there is an allowance for school officials to adjust punishments at their discretion on case-by-case bases. Special education students who are expelled for gun possession may be placed in alternative instructional programs (Skiba et al., 2009/2010).

The Gun-Free Schools Act of 1995 specifies that all states must enact legislation requiring at least a 1-year expulsion, and states are permitted to expand the scope of the law to include other weapons. Although the American Federation of Teachers supported this measure, opposing groups challenged the law as unconstitutional. For example, the Sixth Circuit struck down a zero tolerance policy, reasoning that it would have violated a student's right to substantive due process if he had been suspended or expelled for unknowingly possessing a weapon because a friend left one in the glove compartment of his vehicle (*Seal v. Morgan*, 2000).

As a result of the Gun-Free Schools Act of 1995, states have attempted to implement similar legislation. For example, shortly after the passage of the Gun-Free Schools Act, every state and the District of Columbia enacted some form of zero tolerance policy. Interestingly, some school officials expanded the scope of legitimate expulsions under the act even further to include other types of behaviors such as fighting and drug possession. As a result, zero tolerance policies have been under attack by the American Bar Association, which recently approved a resolution opposing zero tolerance policies in schools (Skiba et al., 2009/2010).

One criticism of zero tolerance policies is that they disproportionately impact students of color. Yet, others argue that zero tolerance actually reduces discrimination because there is less of a chance for favoritism (see Billitteri, 2008). For example, the superintendent's child will be treated in the same manner as any other student who violates such a policy. Nevertheless, opponents of zero tolerance policies argue that they do not effectively balance safety concerns with educational opportunities for all students. To this end, the Justice Policy Institute and the Children's Law Center contend that zero tolerance policies are creating pipelines into the juvenile justice system (Heard, 1997). Others contend that suspension and expulsion rates have unnecessarily increased for minor infractions (Billitteri, 2008). This book explores some of the controversies associated with zero tolerance policies. One chapter debates whether zero tolerance policies are acceptable with respect to drugs, alcohol, and weapons, while another focuses on the controversy surrounding the over-representation of minority students in school disciplinary matters.

In addition to these areas, this book examines controversial topics relating to a variety of other school disciplinary and safety concerns through a point/counterpoint essay format. In so doing, this book discusses topics, including child abuse, suicide prevention, bullying, and classroom management. The remainder of this introductory essay highlights key controversies that are discussed in the following chapters.

DISCIPLINE AND SAFETY ISSUES WITH RESPECT TO SPECIAL POPULATIONS

This book includes chapters on discipline and safety issues related to students from special populations: students struggling with maladaptive behavior, students struggling with emotional behavioral disorders, and students with disabilities who are secluded and restrained. As to maladaptive behavior, there is debate within the education community over the role of teachers in the identification, diagnosis, and treatment of students with internalizing disorders. Internalizing disorders, such as depression and anxiety, often go undetected in the school-age population because the symptoms can be masked with more observable acting-out behaviors. Sometimes, symptoms are overlooked because students simply come off as quiet or reserved. This is a problem that is not likely to go away, though. A staggering number of students, with one study citing as many as 20% to 25%, will struggle with depression before their 18th birthday (Lewinsohn, Hops, Roberts, Seeley, & Andrews, 1993). Therefore, it is not surprising that schools have been identified as a logical place for screening and treatment to occur (Shirk & Jungbluth, 2008). Tensions within this debate revolve around whether teachers specifically would be involved in such efforts and, if so, what their role would look like. The authors of the point and counterpoint essays examine two different sides of the debate concerning the classroom teacher's role in identifying and working with students with internalizing disorders or maladaptive behaviors.

Turning to safety concerns for students with emotional and behavioral disorders (EBDs), experts agree that the best intervention is prevention. Research shows that the earliest possible interventions are needed to halt the destructive progression of such disorders that can occur throughout a child's elementary and secondary school years (Webster-Stratton & Reid, 2004). The positive behavior intervention supports (PBIS) model uses a three-tiered approach to prevention that initially focuses on all students in the school and becomes more selective and intensive as additional services are needed. A number of the early studies conducted on the effectiveness of PBIS strategies provided convincing endorsements of the support system, and the approach was largely adopted in the 1997 reauthorization of the Individuals with Disabilities Education Act (Crimmins & Farrell, 2006). However, this chapter notes the importance of exploring some of the limitations and criticisms of PBIS. These include issues related to treatment fidelity, reliability of office discipline referrals as a measure of school improvement, cost factors, and methodological limitations of the research regarding PBIS.

TEACHER RESPONSIBILITY FOR STUDENT SUICIDE

This book also discusses the growing concern that educators face in their duty to prevent student suicide. Specifically, when addressing the issue of adolescent suicide, experts grapple with the question of whose responsibility it is to stop suicides before they happen. Among those best positioned to assist are parents, friends, primary care physicians, mental health professionals, and teachers. Many argue that because teachers have daily contact with children and often know students well, they may be able to identify the need for intervention before others recognize it. According to proponents of this position, teachers, through their normal daily routines, can easily observe and report students who are contemplating suicide. These individuals add that teachers also have quick access to counselors or psychologists within their schools who can provide all but immediate assistance to needy students.

Engaging teachers as the gatekeepers of adolescent suicide is complicated, though. On the other hand, the point essay maintains that since teachers are already charged with various tasks from teaching content to managing overcrowded classrooms, they cannot carry the heavy burden of preventing all student tragedies associated with suicides. In fact, courts have not found school personnel liable for student suicides as long as they behaved in a reasonable manner.

THE ROLE OF SCHOOL RESOURCE OFFICERS

In the years since the tragic shootings in Columbine, Colorado, law enforcement personnel have become an increasingly more common sight in schools around the country. These law enforcement agents or school resource officers (SROs) are on contract from local departments of law enforcement to help ensure that schools are safe. Although typically funded through state or federal funding, SROs have unique legal and social positions in schools and districts that generate controversies among civil liberties organizations, school boards, administrators, parents, and even students. Specifically, there has been debate regarding the role that SROs should play in public schools. In this book, one chapter debates whether SROs should function strictly as police officers or whether they should be considered more holistically and be integrated into schools in a manner similar to other educational professionals such as counselors, teachers, and resource officers. Both sides offer differing arguments that are sure to serve as food for thought regardless of where one is on this timely issue that has a great impact on student safety.

HARASSMENT AND BULLYING

According to several sources, more than 75% of students have experienced bullying in schools. Such statistics are troublesome considering that peer harassment and bullying can have long-term psychological effects on student victims. Although bullying affects all students, research further confirms that bullies often target those with disabilities and those who are gay, lesbian, bisexual, or transgendered. Sadly, recent student suicides that have been related to bullying in schools have been widespread in the media. As a result, debates surrounding the role that educators should play in addressing bullying in schools abound as an array of organizations have dedicated themselves to examining how to address the dangers of bullying. Among the key organizations here are Stop Bullying Now, the Safe Schools Coalition, and the International Bullying Prevention Association.

Without a doubt, school officials play a role in providing a safe educational environment that is free of peer harassment and bullying. In fact, school boards and educational officials have faced an onslaught of litigation filed on behalf of students who have been bullied or harassed, particularly by peers, in the classroom. The point and counterpoint essays in this chapter debate whether such laws ask too much of classroom teachers and take opposite positions on the issue. The author of the point essay is satisfied that existing laws have done enough to balance the rights of students while not rendering school boards and educators liable too easily for harassment or bullying. Conversely, the counterpoint essay argues that educators and the law need to do more to keep students safe from harassment and bullying at the hands of peers.

CLASSROOM MANAGEMENT

Teachers take on a number of different roles and responsibilities throughout typical school days. Still, perhaps the most important and likely the most demanding task that teachers face is trying to maintain safe, well-managed classrooms. Since it is extremely difficult for teachers to instruct and for students to learn in chaotic and disorderly classrooms, it is hard to overstate the importance of the ability of teachers to create a collaborative learning environment with a strong sense of structure. In fact, a number of researchers have concluded that the effectiveness of classroom teachers is the most important factor within the control of educational officials that impacts student academic achievement (Marzano, Marzano, & Pickering, 2003).

Good classroom management is multilayered. Skilled teachers will carefully consider a variety of elements in setting up and carrying out classroom operations. Early on, teachers often work to state positively the expectations of the collaborative learning environment while explicitly teaching the procedures to be used in their classrooms. The physical space of classrooms can also be arranged in such a way that helps maximize the ability of teachers to supervise students actively while moving throughout their rooms. Although these general practices help students to take comfort in the predictability of classroom operations, teachers also face the daily challenge of finding new ways to engage students with creative lesson planning. After all, students who are engaged in positive learning activities are far less likely to create disciplinary problems. Finally, when discipline problems do arise, skilled teachers are likely to be firm yet positive in redirecting negative student behavior and using a hierarchy of preplanned intervention strategies (Crimmins, Farrell, Smith, & Bailey, 2007). Although the authors of the point and counterpoint essays agree about the importance of strong classroom management, they differ on the place of extrinsic and intrinsic rewards within the context of classroom management.

TEACHER LIABILITY PROTECTION ACTS

Teachers have a duty to supervise their students, and when they breach that duty, they may be held liable. When considering whether teachers can or should be liable for injuries that occur to the students in their care, courts often consider whether educators behaved as a reasonably prudent teacher would have in that situation and whether the injury was foreseeable. Generally, if educators behaved as a reasonably prudent teacher would have in that situation or the injury was not foreseeable, courts refuse to impose liability on them for the actions or omissions. Despite this fact, teachers continue to worry about facing suits when they use reasonable force in disciplining students.

The No Child Left Behind Act includes a section called the "Paul D. Coverdell Teacher Protection Act of 2001" (TPA). The intention behind this part of the act is to protect teachers or other school officials in the event that they injure a student while attempting to impose discipline. To be precise, the law maintains that school officials are immune to suits if students are injured while employees are attempting to "control, discipline, expel, or suspend a student or maintain order or control in the classroom or school." After the federal TPA was enacted, individual states adopted similar laws to protect teachers from liability when they may have injured students during disciplinary matters. Generally, these state laws grant immunity to public school teachers and administrators who injure students when imposing disciplinary sanctions as long as they act in good faith with no intent to harm children.

The No Child Left Behind Act of 2002 adopted portions of the Coverdell Act. Although the goal of the Coverdell Act is to help reduce the number of suits against teachers, the National Education Association (NEA) and other teacher unions have criticized the plan. Specifically, the NEA has complained that the Coverdell Act is not a comprehensive plan to protect teachers from all legal liability. The point essay supports the proposition that educators and school boards benefit from state and federal teacher protection laws. Conversely, the counterpoint essay responds that insofar as teacher protection statutes are constructed so narrowly that they are unnecessary.

DRESS CODE POLICIES

School officials can require students to wear goggles in chemistry class or uniforms in physical education courses, if such requirements are related to health and safety concerns. For the same reason, most public schools may also regulate how the students dress. Of course, students have the right to express themselves with their dress, but these rights are balanced with concerns about school safety. As a way to encourage student safety, some school boards have crafted policies requiring uniforms, while others have chosen to prohibit specified items of apparel often associated with what is referred to as "gang clothing." For example, school boards in districts that have had issues with gang activity, a major issue of school safety, may choose to regulate specified colors or to ban baggy pants or bandanas, or they may choose to implement uniform policies. Even so, it is without question that school policies regulating student dress have remained controversial.

This chapter examines the tensions surrounding student dress code policies. In the point essay, the author argues that school boards can and should adopt dress code policies that focus on student safety. The point essay contends that educational officials have wide latitude in adopting dress code policies as long as such policies do not infringe on students' First Amendment rights. In the counterpoint essay, the author explains how officials can sometimes be overzealous in adopting dress code policies. Although the counterpoint essay agrees that dress code policies are often necessary, this essay argues that educators should focus their time and energy on immediate responses to violence instead of fixating on the particular clothing a student wears to school.

CHILD ABUSE AND NEGLECT

Teachers will likely confront situations where they suspect that one of their students has been abused or neglected. In these situations, teachers are required to report suspected abuse and neglect to the appropriate authority. In addition to their legal obligations, teachers are expected to react sensitively and appropriately when students disclose that they have been victims of abuse. Knowing the signs of abuse and neglect, understanding one's responsibilities, and learning appropriate ways of responding to children who disclose abuse are an important part of teacher preparation programs. As the point essay notes, reporting child abuse and neglect is an ethical and legal obligation for teachers and school personnel. Yet, the counterpoint essay argues that mandating reporting of any and all suspicion of child abuse and neglect does raise concerns because it may require educators to intrude too far into the lives of families, thereby creating even more problems. The counterpoint essay concludes that insofar as it is not clear whether teachers really understand what is involved in reporting child abuse and neglect, perhaps it is best that they not be required to report all suspected incidents.

SUMMARY

The goal of this volume is to frame some of the larger debates with regard to safety and discipline issues that educators face on a daily basis. Thus, the point/counterpoint essay format should hopefully provide readers with different perspectives on the variety of school safety and disciplinary issues that it addresses.

Suzanne E. Eckes
Indiana University

Charles J. Russo
University of Dayton

FURTHER READINGS AND RESOURCES

Billitteri, T. (2008). Discipline in schools. *CQ Researcher, 18*(7), 145–168.

Crimmins, D., & Farrell, A. F. (2006). Individualized behavioral supports at 15 years: It's still lonely at the top. *Research & Practice for Persons with Severe Disabilities, 31*(1), 31–45.

Crimmins, D., Farrell, A., Smith, P., & Bailey, A. (2007). *Positive strategies for students with behavior problems.* Baltimore: Paul H. Brookes.

Heard, J. (1997, March 11). Off-campus crime spells expulsion from school. *Chicago Tribune,* p. 1.

Lewinsohn, P. M., Hops, H., Roberts, R. E., Seeley, J. R., & Andrews, J. (1993). Adolescent psychopathology: Prevalence and incidence of depression and other *DSM-III-R* disorders in high school students. *Journal of Abnormal Psychology, 102,* 133–144.

Marzano, R. J., Marzano, J. S., & Pickering, D. J. (2003). *Classroom management that works: Research-based strategies for every teacher.* Alexandria, VA: Association for Supervision and Curriculum Development.

The National Education Association. Teacher Protection Act. Retrieved from http://www.nea-nm.org/ESEA/TPA.htm

Osborne, A. G., & Russo, C. J. (2009). *Discipline of students with disabilities: Legal issues.* Thousand Oaks, CA: Corwin.

Russo, C. J. (1995). *United States v. Lopez* and the demise of the Gun-Free School Zones Act: Legislative over-reaching or judicial nit-picking? *Education Law Reporter, 99*(1), 11–23.

Shirk, S. R., & Jungbluth, N. J. (2008). School-based mental health checkups: Ready for practical action? *Clinical Psychology: Science & Practice, 15*(3), 217–223.

Skiba, R., Eckes, S., & Brown, K. (2009/2010). African American disproportionality in school discipline. *New York Law School Law Review, 54,* 1071–1112.

Webster-Stratton, C., & Reid, J. M. (2004). Strengthening social and emotional competence in young children—The foundation for early school readiness and success: Incredible Years classroom social skills and problem-solving curriculum. *Infants and Young Children, 17,* 96–113.

COURT CASES AND STATUTES

Dixon v. Alabama State Board of Education, 294 F.2d 150 (5th Cir. 1961).

Goss v. Lopez, 419 U.S. 565 (1975).

Gun-Free Schools Act, 20 U.S.C. Sec 8921 (2000) (repealed 2002).

Individuals with Disabilities Education Act (IDEA), 20 U.S.C. §§ 1400 *et seq.*

Ingraham v. Wright 430 U.S. 651 (1977).

Jefferson v. Ysleta Independent School District, 817 F.2d 303 (5th Cir. 1987).

No Child Left Behind Act, 20 U.S.C. §§ 6301–7941 (2006).

Paul D. Coverdell Teacher Protection Act of 2001, 20 U.S.C. §§ 6731 *et seq.* (2010).

Seal v. Morgan, 229 F.3d 567 (6th Cir. 2000).

Tinker v. Des Moines Independent Community School District, 393 U.S. 503 (1969).

Should all public schools adopt dress code policies that focus on student safety?

POINT: Richard Fossey, *University of North Texas*

COUNTERPOINT: Todd A. DeMitchell, *University of New Hampshire*

OVERVIEW

School officials can require students to wear goggles in chemistry class or uniforms in physical education courses, if they are related to health and safety concerns. Most public schools may also regulate how students dress for the same reason. Of course, students have the right to express themselves with their dress, but these rights are balanced with concerns about student safety. To encourage student safety, some school boards may dictate uniforms, while others may choose to prohibit particular items of apparel. For example, school boards that have had issues with gang activity (a matter of school safety) may choose to regulate specified colors or to ban baggy pants or bandanas, or they may choose to implement a school uniform policy. However, it is without question that school policies regulating student dress have remained controversial.

The first use of a mandatory uniform or dress code policy in a public school district is attributed to the Long Beach Unified School District in California, which introduced its policy in 1994. In an effort to curb gang-related problems, the board required all elementary and middle school students to wear uniforms. Initial reports from principals in the district demonstrated astounding drops in violence that were attributed solely to the newly instituted dress code. An empirical study found, however, that the uniforms were not causally responsible for the dramatic improvements in behavior in Long Beach (Brunsma & Rockquemore, 1998). As a result of conflicting opinions, the debate about school uniforms has raged on—with additional empirical studies showing no positive effects of uniforms on behavior or academics, while principals and parents share anecdotal evidence that they have seen dramatic improvements in school safety. David Brunsma and Kerry Rockquemore (1998) suggested that the implementation of a dress code is purely an external change, and although it may affect the environment of the school, it has no real impact on the behavior of students:

> Instituting a mandatory uniform policy is a change that is immediate, highly visible, and shifts the environmental landscape of any particular school. Changing the landscape is a superficial change, but it attracts attention because of its visible nature. Instituting a uniform policy can be viewed as analogous to cleaning and brightly painting a deteriorating building in that on the one hand it grabs our immediate attention; on the other hand, it is only a coat of paint. (p. 60)

Supporters of school dress code and uniform policies contend that they positively impact attendance, academics, behavior, and school environment. They also argue that students from low-income families benefit from school uniform policies because these students do not stand out because they cannot afford the latest clothing trends. Another claim is that such policies prevent students from particular social groups or gangs from wearing identifiable clothing that set them apart from their peers in any distracting or negative way. Nearly 70% of the 5,500 secondary school principals surveyed at the 1996 National Association of Secondary School Principals conference believed that "requiring students to wear uniforms to school would reduce violent incidents and discipline problems" (Brown, 1998, p. 2). This conference came closely on the heels of both President Bill Clinton's endorsement of uniforms in his 1996 State of the Union Address and a memorandum on the subject that he issued to his Secretary of Education.

Despite the lack of evidence supporting a causal link between dress codes and improved safety, there is strong evidence that associates uniform policies with improved school climate (Murray, 1997). Richard Murray found that the students in his study reported "positive teacher-student relationships, a stronger sense of security, an improved parent and community-school relationship, effective instructional management, an improved outlook on student behavioral values, and a more positive reaction to guidance from teachers and counselors"

(p. 110). In turn, it seems easy to assume that these improved perceptions of climate by the students would result in similarly improved safety.

Whether relying on anecdotal or empirical evidence, uniform and dress code policies seem to have a broad range of support from parents, principals, and even those in the political sector. Although a dress code can be viewed as a "quick fix" that is not a panacea for all manner of school violence problems, it does seem to have some impact on the school climate and potentially on the safety of the students in the school as well. According to supporters, well-crafted dress code policies treat the students fairly and respect their right to express themselves while still instilling order in the school environment (Essex, 2001).

This chapter examines the tensions surrounding student dress code policies. In his point essay, Richard Fossey (University of North Texas) argues that school districts can and should adopt dress code policies that focus on student safety. He contends that school officials have wide latitude in adopting dress code policies as long as such policies do not infringe upon students' First Amendment rights. In the counterpoint essay, Todd A. DeMitchell (University of New Hampshire) explains how sometimes school officials can be overzealous in adopting dress code policies. Although DeMitchell believes that dress code policies are often necessary, school officials should focus their time and energy on immediate responses to violence instead of fixating on the particular clothing a student wears to school.

Suzanne E. Eckes
Indiana University

POINT: Richard Fossey
University of North Texas

This essay argues that public school boards and officials may adopt dress code policies requiring students to adhere to school-mandated standards of dress as a means of promoting safety and order without violating students' First Amendment rights. Although scholarly research about the impact of student dress codes on safety does not consistently support the view that dress codes have a positive impact on safety (DeMitchell & Paige, 2010), many educators believe student dress codes are beneficial. Also, some studies have demonstrated the positive impact that dress codes may have on school climate (Murray, 1997).

As we will discuss, an important opinion from the Fifth Circuit upheld a school board's student dress code without requiring officials to support their stance with statistical evidence. Rather, the Fifth Circuit reasoned that school officials, not courts, are in the best position to judge the value of student dress codes and that some of the benefits of such codes are not measurable through quantitative means (*Palmer v. Waxahachie Independent School District*, 2009). In light of this case, the point essay argues why school officials should be given more leeway; then the counterpoint essay recommends monitoring student dress in order to promote safe school environments.

SCHOOL DRESS CODES AND THE FIRST AMENDMENT

In *Tinker v. Des Moines Independent Community School District* (1969), the U.S. Supreme Court held that students in the public schools have a constitutional right of free expression that they do not give up when they enter the school environment. That famous case involved students who protested the Vietnam War by wearing black armbands while at school. School authorities suspended the students for wearing the armbands, and the students sued, arguing that the board's ban on their black armbands violated their constitutional right to free speech under the First Amendment.

In a landmark decision, the Supreme Court ruled that school officials could not ban controversial student speech simply because it might make some people uncomfortable. Unless student speech threatened to create a substantial disruption in the school environment or interfered with the rights of other students, the Court found that students have a constitutional right of expression under the First Amendment that school authorities cannot suppress.

Tinker involved the right of students to express themselves on an important social and political issue of the day—the war in Vietnam. The Supreme Court's ringing endorsement of the constitutional right of expression of students in public schools is recognized today as one of its most important constitutional pronouncements. Indeed, in the more than 40 years that have passed since *Tinker*, students have invoked it in hundreds of cases to support their claim that school officials suppressed their constitutional right of expression. A small number of these cases have involved disputes between school officials seeking to implement dress codes to promote school safety and students who challenged these codes on First Amendment grounds.

In a case out of New Mexico, for example, educational officials from a local high school imposed a rule against students wearing sagging pants to school based on their concern that sagging pants were associated with gang activities. A student challenged the rule, claiming a constitutional right to wear sagging pants, which, he contended, expressed his identification with "hip hop" style (*Bivens v. Albuquerque Public Schools,* 1995). A federal trial court rejected the student's arguments and upheld the school board's dress code, noting that students' free speech rights had to be balanced against "the need to foster an educational atmosphere free from undue disruptions to appropriate discipline" (p. 559). In addition, the court was unconvinced that the wearing of sagging pants constituted a form of speech that was protected by the First Amendment.

In *Jeglin v. San Jacinto Unified School District* (1993), the court considered a California school board's adoption of a dress code that required student clothing for all elementary, middle, and high school students to "be free of writing, pictures or any other insignia which identifies any professional sports team, college, or group advocating or participating in disruptive behavior" (p. 1463). One student was specifically told not to wear T-shirts advertising sports teams from Los Angeles. The board justified the dress code on the grounds that student clothing advertising professional sports teams was associated with gang affiliations.

A group of students sued the school board, arguing that its dress code violated their constitutional rights under the First Amendment. A federal trial court, after reviewing the evidence, determined that the board had not shown a gang presence in the elementary schools and that the evidence of gang activity in the middle schools was negligible. Therefore, the court struck down the dress code in the elementary and middle schools but allowed it to be enforced in the high schools where student gangs were actually operating. This case suggests that although school officials have leeway in adopting dress code policies, they must be sure to consider the First Amendment when adopting these policies.

Some school boards and officials have enacted grooming codes prohibiting male students from wearing long hair as a means of promoting safety and order. Not surprisingly, these codes have been also attacked on constitutional grounds. The courts have ruled inconsistently in these cases, sometimes finding that students have a constitutionally protected interest in choosing their hair length and sometimes siding with school authorities.

In a 1972 decision, Chesley Karr, a high school student in Texas, filed suit in federal court, arguing that his school board's grooming policy violated the First Amendment. The Fifth Circuit upheld the grooming policy, which the board adopted as a means of achieving "the elimination of classroom distraction, the avoidance of violence between long and short haired students, the elimination of potential health hazards, and the elimination of safety hazards resulting from long hair in the science labs" (*Karr v. Schmidt,* 1972, p. 617). Rejecting Karr's claim, the Fifth Circuit ruled that high school students have no constitutional right to challenge school grooming codes. In the court's view, there were "strong policy considerations in favor of giving local school boards the widest possible latitude in the management of school affairs" (p. 615). The court added that the board's justifications for its grooming rules were rational and did not violate the student's constitutional rights.

Finally, *Tinker* has been invoked again and again by students who have claimed a First Amendment right to proclaim messages on their clothing—usually their T-shirts. The courts have not ruled consistently in these cases, sometimes deciding that T-shirt messages are constitutionally protected and sometimes granting school officials the authority to ban specific messages.

In the key case of *Palmer v. Waxahachie Independent School District* (2009), however, the Fifth Circuit upheld the student dress policy of a board in Texas banning all messages on student clothing, finding that the policy furthered the board's important governmental interest in promoting school safety. *Palmer,* which is discussed below, sets forth a sensible approach for resolving constitutional challenges to student dress codes in public schools. If the Fifth Circuit's approach is adopted by other federal courts, much of the constitutional litigation brought by students and their parents challenging school dress codes is likely to come to an end.

PALMER V. WAXAHACHIE INDEPENDENT SCHOOL DISTRICT: A SENSIBLE APPROACH TO SCHOOL DRESS CODES

Paul Palmer, a high school student at Waxahachie High School in Texas, first ran into trouble with school authorities over the board's dress code in

September 2007 when he wore a shirt to school that simply said, "San Diego." Mr. Johnson, the school's vice principal, told Palmer that his shirt violated the dress code, which did not allow printed messages on T-shirts. Palmer called his parents, who brought him a replacement shirt to wear that proclaimed the message "John Edwards for President." Vice Principal Johnson told Palmer that the replacement shirt was also unacceptable because it too contained a message. Palmer appealed Johnson's decision to the principal and the superintendent, both of whom agreed with the vice principal.

Palmer sued the school board, arguing that its dress code violated his right to freedom of speech under the First Amendment. After he filed suit, the board adopted an amended dress code, which was stricter than the one Palmer had originally challenged. The revised policy prohibited T-shirts and polo shirts with messages, shirts with sports team logos, and clothing with university messages. The amended code permitted messages on students' clothing pertaining to school-sponsored curricular clubs and organizations, athletic teams, and "spirit" collared shirts or T-shirts, so long as these messages were approved by the campus principal. The amended policy also permitted logos smaller than two inches by two inches.

Waxahachie school officials explained to the court that the school board had adopted a stricter dress code because teachers were spending too much time enforcing the old code and the board believed the amended code would be easier to enforce. The board added that it had banned clothing referencing professional sports teams based on a belief that it had been used to signal gang affiliation. The board also informed the court that it considered enacting a school uniform code but decided on a dress code instead in order to give students some freedom in choosing their clothing.

In response to the school board's amended code, Palmer presented three shirts to it for approval. The first shirt was the original "John Edwards for President" T-shirt. The second was a polo shirt proclaiming "John Edwards for President." The third shirt proclaimed "Freedom of Speech" on the front and the text of the First Amendment on the back. The Waxahachie School District rejected all three shirts.

Palmer renewed his suit against the Waxahachie School District, arguing that the amended dress code also violated his right to freedom of speech under the First Amendment. He thus sought a preliminary injunction barring the board from implementing its amended dress code. After a federal trial court in Texas denied Palmer's motion, he appealed to the Fifth Circuit.

At the Fifth Circuit, Palmer argued that he was entitled to an injunction against the school board because his shirt messages were not censorable under any of the standards articulated by the Supreme Court for regulating student speech. First, Palmer claimed that since the messages on his shirts were not disruptive, they could not be banned under *Tinker*. He next maintained that since the messages were not lewd or vulgar, they could not be barred under the Supreme Court's holding in *Bethel School District No. 403 v. Fraser* (1986). The student then contended that since the messages were not school sponsored, they could not be censored under the Supreme Court's rationale in *Hazelwood School District v. Kuhlmeier* (1988). Finally, Palmer asserted that insofar as the messages did not advocate illegal drug use, the Supreme Court's rationale in *Morse v. Frederick* (2007) was inapplicable.

Unfortunately for Palmer, the Fifth Circuit rejected his arguments as unpersuasive. The court pointed out that it had previously upheld the student uniform code for a school board in Louisiana on the basis that it was content-neutral and furthered important or substantial governmental interests (*Canady v. Bossier Parish School Board*, 2001). The Fifth Circuit explained:

> [S]chool regulation of student speech can be justified on five—not just four—grounds. If the speech is disruptive (*Tinker*), lewd (*Fraser*), school-sponsored (*Hazelwood*), or promoting drug use (*Morse*), schools may in some instances restrict specific student speech. Student speech can also be regulated so long as the regulation is viewpoint- and content-neutral (*Canady*). (p. 509)

Going to the heart of the matter, the Fifth Circuit reasoned that the student dress code was content-neutral. Thus, the Fifth Circuit would uphold the code against a constitutional challenge if the school board could show that the code furthered its important governmental interests.

In its analysis, the court pointed out that the school board justified its dress code as a means "to maintain an orderly and safe learning environment, increase the focus on instruction, promote safety and life-long learning, and encourage professional and responsible dress for all students" (p. 510). The court also acknowledged that the board viewed the dress code as a way to reduce the administrative time spent enforcing its code and that the code reasonably allowed student clothing promoting school activities.

According to the Fifth Circuit, the school board articulated acceptable justifications for its dress code that qualified as important governmental interests. In particular, the court focused on the board's belief that the dress code would help provide a safer and more orderly learning as a necessary precondition for creating such a safer school environment. In addition, the court acknowledged "[t]he benefits for the school, such as reducing time spent enforcing the code and promoting school spirit, are also important in promoting better education" (p. 511).

In language that was very friendly toward public school boards in general, the Fifth Circuit emphasized that in previous cases it had "properly set a low bar for the evidence a board must submit to show its dress code meets its stated goals" (p. 511). The court asserted that statistical evidence that the dress code was advancing its goals was not necessary to show that the code was advancing important governmental interests. The court did indicate that "evidence of improvements in other boards that have adopted the same or a similar dress code [would have] support[ed] the district's decision" (p. 511).

Going even further to accommodate the school board, the Fifth Circuit added that it would not require statistical or scientific evidence to uphold a school dress code since "improvements in discipline or morale cannot always be quantified" (p. 511). The court thus accepted the sworn testimony of school administrators or teachers as sufficient to establish that the dress code was an effective means of advancing [for variety] the board's important governmental interests. After all, the court reasoned, "The District and its administrators—not federal judges—are in a better position to formulate a dress code, and we are understandably hesitant to question their stated justifications" (p. 511).

In explaining its rationale, the Fifth Circuit noted that the assistant superintendent testified that the school board had examined more than 40 dress codes in other districts and that officials went so far as to visit other systems to help determine which kind of dress code would have been best for Waxahachie. In addition, the court remarked that the board reviewed data from other school systems regarding the impact of dress codes. The Fifth Circuit concluded that this "is more than enough to show that the District justified its important government interests with factual support" (p. 511).

Palmer attempted to undercut the school board's justification for its dress code by pointing out that its stated interests were undermined by the fact that educators allowed students to wear pins, buttons, and wristbands proclaiming various kinds of messages while permitting them to display bumper stickers communicating messages. The Fifth Circuit was not persuaded by this argument, finding the board's distinction between messages on clothing and messages on buttons and pins was reasonable:

> Because shirts are large and quite visible, banning them while allowing buttons would cause less distraction and promote an orderly learning environment. Buttons and pins are also less prominent than are shirts and therefore require less attention from and regulation by teachers. Another District goal—promoting professional and responsible dress—still functions as well, because students are prepared for a working world in which pins and buttons may be appropriate at work but large, stark political messages usually are not. (p. 512)

In addition, reemphasizing a theme that it had already articulated, the Fifth Circuit declared that even if it considered the school board's distinction between messages on clothing and messages on buttons to be odd, it would still defer to the reasoning of educators insofar as "we recognize that the teachers and administrators who establish these rules know better than we do how the distinction will function in schools" (p. 512). In short, the court concluded that "[t]he determination of where to draw the line on dress code decisions properly rests with the school board, rather than with the federal courts" (p. 512, internal citation omitted).

COURTS SHOULD DEFER TO SCHOOL BOARDS WITH REGARD TO STUDENT DRESS CODE DECISIONS

Palmer v. Waxahachie Independent School District offers strong judicial support for school officials who wish to adopt a student dress code to build a safer and more secure school environment. In *Palmer,* the Fifth Circuit ruled that a student dress code banning messages on clothing promotes important governmental interests and that educators need not offer statistical evidence to show that their dress codes in fact further such an interest. *Palmer* is a sensible decision that provides a model for other federal, and state, courts to follow when analyzing constitutional challenges against the student dress codes enacted by school boards.

As commentators have pointed out, research does not always support the positions of boards and officials that student dress codes can help make schools safer. Even so, the Fifth Circuit was right to acknowledge that some of the benefits of student dress codes cannot be established by statistics alone and that, in any event, educational administrators, not the courts, are in the best position to evaluate whether particular dress codes help promote safe school environments. The counterpoint essay's approach simply does not afford school officials enough flexibility and discretion in making these important determinations in their districts.

COUNTERPOINT: Todd A. DeMitchell
University of New Hampshire

An appellate court in Illinois aptly and succinctly captured the concern about safety within the schoolhouse gate. The court wrote:

> We long for the time when children did not have to pass through metal
> detectors on their way to class, when hall monitors were other children,
> not armed guards, when students dressed for school without worrying
> about gang colors. Those were the days when sharp words, crumpled
> balls of paper, and, at worst the bully's fists were the weapons choice.
> (*People v. Pruitt*, 1996, p. 545)

Indeed, we long for that sense that children are safe at school. In fact, the concern for safety, Todd A. DeMitchell and Casey Cobb (2003) concluded, has resulted in the development of a new, fundamental value in educational policy making—security. Security is different from safety, which often focuses on the liability for injury and school discipline. Safety regulations are found in chemistry laboratories, the use of trampolines, playground rules, and other places where there is a possibility of harm from negligent acts. Disciplinary policies are typically aimed at disruption, fighting, and rowdy behavior, whereas security policies are aimed at protecting students from grievous injury and death. Examples of security policies include the use of magnetometers, erection of gun- and drug-free zones around schools, condom availability policies, and after the Columbine shootings, policies targeting Marilyn Manson T-shirts and black trench coats, as well as gang-related policies.

This counterpoint essay focuses on the intersection of safety and security by discussing the section of dress codes aimed at both safety and security. Specifically, this essay examines issues surrounding gang-related clothing and generalized dress codes directed at preventing violence. This counterpoint essay does not discuss dress codes that concern immodest clothing such as sagging pants or that address clothing advertising alcohol or drugs. These are generally good policies. This essay also does not address dress code restrictions specifically directed at dangerous apparel such as choke chains, spiked bracelets, or inappropriate shoes such as flip-flops. These too are generally good policies for schools to have and to enforce. Restrictions on T-shirts targeted at gays and lesbians and religion are also left for another day since they deserve their own discussion about the conflict between free speech and personal harm.

GANG-RELATED CLOTHING RESTRICTIONS

Gang activity at school can negatively impact the safety of all students. A growing number of states has passed legislation aimed at curbing gang activity at schools by imposing dress code restrictions on wearing gang-related apparel. For example, Iowa passed the following school dress code statute:

> The general assembly finds and declares that the students and the administrative and instructional staffs of Iowa public schools have the right to be safe and secure at school. Gang-related apparel worn at school draws attention away from the school's learning environment and directs it toward thoughts and expressions of violence, bigotry, hate, and abuse. (Iowa Code § 279.58)

However, although the argument that a ban on gang apparel as part of a dress code promotes safety, one must consider whether dress codes are effective. A 2002 Education Commission of the States Policy Report by Wendell Anderson, "School dress codes and uniform policies," found that empirical research on the efficacy of dress codes offers no strong support for dress codes. The report concludes with a quote from a research report; in the absence of longitudinal research, for the research on dress codes and school uniforms, "the results remain anecdotal and unproven" (p. 10).

School officials must take reasonable steps to safeguard their students from foreseeable harm. These steps must comport with the constitutional freedoms that students bring with them when they enter the schoolhouse gate while recognizing that the rights of students are not coextensive with those of adults. In an effort to combat violence, many states allow school boards to enact regulations targeting gang-related apparel. These are intended to reduce the likelihood of violence by restricting the display of symbols associated with gang membership so that a gang member cannot outwardly identify himself or herself as a part of a gang. In addition, these regulations protect nongang students from being mistakenly targeted by gang members as a rival. The following is an example of a gang-related dress code for elementary school students from the Parma City School District, Ohio: "The presence of any apparel, jewelry, accessory, notebook, or manner of grooming, which by virtue of its color, arrangement, trademark, or any other attribute, denotes membership in a group or gang is prohibited" (Board of Education Policy, 5511A).

It is interesting to note that the secondary gang-related section for secondary school students is slightly different. It reads as follows: "Inappropriate insignias, emblems, and/or gang-related colors shall not be worn during the school day or at school functions." It is unknown as to why the difference in policy. The elementary school student policy is more explicit in defining the restrictions.

The questions raised by gang-related dress code restrictions are two-fold: First, are they effective or do they just target gang wannabes, while real gang members find subtle new ways of identification of membership? Second, do they violate the constitutional rights of students? Whether the gang-related dress codes are effective in curbing violence at school is beyond the scope of this discussion. The second issue of constitutional violations is discussed because if policies violate students' constitutional rights, then their effectiveness does not matter because they are unconstitutional and therefore void.

In addition to the issue of free speech, a major concern about gang-related dress codes is whether they violate the substantive due process rights of students. Under the Fourteenth Amendment, public school boards and officials may not adopt rules or regulations that violate the substantive due process, or property, rights of their students. An important aspect of substantive due process is vagueness. The "void for vagueness" doctrine of the Fourteenth Amendment forbids arbitrary and discriminatory enforcement. A regulation is void on its face when it is so vague that persons of common intelligence must necessarily guess at its meaning and its application. In other words, a regulation or policy violates due process guarantees if a reasonable person would not know what to refrain from doing or not know what must be done in order to follow the law, rule, or regulation. If it does not meet this standard, it is vague. If the rule is vague, it does not provide fair notice or warning. A second substantive due process consideration is whether the regulation or policy is overbroad, sweeping in protected activity, and thus rendering the protected activity unprotected. Comporting with the requirements of substantive due process is a challenge for gang-related dress codes.

The Rosary as Gang Apparel

An example of a gang-related dress code policy that ran afoul of substantive due process can be found in New Caney High School in Montgomery County, Texas. The policy prohibited gang-related attire. Under the enforcement of the policy, the wearing of rosaries outside of the shirt was considered gang-related apparel. However, rosaries were not specifically listed as gang apparel. A police officer identified that gang members wore rosaries and therefore did not want any student wearing a rosary outside of the shirt at school. Even though school authorities stated that two students who wore rosaries to school were not members of a gang, they were told by police officers that for their safety they could not wear their rosaries where they could be seen. The students brought suit in a federal trial court.

The court, in *Chalifoux v. New Caney Independent School District* (1997) in addressing the void for vagueness doctrine, found that the policy—"Any attire which identifies students as a group (gang-related) may not be worn to school or school-related activities"—violated the substantive due process rights of the students because it was vague. This definition, the court asserted, revealed little about what conduct was prohibited. Without a definition, the court explained, students did not receive notice of prohibited conduct such as wearing a rosary on the outside of the shirt. In addition, the court observed that the gang-related dress code placed too much discretion to define violations of the ban on gang-related apparel in the hands of school officials.

At the same time, the court ruled that the policy was overbroad. In other words, although the policy was aimed at reducing gang identity on campus, it infringed on First Amendment rights of speech and religion of third parties who were not gang members. Here the court decided that the policy was overbroad because not all gang members wore rosaries and not all individuals who wore rosaries were gang members.

Tattoos

Brianna Stephenson, as an eighth-grader, tattooed a small cross between her thumb and index finger. The cross was not intended as a religious symbol or as gang identification. Brianna did not have a record of disciplinary problems; in fact her teacher considered her to be "conscientious and diligent." For 30 months, she wore the tattoo without incident. That changed when her high school experienced an increase in gang activity.

The school board, in response to Brianna's wearing the tattoo, developed the "Proactive Disciplinary Position K-12." The policy stated, in pertinent part, that "[g]ang related activities such as display of 'colors,' symbols, signals, signs, etc., will not be tolerated on school grounds." Soon after the policy was implemented, a school counselor with whom Brianna was meeting saw the tattoo and informed the associate principal. It was determined that the tattoo of the cross was a gang symbol even though there was no evidence that Brianna was involved in gang activity and no other student filed a complaint about her tattoo being a gang symbol. Brianna was suspended for 1 day. In the subsequent meeting with Brianna and her parents, the associate principal informed them if Brianna did not remove or alter the tattoo, she would face a 10-day suspension.

Brianna, concerned that altering the tattoo would make it bigger and the school authorities and others could consider the alteration to be a gang symbol, decided to undergo laser treatment to remove the tattoo, leaving a scar in place of the tattoo. Brianna then filed suit after the removal of the tattoo arguing in part that the gang-related policy violated her due process because the policy was vague.

The case found its way to the federal Court of Appeals for the Eighth Circuit (*Stephenson v. Davenport Community School District*, 1997). The Eighth Circuit appellate court struck down the policy as void for vagueness. The court noted that the fact that the term *gang* was not defined rendered the policy defective. The court asserted that the school's policy prohibiting colors, symbols, signals, and signs is not adequately explained. Consequently, the court was of the opinion that the policy failed to provide adequate notice of what conduct is prohibited. In addition, as in *Chalifoux* discussed above, the court noted that the policy provided virtually unfettered discretion for school authorities and police officers to define gang-related activity and symbols in any way they choose. Insofar as the term lacks a working definition, the court concluded that it failed to provide meaningful guidance for educators who enforced the policy.

Discussion: Dress Code Response to Gangs

School administrators certainly have a legal and a professional duty to take reasonable steps to respond to the violence associated with gang activity at school. The question is whether dress codes aimed at gang-related apparel are reasonable and viable. Given the possibility that such dress codes may be constitutionally vague, are they a workable approach? Does a gang-related dress code provide sufficient notice and definition of what is prohibited? Once a restriction is in place, many gangs morph their identifying symbols and signs for the specific purpose of keeping them secret from authorities, raising the question of effectiveness. A better approach is to focus energy and resources for immediate responses to any acts that endanger or tend to endanger students or staff. It is the response to a violent, or intimidating, act that is most important, not the response to the color of the clothes of the individual.

VIOLENCE AND T-SHIRTS

School boards and officials should and do have the authority to restrict clothing that promotes and glorifies violence. However, officials go overboard when they restrict clothing that has only benign depictions of weapons. For example, school policies banning T-shirts displaying pictures of weapons restrict such depictions as "Washington Crossing the Delaware" in which he has a sword at his side. Similarly, pictures on T-shirts of the Marine Corps Creed with a picture of an M16 rifle (see *Griggs v. Ft. Wayne School Board,* 2005) do not glorify or promote violence; instead, this picture promotes a vital part of our national security.

An example of a dress code on violence run amuck occurred in Coventry, Rhode Island, in 2010. David Morales, age 8, designed and wore to school a camouflage hat with little plastic army men glued to it to honor the men and women serving in the armed services. David was told to take the cap off because it violated the policy on weapons at school. It is highly doubtful that the students at his school had a heightened risk of harm because of the five plastic soldiers on David's hat. Real threats should occupy the time, resources, and energy of educators. A rigid, unreasonable response to guns on campus dilutes the power of the message about needed restrictions.

PROMOTION OF GUN USE

Jack Jouett Middle School in Albemarle County, Virginia, had a dress code policy prohibiting "messages on clothing, jewelry, and personal belongings that relate to . . . weapons." One day Alan Newsom, a 12-year-old student at the school, wore a purple T-shirt depicting three black silhouettes of men holding rifles superimposed on the letters "NRA" positioned above the phrase "SHOOTING SPORTS CAMP." Elizabeth Pitt, the assistant principal, on seeing the T-shirt, thought of the shootings at Columbine High School. She also thought the students might interpret the T-shirt as promoting the use of guns in contradiction to the school's message that "Guns and Schools Don't Mix." After a discussion with Pitt, Newsom turned his T-shirt inside out so that the writing and picture could not be seen. The following academic year, he filed suit seeking a preliminary injunction to stop the enforcement of the dress code policy.

Newsom lost at the federal district court level but appealed to the Fourth Circuit Court of Appeals, which remanded the case with instructions to grant the student's request for a preliminary injunction. The court examined the question of whether the dress code policy section pertaining to weapons was overbroad, sweeping protected speech into its prohibitions. It found that there was a dearth of evidence demonstrating a connection between the nonviolent and nonthreatening message of the T-shirt and a disruption at school. In an interesting twist, the court noted that the dress code would have prohibited students from wearing clothing depicting the State Seal for the Commonwealth of Virginia because the seal shows a woman standing with one foot on the chest of a vanquished tyrant and holding a spear. The court commented that since the spear is a weapon, showing it would have violated the school's dress code. Similarly, the court acknowledged that the symbol of the University of Virginia's mascot is a Cavalier with two crossed sabers. As such, the court added that students would have violated the dress code had they worn a shirt depicting the mascot. Accordingly, the Fourth Circuit vacated the order denying the student's request to enjoin the enforcement of the school dress code section on weapons.

CONCLUSION

As the point essay argument asserts, school dress codes focusing on safety are appropriate. Conversely, as this counterpoint essay asserts, such dress codes are not appropriate in all situations. Clothing that is dangerous should be banned. Clothing that has messages of drug and alcohol use can be appropriately restricted. Clothing that spews hate and calls for violence should be beyond the pale of what is acceptable at school. However, clothing restrictions must comport with the requirements of substantive due process, giving students fair warning of what is proscribed. Educators must seek clarity on what is prohibited. Restrictions must be reasonable. Knee-jerk policies banning gang-related apparel may not serve the worthy goals and may only snare nongang members in the sticky threads of undeserved discipline. Dress codes seeking safety for students must balance what is a real threat to safety and what is a reflexive, unthinking response.

Dress codes that are directed at making students safe represent a powerful argument for their adoption. Nevertheless, the question of whether dress codes clearly address the problems effectively is a major challenge. At the same time, it is important to keep in mind that dress codes are not cost-free. Policies must be consistently and fairly enforced. The already stretched resources of school systems may be better used in enacting policies designed and shown to improve the safety of students rather than in policing what they wear. Some have dubbed this activity as the work of the "Fashion Police." Although we may long for the world of the school the court in *People v. Pruitt* (1996) lamented losing, we cannot try to recapture it through policies that have constitutional defects and questionable effectiveness.

FURTHER READINGS AND RESOURCES

Anderson, W. (2002, Fall). *School dress codes and uniform policies.* Policy Reports. Education Commission of the States. Retrieved September 12, 2010, from http://www .ecs.org/html/offsite.asp?document=http%3A%2F%2Feric%2Euoregon%2Eedu%2F pdf%2Fpolicy%5Freports%2Fpolicy%2520report%2520dress%2520code%2Epdf

Brown, T. (1998). *Legal issues and the trend towards school uniforms.* Retrieved from ERIC database.

Brunsma, D., & Rockquemore, K. (1998). Effects of student uniforms on attendance, behavior problems, substance use, and academic achievement. *Journal of Educational Research, 92*(1), 53–62.

Darden, E. C. (2009, November). What not to wear. *American School Board Journal, 196,* 44–45.

DeMitchell, T. A., & Cobb, C. (2003). Policy responses to violence in our schools: An exploration of security as a fundamental value. *Brigham Young University Education and Law Journal,* 459–484.

DeMitchell, T. A., & Paige, M. A. (2010). School uniforms in the public schools: Symbol or substance? *Education Law Reporter, 250,* 847–879.

Essex, N. (2001). School uniforms: Guidelines for principals. *Principal, 80*(3), 38–39.

Fossey, R., Eckes, S., & DeMitchell, T. A. (2010). The end of the t-shirt wars in the public schools? *Palmer v. Waxahachie Independent School District. Teachers College Record.* Retrieved from http://www.tcrecord.org ID Number: 15775

Institute for Intergovernmental Research. (n.d.). *Gang-related legislation: Gang-related clothing, dress codes, school uniforms.* Retrieved June 20, 2011, from National Gang Center website: http://www.nationalgangcenter.gov/Content/HTML/Legislation/gang_relatedclothing.htm

Murray, R. (1997). The impact of school uniforms on school climate. *NASSP Bulletin, 81*(593), 106–112.

Shirk, S. R., & Jungbluth, N. J. (2008). School-based mental health checkups: Ready for practical action? *Clinical Psychology: Science & Practice, 15*(3), 217–223.

Stewart, R. M., Benner, G. J., Martella, R. C., & Martella-Marchand, N. E. (2007). Three-tier models of reading and behavior: A research review. *Journal of Positive Behavior Interventions, 9*(4), 239–253.

Sugai, G., & Horner, R. H. (1999). Discipline and behavioral support: Practices, pitfalls, and promises. *Effective School Practices, 17*(4), 10–22.

Todd, A. W., Campbell, A. L., Meyer, G. G., & Horner, R. H. (2008). The effects of a targeted intervention to reduce problem behaviors: Elementary school implementation of check in-check out. *Journal of Positive Behavior Intervention, 10*(1), 46–55.

Walker, H. M., Golly, A., McLane, J. Z., & Kimmich, M. (2005). The Oregon First Step to Success replication initiative: Statewide results of an evaluation of the program's impact. *Journal of Emotional and Behavioral Disorders, 13*(2), 163–172.

COURT CASES AND STATUTES

Bethel School District No. 403 v. Frazer, 478 U.S. 675 (1986).

Bivens v. Albuquerque Public Schools (D.N.M. 1995).

Canady v. Bossier Parish School Board, 240 F.3d 437 (5th Cir. 2001).

Chalifoux v. New Caney Independent School District, 976 F. Supp. 659 (S.D. Tex. 1997).

Griggs v. Ft. Wayne School Board, 359 F. Supp. 2d 731 (N.D. Ind. 2005).

Hazelwood School District v. Kuhlmeier, 484 U.S. 260 (1988).

Jeglin v. San Jacinto Unified School District, 827 F. Supp. 1459 (C.D. Calif. 1993).

Karr v. Schmidt, 460 F.2d 609 (5th Cir. 1972).

Morse v. Frederick, 551 U.S. 393 (2007).

Palmer v. Waxahachie Independent School District, 579 F.3d 502 (5th Cir. 2009), cert. denied, 130 S. Ct. 1055 (2010).

People v. Pruitt, 662 N.E.2d 540 (Ill. App. Ct 1996).

School Dress Code Policies, Iowa Code § 279.58 (2009).

Stephenson v. Davenport Community School District, 110 F.3d 1303 (8th Cir. 1997).

Tinker v. Des Moines Independent Community School District, 393 U.S. 503 (1969).

Are zero tolerance policies acceptable with respect to drugs, alcohol, weapons, where student safety is concerned?

POINT: Aimee Vergon Gibbs, *Dickinson Wright, PLLC, Detroit, Michigan*

COUNTERPOINT: Charles B. Vergon, *Youngstown State University*

OVERVIEW

In response to a growing tide of student substance abuse in and around schools in the form of drugs and/or alcohol, along with weapons-related violence, many American school boards have adopted zero tolerance policies in attempts to reduce, if not eliminate, these problems. Putting aside, for a moment, the wisdom of such a draconian approach and whether such zero tolerance policies should be reserved for zero tolerance offenses, meaning that it should be applied only for significant transgressions, it is clear that such an approach has led to controversy and litigation. In fact, when courts review challenges to zero tolerance policies, they look to ensure that school officials acted with appropriate discretion in disciplining students. Moreover, although courts seem to be taking a dim view of zero tolerance policies as a one-size-fits-all approach to a serious problem that does not place enough discretion in the hands of school officials, the judiciary continues to reach mixed results when students and/or their parents file suit challenging their having been disciplined under such policies.

In a high-profile case from Tennessee, for example, the Sixth Circuit invalidated the proposed suspension of a high school student under a zero tolerance policy after a hunting knife was discovered in the glove compartment of his car. The court ruled that since the knife did not belong to the student, and was put in the glove compartment by a passenger, his being excluded from school under a provision allowing educators to discipline students even if they did not knowingly possess weapons was not rationally related to a legitimate interest of the school board (*Seal v. Morgan,* 2000).

A year earlier, an intermediate appellate court in Pennsylvania struck down the proposed suspension of a middle school student for coming to class with a Swiss Army knife in his pocket. The facts of the case revealed that the student found the knife on the floor in a hallway but forgot to turn it in to someone in the school office before going to his class. The court reasoned that the policy was invalid because it ignored the clear legislative intent that zero tolerance policies should not be applied blindly (*Lyons v. Penn Hills School District,* 1999). In yet another case, a federal trial court in Mississippi overturned the expulsion of a student with a disability for bringing a Swiss Army knife to school but otherwise agreed that a school board had the authority to enact such a rule (*Colvin ex rel. Colvin v. Lowndes County, Mississippi, School District,* 1999).

Nevertheless, the Fourth Circuit affirmed that officials in Virginia could suspend a student who had a knife in his locker even though he took it from a classmate who was suicidal (*Ratner v. Loudoun County Public Schools,* 2001, 2002). The court was satisfied that school officials gave the student sufficient due process before suspending him under the board's zero tolerance policy. Similarly, an appellate court in Florida rejected the claim of a student who challenged his suspension for bringing a gun to school in violation of a zero tolerance policy (*D.K. ex rel. Kennedy v. District School Board Indian River County,* 2008). The court dismissed the claim on the basis that since the student was subject only to suspension, not expulsion, it lacked the authority to intervene.

With respect to zero tolerance policies on alcohol and drugs, an illustration of the need for a more nuanced law can be seen in a change in the language of the Individuals with Disabilities Education Act (IDEA, 2004). This modification essentially rejects the zero tolerance approach for students with disabilities and reflects the notion that mere possession of drugs is an insufficient basis on which to discipline students with disabilities. The change came about in response to incidents wherein students with disabilities were disciplined for acting as "mules," unknowingly carrying drugs for others. Congress modified the IDEA so that now, students with disabilities can be disciplined only "for knowing possession, use, sale, or solicitation of drugs 20 U.S.C.A. § 1415(k)(1) (G)(iii)."

Against this backdrop, the point and counterpoint essays in this chapter take different approaches to the appropriateness of zero tolerance policies. The author of the point essay, Aimee Vergon Gibbs (Dickinson Wright, PLLC, Detroit, Michigan), begins by briefly tracing the history of zero tolerance policies in the United States in order to place them in context. She then argues that the use of zero tolerance policies has aided significantly in reducing drug and alcohol use as well as the use of weapons among students. Gibbs concludes that the impact of zero tolerance policies must be examined over the long haul because although they have not eliminated all of the problems they were intended to address, they have contributed greatly to making schools safer learning environments.

Conversely, Charles B. Vergon's (Youngstown State University) counterpoint essay maintains that zero tolerance policies have not only failed to stem the tide of drug, alcohol, and weapons use in schools, but they also have been an insufficient and ineffective approach resulting in an array of unintended negative consequences. More specifically, he contends that since zero tolerance policies are typically applied without consideration of the context or circumstances involving infractions, particularly involving weapons, they have led to rigid and disproportionate punishments that, in excluding students, ultimately do children more harm than good.

As you read these essays, ask yourself two questions. First, do you think that one-size-fits-all zero tolerance policies really make sense, or do they deprive educational leaders of the discretion to discipline students in ways that are proportionate to their offenses? Second, regardless of whether you agree with the use of zero tolerance policies, can you think of a better disciplinary tool that educational leaders can adopt in trying to ensure that schools remain safe and orderly learning environments that are free from drugs, alcohol, and weapons?

Charles J. Russo
University of Dayton

POINT: Aimee Vergon Gibbs
Dickinson Wright, PLLC, Detroit, Michigan

In the past 2 decades, federal and state governments have become increasingly concerned with school crime and student drug use. During this time, officials at these agencies have implemented a variety of measures to address and reduce the detrimental and often deadly implications of weapons and drugs, in particular in schools. Of course, student use of alcohol has also created problems. The notion of "zero tolerance" in the context of education refers to a disciplinary philosophy and policy in which violation of certain rules subjects the offending student to mandatory, predetermined punitive exclusion from school.

The majority of public schools have established some version of zero tolerance policies in order to address and combat serious offenses, including student possession of weapons, alcohol, and drugs at schools. The objective behind zero tolerance policies is to deter dangerous student misconduct through the consistent application of strict disciplinary measures. The development, implementation, and application of zero tolerance policies have been subject to heated debate since their inception, with much controversy concerning the efficacy of such policies. However, what is not subject to debate is the essential need for comprehensive and effective prevention of student violence and drug use. This point essay discusses and debates the efficacy of zero tolerance policies operated in the schools.

HISTORICAL BACKGROUND

As part of this debate, it is important to understand the historical development of zero tolerance policies. The term *zero tolerance* was initially used in the 1980s in connection with the "war on drugs." The policy became law when Congress passed the Drug-Free Schools and Campuses Act of 1989, which banned the unlawful use, possession, or distribution of drugs and alcohol by students and employees on school grounds and college campuses. The Drug-Free Schools and Campuses Act required all educational institutions receiving federal funding to establish disciplinary sanctions for violations or risk forfeiture of their federal funding. To maintain funding, therefore, the majority of the schools and colleges implemented zero tolerance laws concerning drug and alcohol possession.

In the early 1990s, the federal zero tolerance policy framework was expanded to include sanctions for possession of weapons on school grounds.

Specifically, Congress legislated zero tolerance of weapons by passing the Gun-Free Schools Act of 1994 (GFSA), which mandated a 1-year expulsion of any student found in possession of a gun, but the U.S. Supreme Court invalidated this requirement in 1995 (Russo, 1995). The reauthorized GFSA required that all recipients of federal funding for education purposes adopt policies governing weapons possession on school premises. Among the state and local policy features required by the GFSA were the following:

- A calendar-year expulsion of any student who brings a weapon to school.

- Case-by-case review of expulsion to ensure appropriateness of sanction and to reconcile with IDEA guarantee of free and appropriate education for students with disabilities.

- Criminal justice system referral of any student who brings a weapon to school.

- Assurances of compliance and reports of weapons incidents to state education agencies and annually by state agencies to the U.S. Department of Education.

As might have been anticipated given the federal funding stipulations, states and local school boards almost universally adopted zero tolerance policies prohibiting students from bringing weapons, alcohol, and drugs to school or school-related activities or events. Further, as one might also have expected, variations in the content of such policies and the procedures for implementing them emerged among the states. Therefore, what constitutes a "weapon," or what behavior and conduct will result in automatic suspension or expulsion, for example, may differ among states and even local districts. Even so, what remains consistent on a national level is the need for disciplinary policies to ensure school safety and promote the well-being of students at school.

IMPACT OF ZERO TOLERANCE POLICIES

Ensuring student safety in school is the most basic and fundamental concern of educators, administrators, and parents, students, and community members. Although student misconduct has arguably decreased over the past 20 years, its severity has escalated dramatically as evidenced by the number of school shootings, warranting the strict application of zero tolerance policies currently in effect in most schools.

Zero Tolerance for Weapons

Since the early 1990s, schools have witnessed unprecedented acts of violence. The 1990s brought the first substantial number of school-based homicides, more than 251 fatalities between the 1992–1993 and the 1998–1999 school year according to the National Center for School Safety. Of the 251 school-related violent deaths, 78% were the result of shootings, 13.5% of stabbings, 4.4% of beating or kicking, less than 2% from strangling or suffocation, and approximately 3% from unknown causes. Further, in the year 1996 alone, students ages 12 through 18 years were victims of approximately 255,000 incidents of non-fatal serious violent crimes at school. The violence is not just aimed at students. Between the period of 1992 to 1996, teachers were victims of 1,581,000 nonfatal crimes at school, including 962,000 thefts and 619,000 violent crimes such as rape or sexual assault, robbery, and aggravated and simple assault. Similarly disconcerting is the percentage of students who reported feeling unsafe while they were at school in the 1990s. From 1989 to 1995, the percentage of students who sometimes or most of the time feared they were going to be attacked or harmed at school had risen 3%, from 6% to 9%, which represented 2.1 million students during the relevant time period.

The 1990s were also witness to numerous highly publicized school shootings that contributed to parents' and students' fears about the ability of our educational system to keep students safe in school. In 1992, Eric Houston phoned the principal of Lindhurst High School in Olivehurst, California, threatening to bring a gun and "shoot up a school rally." Although the pep rally was cancelled, Eric Houston entered the school with a 12-gauge shotgun and a sawed off .22 caliber rifle and killed four people and held 80 others hostage for over 8 hours. Also in 1992, six students were wounded by gunfire in a crowded hallway at Palo Duro High School in Texas. A year later, a student shot his English teacher and the head custodian at East Carter High School in Kentucky and then held classmates hostage before surrendering. These are only some examples of the school violence that plagued our nation's schools in the 1990s. Between 1992 and 1995, there were 101 homicides in schools in the United States. Moreover, everyone can recall the terrifying images of Columbine, Colorado, students fleeing their high school as fellow students Eric Harris and Dylan Klebold shot and killed 11 students and 1 teacher, and injured another 21 students. This senseless type of mass random violence in the school setting not only physically endangers students but also leads to an environment of fear and intimidation.

As a result of these and other violent incidents occurring in schools across the nation and being played out on the national news, public concern regarding the safety of students was particularly understandable in the 1990s and served as the impetus behind the development and proliferation of zero tolerance policies. Although the number and proportion of schools affected by such tragic killings may be relatively small, any incident that suggests schools are no longer safe-havens, but microcosms of the violence in the neighborhoods in which they are embedded, causes alarm. Consequently, the adoption of zero tolerance weapons policies to rid the schools of guns was appropriately focused. Something had to be done quickly and swiftly to ensure student safety and to send the message that school violence would not be tolerated.

Impact of Zero Tolerance Policies on Weapons

Zero tolerance policies involving weapons serve two critical objectives. The first is to deter students from bringing weapons to school grounds through the consistent application of mandatory and stringent punishment. The second objective is to intervene in cases where students violate the weapons ban and hold them accountable by excluding them from school to ensure the protection and safety of the other students. As a result of the escalation in severity of school violence in the early 1990s, zero tolerance policies were crafted to be a just, predictable, and swift response to what had become a deadly crisis in schools. The decline in school homicides and other forms of violence in schools confirms that they have served their purpose. According to the National Center for Education Statistics, homicide rates in schools peaked in 1993–1994, and they have not returned to those levels since. Additionally, the number of crimes in schools per 1,000 students decreased from 155 in 1993 to 102 in 1997, and there were declines in the number of students carrying weapons to school and student fights during this period. According to the National Crime Victimization Survey, Bureau of Justice Statistics, the annual rate of serious violent crime in 2007 (40 per 1,000 students) was less than half of the rate in 1994.

Enforcement

Zero tolerance policies governing weapons have been reasonably implemented and enforced on the whole. Although the length of the discipline is proscribed by the GFSA as a calendar year if a student violates the zero tolerance weapon policy, the GFSA itself acknowledges that there is a high degree of factual variation in student misconduct cases, some of which should affect the consequences imposed on the students. The legislation specifically calls for the "case-by-case review" of exclusions to ensure the appropriateness of the sanction and to reconcile with IDEA's guarantee of free and appropriate education for students with disabilities. Most education administrators are highly educated, skilled professionals whose primary goal and concern is to provide students with sound education in a safe environment.

Such individuals are fully capable of assessing and implementing proper disciplinary measures in proportion to the student misconduct. This assessment is borne out by the actual percentage of GFSA weapons cases that are modified by school district superintendents. According to a U.S. Department of Education report prepared for Congress, 44% of some 3,500 GFSA weapons-related expulsions were modified and reduced in the 1996–1997 school year. The appropriate exercise of discretion is also confirmed by the fact that discipline imposed under zero tolerance policies has only been infrequently challenged in court and, when challenged, found in 75% of those cases not to be unreasonable, arbitrary, or capricious, according to a study by Charles B. Vergon appearing in the proceedings of the Education Law Association.

Zero Tolerance for Drugs and Alcohol

Drugs and alcohol have been a prominent part of youth culture for many years. This is evident from the findings from the annual Youth Risk Behaviors Studies and the U.S. Supreme Court's taking of judicial notice of the problem without requiring proofs in its 2002 judgment in *Board of Education of Independent School District No. 92 of Pottawatomie v. Earls,* wherein it upheld drug testing for students who are involved in extracurricular activities.

According to the annual reports conducted by the U.S. Department of Health and Human Services surveying drug use, alcohol usage reported as at least one drink of alcohol in the preceding 30 days among high school students remained steady from 1991 to 1999 and then decreased from 1999 to 2009. Significantly, there was a reported 50% decline of the number of students who reported drinking on school premises in 2007 as contrasted with 1995. Similarly, although illicit drug use among students still occurs, the percentages of students who use such drugs have been significantly reduced. In 2009, the percentage of students using marijuana was 21%; prescription drugs without a prescription, 20%; inhalants, 12%; hallucinogenics, 8%; ecstasy, 7%; and cocaine, 2%. These statistics indicate a downward trend in usage, as students' use of all drugs has declined substantially between 1991 and 2009, except for inhalants.

Given the prevalence of illicit drug and alcohol among school-age youth and the harmful consequences associated with their continued use, school officials needed to take an aggressive stance to discourage their use. Zero tolerance policies are one such strategy, often combined with various means of surveillance in the form of school drug-testing regimes for students who participate in interscholastic athletics and other interschool activities, as well as those who drive to school. Zero tolerance policies impose clear strict rules against possession of alcohol and drugs on school property and further ensure the safety of other students. Zero tolerance and related zero tolerance initiatives have led to the decline in usage by high school students of all forms of drugs except inhalants between 1991 and 2009.

CONCLUSION

Evaluation of the efficacy and impact of most policies must be done from a longitudinal perspective. This holds especially true for policies such as zero tolerance, which require the implementation of an intergovernmental policy in a complex social organization, such as the nation's schools. Opponents of zero tolerance policies, such as those reflected in the counterpoint essay, and those who contend that zero tolerance policies are an ineffective method of maintaining student safety, fail to acknowledge and assess the outcome on a longitudinal basis. These critics therefore fail to recognize that the deterrent effects and general increase in student safety are incremental results realized from the application of zero tolerance policies over several years rather than instantaneously. Thus, the reduction in violent acts and drug and alcohol usage that became evident only after several years following the enactment of the zero tolerance policy may still be appropriately attributable to it.

Additionally, even though guns and drugs have not been totally eliminated from schools, their presence is far less than would have been the case in the absence of the adoption of zero tolerance policies that impose stringent and unambiguous discipline on students for the possession of weapons, drugs, or alcohol on school grounds. This is supported by the fact that drug use and violence in society generally have increased over the past 2 decades at an alarming rate, while there has been decrease of such behavior in the schools. In summary, the arguments of the counterpoint essay notwithstanding, zero tolerance policies have contributed to a decrease of school violence and student possession of drugs and alcohol at school. Overall, serious incidents in schools significantly declined starting in the 1990s; homicide rates in schools peaked in 1993–1994, and they have not returned to those levels since; and most forms of drug usage among high school students has declined over the past 2 decades.

COUNTERPOINT: Charles B. Vergon
Youngstown State University

Nearly a half-century of governmental policy initiatives to correct a variety of national social problems has taught us that federal policy may not always achieve the objectives policymakers intended. All too frequently policies are accompanied by unintended consequences that are most often negative. The adoption and implementation of zero tolerance policies at the local and state level, spurred in part by the Gun-Free Schools Act of 2004 (GFSA), are a reminder of these lessons.

In contrast to the point essay argument in favor of zero tolerance policies, this counterpoint essay maintains that the failure of zero tolerance policies to decrease school violence and student drug and alcohol use, as well as the numerous unintended negative consequences that emanate from such policy making, renders their use an inefficient, ineffective, and often detrimental approach to promoting student and school safety.

INEFFECTIVENESS OF ZERO TOLERANCE POLICIES
Zero Tolerance for Weapons

No one can argue with the objectives underlying "zero tolerance" policies that take a tough stance against school violence and student drug and alcohol use. However, as with many other policies evolving out of popular sound bites such as "zero tolerance," the policy design, implementation, and outcomes are less positive. Thus, although the adoption of the GFSA and its zero tolerance provisions may have been "good politics," there is little evidence that it has accomplished its intended objectives. In fact, there is a general lack of empirical data to show that zero tolerance policies actually prevent or in any way deter students from bringing weapons, alcohol, or drugs to school. Although the incidents of student deaths at school may have decreased since the 1990s, there remains significant misconduct and disciplinary problems at schools.

Additionally, although it is true that the number of school homicides has declined between 1992 and the present, the number did not change appreciably between 1992 and 1998, consistently falling between 28 and 34 homicides annually with no consistent downward or upward trend. It is also important to note that one of the most publicized and deadly school shootings, the massacre in Columbine, Colorado, occurred in 1999, a full four years after the enactment and implementation of zero tolerance policies. Only since 2000 has a consistent and substantial drop in school-related homicides been recorded, negating the suggestion that the change can be attributable exclusively or even primarily to the adoption of a zero tolerance weapons policy 6 years earlier.

A similar pattern persisted with respect to the percentage of 9th- to 12th-grade students who reported carrying a gun to school during the previous 30 days. Although the proportion declined from 1993 (11%) to 2007 (6%), there was no precipitous decline in the mid-1990s when the zero tolerance policies went into effect. Nor did the percentage of 9th- to 12th-grade students who indicated they were threatened or injured with a weapon at school change appreciably between 1993 and 2003. In fact, the proportion actually rose from 7.3% to 9.2% over this time period, according to the National Center for Educational Statistics, Indicators of School Crime and Safety Report, further negating the claimed beneficial effects of the 1994 GFSA zero tolerance weapons policy.

Zero Tolerance for Drugs and Alcohol

Drug and alcohol use among adolescents has been a concern of parents, educators, and policymakers for decades, years before the concern regarding firearms arose. Yet according to the Centers for Disease Control and Prevention's 2009 Youth Risk Behavior Survey results, there was little change in alcohol or drug use at school between 1991 and 1999. Declines, when they have occurred, have been most evident since 2003.

In the case of alcohol, the same percentage of 9th- to 12th-grade students (4.2%) reported consuming it at school in 1993 as in 2003. Marijuana use at school actually increased slightly during that time from 5.6% to 5.8% of the 9th- to 12th-grade population. Since 2003, there has been a general downward trend in most forms of youth drug use, including the recently more prevalent inhalant, prescription, and over-the-counter drug misuse.

Tellingly, though, the proportion of secondary school students reporting that drugs were available to them on school premises remained virtually unchanged between 1993 (24%) and 2007 (22%). According to the 2009 Youth Risk Behavior Survey, there is consequently a discernible difference in the level of continuing availability of drugs at school as contrasted to the recent declining use of drugs by 9th- to 12th-grade students. This discrepancy may be most readily explained by the growing proportion of schools that provide alcohol and drug prevention programs at school (upward of 80% of schools) as contrasted to the impact of the adoption of a zero tolerance policy.

It seems, therefore, that despite the creation and proliferation of the zero tolerance policies, school violence and student use of drugs and alcohol still represents a substantial and direct threat to school safety. In fact, the reliance on such a simplistic policy solution may have actually forestalled, at least temporarily, the adoption of more effective approaches to foster safe and orderly schools.

UNINTENDED CONSEQUENCES: NUMEROUS AND NEGATIVE

Not only is evidence lacking that zero tolerance policies accomplished what policymakers intended, there is also substantial evidence that they are having harmful unintended consequences for the children they were intended to protect. These unintended consequences flow from a variety of causes, but they have uniformly negative implications for children. These causes include the following.

1. *The rigid application of zero tolerance policies with respect to "weapons" has contributed to absurd results that are harmful to children and that compromise the credibility of public schools and school officials.*

Because of their mandatory language and predetermined consequences, zero tolerance policies are frequently applied literally and without regard to the intentions underlying the policy. When this is done, zero tolerance policies negate the exercise of professional discretion by school administrators, frequently leading to absurd and highly inappropriate consequences for students. Although the language of the GFSA statute itself authorizes local case-by-case review of calendar-year exclusions by local superintendents to ensure the appropriateness of sanctions, recent history is replete with numerous instances in which such discretion was not exercised, and policies were enforced in ways that can only be described as lacking common sense.

Generally, zero tolerance policies when applied as a blanket policy for student misconduct are unjust and unfair because they are applied without consideration of the context or circumstances surrounding the presence of the weapon, such as the instrument itself, the age of the student, the explanation for the presence of the weapons, and the student's intent to use the object as a weapon or do harm. Examples of the overly rigid application of zero tolerance policies are numerous and notorious:

- Four kindergarteners suspended for "making threats" by pretending their fingers were guns while playing cops and robbers at recess.

- A kindergarten student suspended for bringing a toy ax to school that was part of his fireman costume for Halloween.

- A fifth-grader during lunch discovered that her mother packed a plastic knife in her lunch to cut an apple and immediately turned it into her teacher. The child was expelled.

- A seventh-grader, after watching the movie *October Sky,* made a rocket out of a potato chip canister and brought it to school. The student was suspended when school officials classified the rocket as a weapon.

- A 14-year-old girl was strip searched and suspended because she gave a classmate a tablet of Midol.

- A senior was suspended for asking students to vote on whether certain administrators most resembled Big Bird, a witch, or a dead body. School officials alleged that the poll constituted a death threat.

- A high school senior was suspended for violating a school rule banning the use of alcohol after he took a swig of Listerine.

As can be expected, such rigid and disproportionate punishment is not only an ineffective method of altering students' behavior but also harms the future educational success of the student. Such absurd results create distrust in children and undermine parental support and community confidence in public schools and the judgment of school officials, at a time in history when this can be least well afforded.

2. Rather than deterring misconduct warranting serious disciplinary consequences, zero tolerance policies have actually increased the proportion of students that are excluded from school.

The adoption of zero tolerance policies for a wide array of school misconduct has been accompanied by a precipitous increase in the number of students being suspended from school once or more in a given school year. According to the U.S. Department of Education's National School Civil Rights Survey, the number of students suspended rose from 2.35 million in 1992, 3 years preceding the national adoption of zero tolerance policies, to 3.36 million in 1997, an increase of 43% 3 years after the adoption of the GFSA.

This dramatic increase was not attributable to school officials for the first time holding students accountable for weapon or drug possession, since school policies have for decades called for such sanctions. Nor is it plausible to contend that the rise in suspensions reflected a new tidal wave of such serious misconduct—precisely the two types of misconduct that the stringent zero tolerance law was designed to deter. In fact, even if there had been no prior suspensions or expulsions for possession of firearms prior to the adoption of zero tolerance laws, there would have been fewer than 17,000 additional suspensions in the 1996–1997 school year according to the National Center for Educational Statistics' School Crime and Safety data. And although an initial escalation in the number of suspensions and expulsions might be anticipated in conjunction with the adoption of such a zero tolerance policy until its deterrent effect might take hold, the number of students suspended once or more in a school year has never receded to less than 3 million students, let alone returned to the 2.35 million student level observed prior to the introduction of the GFSA zero tolerance policy.

Rather, as states and localities responded to the GFSA, many of them broadened the application of the zero tolerance policy to include a wide array of student misconduct, often requiring or authorizing the use of suspensions from school, even if not mandating the same calendar-year expulsions called for by the GFSA. The consequences of excluding large numbers of students for conduct that does not threaten the safety of students or schools are numerous and profound. Suspensions have been shown to be associated with deteriorating academic performance, retention in grade, and ultimately dropping out of school. In addition, numerous studies suggest that the likelihood of the student's engagement in criminal conduct increases when they are out of school, as does the likelihood of future incarceration. In these ways, then, zero tolerance policies that are not narrowly focused on serious threats to school safety have harmful effects on students that are impossible to justify.

Finally, the exclusion of students from school for all but the most serious offenses where safety necessitates such removals may in fact perpetuate the very type of misconduct it seeks to deter. Students excluded from school are effectively removed from structured environments supervised by adults with specialized training to promote their growth and development into responsible citizens, the primary purpose for which the system of universal public education was established in the United States. In fact, to the extent that reductions in school homicides, weapons possession, and drug usage at school has declined since 1994, it may be attributed not to the banishment of students from school but to the adoption of a host of school-based education and prevention programs.

3. Zero tolerance policies have actually increased the disproportionate exclusion of students of color rather than reduced educational inequality as the policy's proponents promised would happen.

A claim made in support of zero tolerance laws has been that they would ensure consistent application of school sanctions and eliminate historic contentions that students of color were often disciplined more often and harshly than their White peers. Although seemingly a plausible policy outcome, particularly since possession of a weapon or drugs represents a fairly objectively determinable violation of school rules, as contrasted to a subjectively determined one, this benefit has not materialized. In fact, the opposite has occurred. The number of students of color who were suspended increased between 1992 and 1994 from 113 to 143 students per 1,000, or by 27%, exceeding the rate of increase among White students that climbed from 45 to 55 students per 1,000 as GFSA-inspired zero tolerance policies took effect. The substantially disproportionate rate at which students of color are excluded from school persists to the present day nationally and in the vast majority of states and school districts.

The worsening of educational opportunities for this group of already at-risk students is not attributable to their disproportionate violation of school rules governing weapons or drugs. Rather, it is attributable to schools sweeping within the boundaries of zero tolerance policies a host of less serious, and often highly, subjective offenses, such as "disrespect" or "insubordination." Compelled absences associated with overly and unnecessarily broad school zero tolerance policies unquestionably contribute to the racial achievement gap and the differential dropout rate that plagues not only students of color but also schools, communities, and the national interest.

4. *The extension of the police referral requirement in GFSA to non-weapons-related school offenses, including various forms of minor misconduct for which schools have established means to correct, has devastating and potentially life-long consequences for children.*

As a condition of receiving federal assistance, the GFSA requires school officials to report to local law enforcement or juvenile justice authorities the identity of any student found in possession of a firearm at school. But zero tolerance policies and the extension of the referral to law enforcement provision of the GFSA by local school officials to include minor forms of misconduct at school is creating what is referred to as a "school-to-prison pipeline." The American Civil Liberties Union and the NAACP Advancement Project cite instances where schools rely on suspensions and police involvement, including arrests, to handle discipline problems like bringing cell phones and iPods to school, smoking cigarettes, and skipping class—offenses that traditionally have been cause for a visit to the principal's office rather than to jail.

This "school-to-prison pipeline" has gained national attention as several instances have become highly publicized to show the overzealous application of zero tolerance policies. For example, one student who had been diagnosed with a hyperactive disorder was referred to the police after he told kids in the lunch line not to eat all the potatoes or he would "get them." The 12-year-old was incarcerated for 2 weeks while awaiting trial for making "terroristic threats." In another instance, a 6-year-old Florida girl was handcuffed and transported to the county jail for throwing a tantrum in her kindergarten class.

Although such examples have captured most of the media attention, the involvement of police in the management of minor schoolhouse misconduct is not an isolated phenomenon. In the state of Florida, for instance, the Advancement Project found nearly 27,000 school-related referrals to the state department of juvenile justice during the 2004–2005 school year. Thus, the schools have largely abdicated not only their scope of authority but also their responsibility to teach young children socially appropriate behavior using conventional methods such as denial of privileges, detentions, counseling, and in and out-of-school suspensions of a limited duration. Instead students are branded as criminals with consequences that may be life-long, even though their offenses, such as cell-phone possession, insubordination, or skipping a class, would never constitute a criminal offense if engaged in by an adult.

CONCLUSION

The arguments of the point essay aside, the failure of zero tolerance policies to decrease school violence and student drug and alcohol use, as well as the numerous unintended negative consequences that emanate from such policy making, renders zero tolerance an ineffective and often detrimental approach to promoting student and school safety.

What educational leaders need for all but the most serious forms of student misconduct are more preventive rather than exclusionary responses. School-based interventions are more likely to be successful in promoting school safety than is the exclusion of youth from the one institution where they find structure, consistent adult supervision by those trained in child and youth development, and educational programs that seek to prevent the problem before it occurs or provide interventions to lessen the possibility of its reoccurrence.

FURTHER READINGS AND RESOURCES

American Psychological Association Zero Tolerance Task Force. (2008). Are zero tolerance policies effective in the schools? An evidentiary review and recommendations. *American Psychologist, 63*(9), 852–862.

Baum, K., Dinkes, R., Kemp, J., & Snyder, T. D. (2009, December 10). *Indicators of school crime and safety: 2009*. Washington, DC: National Center for Education Statistics, Bureau of Justice Statistics. Retrieved from http://bjs.ojp.usdoj.gov/index.cfm?ty=pbdetail&iid=1762

Boylan, E., & Weiser, J. (2002). *Survey of key education stakeholders on zero tolerance student discipline policies*. Newark, NJ: Education Law Center.

Casella, R. (2003). Zero tolerance policy in schools: Rationale, consequences, and alternatives. *Teachers College Record, 105*(5), 872–892.

Centers for Disease Control and Prevention. (2010, June 4). *Youth risk behavior surveillance—United States, 2009* (MMWR Surveillance Summaries No. SS-5). Retrieved June 17, 2011, from http://www.cdc.gov/mmwr/pdf/ss/ss5905.pdf

Martin, R. (2001, February). *ABA Juvenile justice policies: Zero tolerance policy report*. Chicago: American Bar Association.

NAACP Florida State Conference and Advancement Project. (2006). *Arresting development*. Retrieved September 2010 from http://www.advancementproject.org/sites/default/files/full%20report.pdf

National Institute on Drug Abuse. *Monitoring the Future study*. Retrieved from http://www.monitoringthefuture.org

Russo, C. J. (1995). *United States v. Lopez* and the demise of the Gun-Free School Zones Act: Legislative over-reaching or judicial nit-picking? *Education Law Reporter, 99*(1), 11–23.

U.S. Department of Education. (2002, July). *Report on state/territory implementation of the Gun-Free Schools Act*. Washington, DC: Author.

U.S. Department of Education. (2004, January). *Guidance concerning state and local responsibilities under the Gun-Free Schools Act*. Washington, DC: Author.

U.S. Department of Education, Office for Civil Rights. (2006). *Civil rights data collection*. Retrieved from http://ocrdata.ed.gov [multiple years comprise the collection]

U.S. Department of Health and Human Services. (2009). *National Survey on Drug Use and Health: Summary of national findings*. Available from http://oas.samhsa.gov

U.S. Department of Justice, Bureau of Justice Statistics. (2007). *National Crime Victimization Survey*. Retrieved May 4, 2011, from http://bjs.ojp.usdoj.gov/index.cfm?ty=dcdetail&iid=245

Court Cases and Statutes

Board of Education of Independent School District No. 92 of Pottawatomie v. Earls, 536 U.S. 822 (2002), on remand, 300 F.3d 1222 (10th Cir. 2002).

Colvin ex rel. Colvin v. Lowndes County, Mississippi School District, 114 F. Supp.2d 504 (N.D. Miss. 1999).

D.K. ex rel. Kennedy v. District School Board Indian River County, 981 So. 2d 667 (Fla. Dist. Ct. App. 2008).

Drug-Free Schools and Campuses Act of 1989, 20 U.S.C. § 1145g.

Gun-Free Schools Act, 20 U.S.C. § 7151 (2004). GFSA originally enacted as part of Goals 2000: Educate America Act (Public Law 103–227), reauthorized in Improving America's Schools Act of 1994 (Public Law 103–382), and again as part of No Child Left Behind Act of 2001 (Public Law 107–110).

Gun-Free Schools Act of 1994, 20 U.S.C. § 8921.

Individuals with Disabilities Education Act, 20 U.S.C.A. § 1415(k)(1)(G)(ii).

Lyons v. Penn Hills School District, 723 A.2d 1073 (Pa. Commw. Ct. 1999).

Ratner v. Loudoun County Public Schools, 16 Fed.Appx. 140 (4th Cir. 2001), cert. denied, 534 U.S. 1114 (2002).

Seal v. Morgan, 229 F.3d 567 (6th Cir. 2000).

3

Should zero tolerance policies be abolished because students of color are overrepresented when schools adopt such policies?

POINT: Spencer C. Weiler, *University of Northern Colorado*

COUNTERPOINT: Luke M. Cornelius, *University of North Florida*

OVERVIEW

As debated in Chapter 2 regarding zero tolerance for drug use and violence, many school boards in the United States have adopted zero tolerance policies in attempts to reduce, if not eliminate, the thorny problems that these policies address. Putting aside, for a moment, the wisdom of such a far-reaching approach and whether it should be reserved for major offenses, courts have increasingly taken a dim view of zero tolerance policies as a "one-size-fits-all" approach to a series of serious problems that do not place enough discretion in the hands of school officials.

Although debates about the future of zero tolerance policies ebb and flow, their implementation has led to what can only be described as unintended consequences. In other words, in the wake of the adoption of zero tolerance policies, the disproportional rate at which students of color, or minority students, are suspended and expelled from public schools in the United States is simply astounding.

As reported by the National Center for Educational Statistics (NCES), 15.6% of Whites were suspended and 1.0% were expelled in 2007. Conversely, African Americans were suspended and expelled at rates of 42.8% and 12.8%, respectively. Moreover, 21.9% of students who are Hispanic were suspended and 3.0% were expelled (NCES, 2010, Table 17b). Taking this one step further, if one filters these data by gender, the disproportionality becomes even more evident. Among African Americans males, 49.5% were suspended and 16.6% expelled, compared with 29.6% and 3.1% for Hispanics but only 21.3% and 1.3% for Whites.

The presence of these striking national data on the disproportionate rate at which children of color are suspended and expelled notwithstanding, the relative scarcity of reported litigation directly involving minority students and zero tolerance policies suggests that the courts, not to mention educational officials, have yet to address the situation adequately or comprehensively. Thus, there is a need to get a handle on the relationship between zero tolerance policies and discipline of minority students in a way that helps both individual students and school systems.

Against this backdrop of data that can lead to divergent interpretations, the point and counterpoint essays in this chapter take different approaches to the appropriateness of zero tolerance policies that lead to the suspensions and expulsions from school of school children of color. The author of the point essay, Spencer C. Weiler (University of Northern Colorado) takes the position that zero tolerance policies should be abolished because students of color are overrepresented when schools adopt such an approach to discipline. He opposes the use of zero tolerance policies not only because of the disproportionate impact that they have on children who are minorities but also because they fail to alter the behavior of students while resulting in higher rates of dropouts, causing even greater headaches for society as a whole. Instead, Weiler suggests that school officials should adopt approaches such as restorative justice whereby students who violate school rules are required to make amends to those they have offended without having to miss additional time out of school since doing so only places them further behind academically, increasing the risk that they will become dropouts.

Conversely, the counterpoint essay by Luke M. Cornelius (University of North Florida) maintains that the high rates of suspension and discipline for minority children are merely the symptoms, not necessarily the causes, of the ongoing social and racial divisions in American society and schools. He argues that even if one were to assume for the sake of argument that zero tolerance policies have some racial effect, this does not necessarily present a valid argument for abolishing them. Cornelius adds that unlike their status generally, courts have typically refused to invalidate zero tolerance policies in the relatively few cases when they are at issue in the narrower context of their application to racial minorities. Cornelius concludes that since the precise reasons for the disparity in discipline rates in schools are unclear, zero tolerance policies should be left in place because applying more traditional forms of punishment may increase the gap in the pace at which minority and majority students are suspended and expelled.

As you read these essays, ask yourself two questions. First, assuming that zero tolerance policies are permitted to remain in place, is it possible for school officials to enact truly racially neutral rules that take no account of race or ethnicity when suspending and expelling misbehaving students? Second, should school boards adopt policies paralleling the approach that is found in the 2004 reauthorization of the Individuals with Disabilities Education Act (IDEA) with regard to minority students? Put another way, it is worth noting that although neither of the essays in this chapter addressed this issue, nor did they have to, the IDEA now includes language directing school officials to develop policies and procedures to prevent the overidentification or disproportionate representation of students by race and ethnicity in special education settings. Would, then, using such a proportional approach in discipline help avoid some of the statistical imbalances between White and minority students that emerge when school officials apply zero tolerance discipline policies, or would this run the risk of creating greater inequities?

Charles J. Russo
University of Dayton

POINT: Spencer C. Weiler
University of Northern Colorado

I will never forget an incident that occurred when I worked as an assistant principal in a middle school in Virginia. The student body was agitated as a result of drug dogs having swept through the school in the morning. By midday, a student had informed me that a peer had cigarettes. I called the second student into my office and asked him whether I would find anything that should not be there if I were to search his backpack. He told me that I would find a gun, and I subsequently confiscated a replica pellet firearm. In the ensuing investigation, I discovered that no student had seen the gun and that this student, who came from a low socioeconomic background, had brought it to school to sell to another student so he would have money to buy his mother a Christmas present. However, in consulting board policy, I saw that I had only one course of action: I had to refer the student to the board for possible expulsion because of a zero tolerance policy related to weapons possession.

Zero tolerance policies were established to promote safer learning environments for students in public schools and were predicated on the ability of officials to remove those who threaten that safety. William Haft (2000) stated, "expulsion is a necessary tool for achieving and maintaining security" (p. 797). Although this point essay questions the value of zero tolerance policies, particularly as they apply to students of color, this is not to imply that educators should treat major infractions lightly. Rather, school leaders "have a duty to use all effective means needed to maintain a safe and disciplined learning environment" (Skiba, 2008, p. 852). What are effective means for promoting school safety?

This essay presents arguments against the use of zero tolerance policies as a way of promoting school safety, and it explores alternative approaches to discipline children in order to empower officials with the ability to educate all students, including students of color, in safe learning environments. Specifically, this point essay affirmatively answers the question, "Should zero tolerance policies be abolished because students of color are overrepresented when schools adopt such policies?"

BACKGROUND

Discipline has evolved from the use of corporal punishment to the teachers determining and administering the appropriate consequence to administrators handling most school-day infractions. As noted in Chapter 2, the practice first surfaced in the 1980s, but these strict approaches to discipline did not gain popularity with America's public schools until the 1990s. The first zero tolerance policies targeted weapons and drugs at school, but they have since expanded to include "smoking, drinking, fighting, threats, and even swearing" as well as other threats to a safe learning environment (Price, 2009, pp. 544–545).

Zero tolerance policies "are designed to suspend or expel students from public schools for a single occurrence of a proscribed conduct" (Haft, 2000, p. 796; Lospennato, 2009, p. 529). These policies are designed to promote school safety and discipline and have "an inherent aspect of absoluteness for punishment" (Hanson, 2005, p. 302). Yet, zero tolerance policies struggle to distinguish between major and minor infractions and, as a result, treat all infractions the same. For example, zero tolerance policies cannot differentiate between students possessing cough drops or cocaine and the threat that nail files and loaded guns pose to other students.

ZERO TOLERANCE POLICIES AND RACE

This point essay now addresses specific items related to the assertion that zero tolerance policies are not only bad for children of color but are detrimental to all students.

History of Discipline and Race

Historically, discipline in America's public schools does not seem to have been meted out equally or fairly. Twenty years after the U.S. Supreme Court's landmark decision in *Brown v. Board of Education* (1954), minority students were 2 to 3 times more likely to be suspended from school than Whites (Skiba, 2001, p. 176; Skiba & Peterson, 2000, p. 339). Were minority students more apt to commit acts that merited suspension or were they being held to a different standard than White students? It is difficult to answer that question clearly now, but the data seem to indicate that a degree of subjectivity existed in discipline consequences based on race.

One reason why zero tolerance policies gained popularity was in response to reports of unequal treatment of students based on skin color. Zero tolerance policies were considered a way to remove subjectivity from the discipline process associated with specific actions. If zero tolerance policies were successful in removing the subjectivity related to student discipline, then its proponents thought that the percent of children suspended or expelled, regardless of race, would be similar across subgroups.

Current Data on Discipline and Race

It seems that students of color remain more likely to be suspended or expelled from public schools when compared with Whites. Table 3.1 reports the percent of students that were suspended and expelled during 2006, disaggregated by race and gender. This illustrates that males and minorities are most likely to be suspended and expelled from school.

The National Center for Educational Statistics (NCES) also reported that in 2007 21% of White students reported being suspended at least once compared with 49% of all Blacks and 30% of all Hispanics (NCES, 2010). Rebecca Gordon, Libero Della Piana, and Terry Keleher (2001) summarized these data by stating, "African-American and Latino students are more likely to be suspended or expelled from school than their white counterparts" (pp. 165–166).

Explanations for Racial Disparities

Ideally, school officials should administer suspensions and expulsions exclusively based on the severity of actions. However, there is evidence to the contrary. Table 3.2 reports the percent of students based on ethnicity in public schools as well as the percent of the total suspensions and expulsions assigned to each race.

According to these data, although children of color make up 35% of the population, 42.8% of Blacks and 21.9% of Hispanics have been suspended as opposed to 15.6% of Whites. Further, although only 1.0% of Whites were expelled, 12.8% of Blacks and 3.0% of Hispanics were expelled. Since the data

Table 3.1

Suspensions and Expulsions Based on Gender and Ethnicity, 2006

Variable	Percent Suspended	Percent Expelled
Male	9.1%	0.3%
Female	4.5%	0.1%
White	4.8%	0.1%
Black	15.0%	0.5%
Hispanic	6.8%	0.2%
Asian/Pacific Islander	2.7%	0.1%
Native American	7.9%	0.3%

Source: NCES, 2006, Table 28-1.

| Table 3.2 |

Suspensions and Expulsions by Race, 2007

Ethnicity	Total Percentage of Public Education	Percent of Suspensions	Percent of Expulsions
White	58%	15.6%	1.0%
Black	17%	42.8%	12.8%
Hispanic	18%	21.9%	3.0%

Source: NCES, 2007; 2010, Table 17b.

indicate that students of color are suspended and expelled at greater rates than Whites, in the absence of evidence that they are engaging in more acts of misconduct, it seems that some aspect of the current disciplinary system results in excessive punishment for students of color.

INJUSTICE IN THE DISCIPLINARY SYSTEM

It is an embarrassing reality that the racial disparity in discipline predates zero tolerance policies. To the extent that zero tolerance policies have resulted in an increase in the overall number of suspensions and expulsions, this rigid approach makes the racial disparities even more apparent.

Bernadine Dohrn (2001) made two significant points with the following statement, "No child should be punished by being deprived of an education; and all school disciplinary measures must be fair, equitable, and individualized" (p. 106). The first point, that no punishment should deny a child an educational opportunity, is explored in greater detail below. The second point stresses that discipline must be fair, equitable, and individualized. Zero tolerance policies fail to ensure fairness for students of color since they cannot distinguish between major and minor infractions.

Looking at the percent of students suspended and expelled based on race and ethnicity, it seems that zero tolerance policies are not equitable. Further, zero tolerance policies fail to consider individual circumstances when reviewing infractions and their consequences. Zero tolerance policies do not allow administrators to explore the motivations of the actions of minority students resulting in discipline.

The purpose of public education is to promote the development of all students "as lifelong learners, ethical and democratic citizens, and increasingly competent, self-sufficient young people" (National Middle School Association

[NMSA], 2003, p. 1). Schools exist to educate children and to provide them with the skills necessary to become contributing citizens as they mature. Schools should not exist to punish students, particularly students of color. This is not to say that school officials should not punish students. Rather, the point is to stress that discipline is not a core purpose of schools. The focus of discipline in schools should be to ensure that all students enter safe learning environments while helping individuals to correct their behavior.

The fact that minority students are more likely to be suspended or expelled highlights the reality that zero tolerance policies are administered inconsistently. What are the implications of this inconsistency?

IMPACT OF RACIAL DISPARITIES
Failure to Change Behavior

Eric Blumenson and Eva S. Nilson (2003) compared zero tolerance policies to triage units attempting "to protect and better educate one group of children by identifying and excising another" (p. 75; Skiba, 2008, p. 852). The underlying premise of zero tolerance policies, that some students must be eliminated from the system, runs counter to the philosophical makeup of most educators, who strive to do what is best for all children. The problem with zero tolerance policies is that they rely exclusively on harsh punishment as a deterrent despite the lack of evidence that they "can prevent the occurrence of school violence" (Skiba & Peterson, 2000, p. 335).

Zero tolerance policies are ineffective at deterring negative behavior because they are inconsistently administered, thereby sending an unclear message that has damaged children. In failing to deter undesired student behavior, zero tolerance policies excessively punish children of color for correctable behavior. Since zero tolerance policies seem to be targeting minority students, "these failed policies are re-segregating our schools" (Lospennato, 2009, p. 541). Rather than working with students of color who violate zero tolerance policies, educators must suspend or expel these children in order to ensure that schools are safe. However, since these policies actually further alienate and isolate students of color, these separations serves as "potential sources for violent conduct" (Haft, 2000, p. 803).

Increased Dropout Rates for Students of Color

Ronald K. Lospennato (2009) reported that one state, Alabama, "has an average of 417 out-of-school suspensions and 7 expulsions every day" (p. 530). The

NCES data average out to 18,493 suspensions and 567 student expulsions daily (2006). What happens to students of color who are denied opportunities to obtain an education as a result of their actions? There is a strong correlation between discipline resulting in suspensions or expulsions and students dropping out of school (Hanson, 2005, p. 330). One reason for this correlation is that students with excessive numbers of suspensions or long-term expulsions are more likely to be retained and struggle on returning to school. Also, if expelled students receive no instruction during their time out of school, then regression issues develop when they return. Blumenson and Nilson (2003) argued that zero tolerance policies create "an alienated, undereducated class that is getting larger, more despairing, and more entrenched" (pp. 83–84).

The irony of zero tolerance policies is that they reverse "long-standing campaigns aimed at keeping children at risk in school" since their purpose is to remove violating students from school (Blumenson & Nilson, 2003, p. 66). This stands in contrast to Chief Justice Earl Warren's words in *Brown:* "it is doubtful that any child may reasonably be expected to succeed in life if he is denied the opportunity of an education" (p. 493). Zero tolerance policies deny students of color opportunities to succeed in life by withholding chances to attend school as a result of their actions.

Zero Tolerance Policies and Intent

Zero tolerance policies fail to consider intent when doling out severe consequences, which is an important consideration in criminal courts. Instead of trying to evaluate the dangerousness of specific acts, zero tolerance policies deny educators the ability to interpret extenuating factors contributing to infractions. As a result, zero tolerance policies deny students of color opportunities to mature in safe environments without serious risks to their futures. The ultimate indictment of zero tolerance policies is that they treat "the most dangerous students" just like "basically good children who have made an error in judgment" (Hanson, 2005, p. 316).

The School-to-Prison Pipeline for Students of Color

One way zero tolerance policies deny students of color opportunities to an education is manifested in the fact that they "redefine students as criminal, with unfortunate consequences" (Blumenson & Nilson, 2003, p. 86). This connection among schools, the juvenile court system, and detainment facilities is commonly referred to as the school-to-prison pipeline (Price, 2009, p. 542). Lospennato (2009) acknowledged that a multitude of factors contribute to the school-to-prison pipeline, but "zero tolerance policies are primary among" them (p. 529). Although the rate of school crimes remained constant for the last 20 years, the number of juveniles referred to the court system has nearly doubled (Blumenson & Nilson, 2003, p. 71).

Costs to Society

Zero tolerance policies result in increased numbers of dropouts who represent a cost to all of society. Unfortunately, students of color have the highest drop-out rates in America (Gandara & Contreras, 2009, p. 29). Avarita L. Hanson (2005) described the costs that dropouts represent as "supporting an unedu-cated, undereducated, or unskilled person" (p. 338). Zero tolerance policies thus deny an education to students of color who make poor choices at school in a way that "threatens irreparable damage, not only to these individuals but to all of us" (Blumenson & Nilson, 2003, p. 68). Instead of educating all stu-dents to become contributing members of society, zero tolerance policies condemn some students, too often minorities, to an inferior life depending on social support for subsistence. This results in a cost to society since individuals who have not earned high school diplomas are more likely to be unemployed, seek government assistance, and become incarcerated (Alliance for Excellent Education, 2009).

ALTERNATIVE APPROACHES TO STUDENT DISCIPLINE

Given the preceding arguments against the use of zero tolerance policies in public schools, officials should search for new strategies to correct behav-ior, ensure the safety of all, and empower students who erred to learn from their experiences (Lospennato, 2009, p. 541). One approach is commonly referred to as restorative justice. By definition, restorative justice "involves changing relationships by engaging people: doing things WITH them, rather than TO them or FOR them—providing both high control and high support at the same time" (Mirsky, 2003, p. 1). According to Haft (2000), "restorative justice principles hold offenders strictly accountable for their conduct while seeking to repair and restore the integrity of the school com-munity after an offense has occurred" (p. 804). Restorative justice requires offenders to make amends to the offended without necessarily losing out on school time. Instead of just removing students of color from school, such as zero tolerance policies, restorative justice encourages them to learn from their errors.

CONCLUSION

The American Bar Association condemned zero tolerance policies "because they replace individualized, equitable adjudications with dangerous, one-size-fits-all sentences of school expulsion" (Dohrn, 2001, p. 106). Zero tolerance policies fail children of color on a multitude of levels and need to be abolished.

In the case of the student who brought the pellet gun to school, he was expelled and responded by eventually dropping out of school. A child with a great deal of potential lost hope as a result of the prescribed consequences associated with zero tolerance policies. School boards would act with the best interest of students of color in mind if they were to revisit these policies, narrow their scope, and seek alternative approaches to discipline.

COUNTERPOINT: Luke M. Cornelius
University of North Florida

There are many valid reasons to abolish zero tolerance policies. One cannot help but despair when reading cases such as when an 11-year-old girl in Delaware received a birthday cake at school from her grandmother. Inside the box was a plastic cake knife provided by the bakery that the teacher used to cut slices for each student in class and then reported the girl for violating the school's zero tolerance policy. This resulted in the girl's mandatory expulsion for a weapons violation. Across the country, in Texas, an honor student and star athlete was expelled after officials discovered a 10-inch bread knife in his truck that fell out of a box of flatware he had driven to a charity the night before and, leaving for early practice at school while it was still dark, had not noticed it. He was expelled and reassigned to an alternative school. In a well-known case in Tennessee, a student was expelled, but did win reinstatement, after a friend, without his knowledge, placed a knife in his glove box. And the list goes on. Students have been expelled under zero tolerance policies for possessing key chains that were deemed "too long" and even for taking weapons away from suicidal classmates.

At least on an anecdotal level, the result of zero tolerance policies has resulted in a parade of absurd and even outrageous injustices that are hard to defend on a legal or policy level. From a purely legal standpoint, these policies all ignore the well-established principle of "willful and knowing" that is required under criminal law to establish culpability for a possession-based criminal offense.

Many, if not most, zero tolerance policies suffer from significant legal and logical deficiencies often to the detriment of justice for the mere sake of consistency. As such, these policies are difficult to justify and even more difficult to defend; this counterpoint essay will not attempt to do either. However, whatever the problems these policies may have, and whatever the valid reasons for their modification or abolition may be, their application to minorities is not one of them. As the above cited instances demonstrate, neither unequal application of zero tolerance policies nor disciplinary actions based on student race or ethnicity are among the legitimate arguments for the abolition or abandonment of zero tolerance policies in America's public schools. To this end, this counterpoint essay argues that, zero tolerance policies are possibly less discriminatory against students of color than more flexible approaches to discipline. It is the position of this counterpoint essay that zero tolerance policies result, if anything, in more fairness to students of color than other approaches.

DISCUSSION

First there is the issue, as raised in the point essay, of the racial disparity in school discipline. Using the same NCES figures, and allowing for the inherent error and completeness issues present in self-reported data, it does seem that African American students are twice as likely to be suspended as Caucasians, whereas Hispanics are 50% more likely. Of course, the problem with such racial comparisons is that they leave out a great deal of information. Should we be concerned that Whites are suspended and expelled more than Asians, a topic that the point essay did not need to address? Moreover, does this prove anything definitive about zero tolerance policies?

Without knowing whether children were expelled and/or suspended under zero tolerance or other nonmandatory policies, it could be just as likely that the rates for some minority expellees are higher because when school leaders are given the discretion over disciplinary outcomes, they are more prone to take harsher measures against students who are not only minorities but who are also disproportionately disadvantaged in terms of social and economic power as compared with many of their nonminority classmates. Again, it seems necessary to remember that disparities in many areas of racial comparison, from test scores to free and reduced lunch, and from the rate of special education referral to dropout rates, are symptoms, not causes of the ongoing social and racial divisions in America. Even if one assumes arguendo that zero tolerance policies have some racial effect, does this constitute a valid argument for their repeal?

Consider, from the research the FBI presented in its 2010 annual *Report on Crime* that African Americans younger than 18 years old are considerably overrepresented in terms of crime commission as well. Consider that African Americans make up 12.6% of the U.S. population according to the 2010 census, a figure that has been relatively constant in recent decades. Yet African American youth account for 31.6% of all juvenile crimes, 51.6% of violent crimes, and an astounding 58% of all murders. Drug offenses are lower, at only 25.6%, but still more than double the African American population. (Note: The FBI does not currently classify crimes by a Hispanic designation.) It can be argued that minorities are overrepresented in expulsions and suspensions, especially for zero tolerance offenses such as weapons and drug, because a significantly greater proportion of these youth are also engaged in related criminal activities. That many racial and ethnic groups are overrepresented in the criminal justice system is surely one of the great tragedies of our nation. Yet, just because an ethnic group happens to represent a greater proportion of arrests and convictions for crimes committed and arrests does not necessarily mean that the application of neutral standards of justice are discriminatory. Under the opposing assumption, schools should only allow minority students into driver's education classes, as nonminorities comprise 92% of all DUI convictions for persons younger than 18 years old.

Also, is it truly discriminatory to apply zero tolerance sanctions more often for serious misbehavior to students of color? Using the same NCES survey as the point essay, it can be noted that African American and Hispanic students are also significantly more likely to be threatened or injured at school and to be involved in fights. Moreover, the same survey actually reports that larger numbers of both of these groups of students admit they carry weapons in school. It needs to be remembered that not only are members of some ethnic groups more likely to commit both specific crimes and the related offenses under zero tolerance policies, but members of these groups are also much more likely to be victims as well. It should be kept in mind that not only are students who are punished pursuant to zero tolerance policies possibly more likely to be members of disadvantaged racial or ethnic groups, but so also are their schoolmates and potential victims. It can be argued that, given the fact that such policies are most often adopted to protect overall student bodies, if anything, zero tolerance policies may actually have the effect of providing more protection for the majority of students of color.

LITIGATION ON ZERO TOLERANCE INCLUDING RACE

It must be noted here again that the mere overrepresentation of a racial or ethnic group does not automatically render laws and policies imposing discipline unconstitutionally or otherwise discriminatory. If this were the case, courts would be obliged to release hundreds of thousands of convicted felons in order to achieve racial equity in the justice system. Rather, as zero tolerance policies are often upheld by courts around the country, the consistent application of neutral regulations does not constitute discrimination merely because they may have a disparate effect among different student populations.

A good case on this general matter is *Vann v. Stewart* (2006) where a student of undisclosed race challenged his 1-year suspension from school for possessing a pocketknife, a fact that was not disputed. The trial court ruled that the school's application of its policy and standard punishment, after two due process hearings, did not violate either due process or equal protection, even in a situation where school officials could have modified the penalty downward. In *Vann*, the student could not demonstrate that the school board had, or would, apply its policy in an unequal manner toward any other students based on any criteria.

An even starker example of the application of a zero tolerance policy occurred in the Fourth Circuit's affirmation in *Ratner v. Loudoun County Public Schools* (2001). An eighth-grader received a note from a classmate who stated that she had a knife and was suicidal. The student was able to get possession of the knife and then, for reasons that remain unclear, put it in his locker instead of turning it over immediately to school authorities. Once officials became aware of the situation, and after searching the locker, they charged the student with violating the school's zero tolerance policy for weapons. Eventually the student was recommended for suspension for the remainder of the school year. A formal administrative hearing and an appeal to the board's discipline committee sustained the suspension under the zero tolerance policy.

The student and his parents filed suit alleging violations of due process, equal protection, and an Eighth Amendment claim of cruel and unusual punishment. The Fourth Circuit affirmed the dismissal of all claims. The court determined that the board's due process, although imperfect in some respects, met the standards established pursuant to the Supreme Court precedent enunciated in *Goss v. Lopez* (1975). As to equal protection, the court agreed that zero tolerance, although harsh, meant that the student had not been treated differently than any other student possessing a weapon on campus would be. Appling *Ingraham v. Wright* (1977), the only Supreme Court case on corporal punishment, the panel noted that the Eighth Amendment does not apply to ordinary school discipline. In one of the most definitive rulings to date on the legality of zero tolerance policies, the Fourth Circuit found, "However harsh the result in this case, the federal courts are not properly called upon to judge the wisdom of a zero tolerance policy" (p. 142).

Similar results have occurred in other challenges to zero tolerance policies in other federal and state courts. Of particular significance to this question would be the federal court ruling in *Fuller v. Decatur Public School Board of Education* (2000), a high-profile case from Illinois in which students from two rival high schools engaged in a violent fight in the stands that was captured on video. One outcome at one school was that six African American students were charged under the school's zero tolerance policy for violence against staff or students, and each was recommended for expulsion/suspension for 2 years in accordance with that policy.

In *Fuller,* a federal trial court denied the students' due process claims since none of them denied their involvement in the fight and all received adequate notice and fair hearing under board policy. Likewise, the court rejected the students' substantive due process claims alleging that their 2-year penalties were too harsh since none of the participants used or possessed weapons. The court pointed out that the discipline policy, of which each student had notice, imposed a separate zero tolerance policy on violence as distinct from weapons.

The most compelling claim in *Fuller* was that the harsh penalties imposed on the African American students specifically denied them equal treatment on the basis of race. Court-ordered discovery established that since the board's zero tolerance policies were established, 82% of all students who were expelled were African American even though African Americans comprised just under half the district's enrollment. Further evidence of the disparity of the application of zero tolerance policies to minority students, in particular African Americans, came from the Rev. Jesse Jackson and his Rainbow/PUSH organization. However, the court, although not disputing the figures presented, decided that the true test of equal protection under the policy was not the frequency with which it was applied to different racial and ethnic groups. Rather, the court viewed the true measure as whether board officials applied the policy equally to all students who were similarly situated. Applying precedent from other civil rights cases, the court reasoned that statistical evidence of disparate rates of expulsion did not alone demonstrate an equal protection violation. Put another way, the court was of the opinion that the burden on the plaintiffs was to show that the school board demonstrably treated minority students under the policy differently than nonminority students who committed similar offenses. The court concluded that since the expelled students utterly failed to establish any difference in treatment based on race, their claim was without merit.

ANALYSIS

It therefore seems that the test for zero tolerance policies, much like innumerable other demonstrable racial discrepancies in schools, is not whether there is a statistically significant effect, but whether a discrepancy is the result of some unequal treatment. In *Fuller* and other cases, this has never been established. If anything, strict zero tolerance policies, because of their inherent rigidity and lack of administrative discretion, virtually guarantee equal treatment when applied according to district policies. This is because, when zero tolerance policies specify single automatic punishments for violating board rules for weapons, drugs, or violence, they ensure that all students, regardless of their race, gender, or ethnicity, will suffer the same punishment for their violation. Zero tolerance removes discretion from principals, superintendents, and even school board members to evaluate whether a Caucasian student carrying a pen-knife can be treated as having committed a lesser violation than a student of color who possessed a combat knife. If individual students of one racial or ethnic background have a greater frequency of enumerated zero tolerance offenses than others, then any discrepancy will be the result of individual transgressions and not attributed to differential treatment on the basis of race.

In point of fact, the individual cases and examples of overly harsh, or even absurd, applications of zero tolerance policies do serve the purpose of helping to establish their racial and ethnic neutrality. With the sole exception of *Fuller,* each example put forth in this counterpoint essay involved children who were either Caucasian or where race was not raised as an issue. However, the fact that the same policies might apply to an 11-year-old Caucasian female with a plastic cake knife as would apply to a 16-year-old male African American or Hispanic male with a more serious weapon serves to demonstrate the inherent fairness of these policies.

When school administrators and boards are allowed discretion in imposing discipline to serious threats to school safety, they are inherently in a position to not only apply their professional judgments to the seriousness of offenses but also to other factors, including their own potential conscious or subconscious bias toward students based on their personal characteristics. Under zero tolerance, assuming that explicit policies are applied openly and in good faith, nonminority students from advantaged backgrounds will receive precisely the same punishment for facial violations as extremely disadvantaged children of color. As previously conceded, zero tolerance policies can be criticized on many levels, but unequal application based on race and ethnicity is not one of them.

This brings the argument back to the statistical assertion raised in the point essay that zero tolerance policies are either responsible for or contribute to the apparent racial and ethnic inequality in student discipline and suspension and/or expulsion rates as reported by the NCES data. The point essay argued that this presents evidence of the racial bias of zero tolerance policies. Of course, it must again be noted that these data cannot be further broken down to evaluate what, if any, effect zero tolerance may have on these variances. However, based on the previous discussion of the neutrality inherent in any strict and inflexible policies, such as zero tolerance, it can be just as easily argued that replacing zero tolerance policies with more traditional discretionary ones would actually result in an *increase* in the disparity between minority and nonminority outcomes under school discipline. Certainly much in the history of America and its public schools suggests that this result is not improbable.

CONCLUSION

In sum, it is important to keep in mind that student discipline outcomes by race, much like many other outcomes such as test scores and eligibility for at-risk programs, are not the result of the policies themselves, but the result of larger and deeper social, economic, and cultural issues that are well documented. Even if it can be shown that zero tolerance policies do, in fact, have a demonstrably unequal application on students of color, it must be remembered that such a disparity is merely a symptom of far deeper and entrenched issues and not an inherent cause of them. There are many good, valid, and even essential reasons why zero tolerance policies should be reformed or rescinded. However, the alleged unequal application of zero tolerance policies to children of color is not one of these reasons.

FURTHER READINGS AND RESOURCES

Alliance for Excellent Education. (2009, August). The high cost of high school dropouts: What the nations pays for inadequate high schools. *Issue Brief.* Retrieved from http://www.all4ed.org/files/HighCost.pdf

Ayers, W., Ayers, R., & Dohrn, B. (2001). Introduction: Resisting zero tolerance. In W. Ayers, B. Dohrn, & R. Ayers (Eds.), *Zero tolerance: Resisting the drive for punishment in our schools* (pp. xi–xvi). New York: The New Press.

Blumenson, E., & Nilson, E. S. (2003, Spring). One strike and you're out? Constitutional constraints on zero tolerance in public education. *Washington University Law Quarterly, 81,* 65–117.

Dohrn, B. (2001). "Look out kid/it's something you did": Zero tolerance for children. In W. Ayers, B. Dohrn, & R. Ayers (Eds.), *Zero tolerance: Resisting the drive for punishment in our schools* (pp. 89–113). New York: The New Press.

Editorial: Zero judgment. (2010, January 9). *The South Florida Times.* Retrieved June 17, 2011, from the Florida Department of Juvenile Justice website: http://www.djj.state.fl.us/zero-tolerance/press.html

Gandara, P., & Contreras, F. (2009). *The Latino education crisis: The consequences of failed social policies.* Cambridge, MA: Harvard University Press.

Gordon, R., Piana, L. D., & Keleher, T. (2001). Zero tolerance: A basic racial report card. In W. Ayers, B. Dohrn, & R. Ayers (Eds.), *Zero tolerance: Resisting the drive for punishment in our schools* (pp. 165–175). New York: The New Press.

Haft, W. (2000). More than zero: The cost of zero tolerance and the case for restorative justice in schools. *Denver University Law Review, 77,* 795–812.

Hanson, A. L. (2005). Have zero tolerance school discipline policies turned into a nightmare? The American dream's promise of equal educational opportunity grounded in *Brown v. Board of Education. UC Davis Journal of Juvenile Law & Justice, 9,* 289–378.

Insley, A. C. (2001). Suspending and expelling children from educational opportunity: Time to reevaluate zero tolerance policies. *American University Law Review, 50,* 1039–1074.

Klehr, D. G. (2009). Addressing the unintended consequences of No Child Left Behind and zero tolerance: Better strategies for safe schools and successful students. *Georgetown Journal of Poverty Law and Policy, 16,* 585–610.

Lospennato, R. K. (2009). Multifaceted strategies to STOP the school-to-prison pipeline. *Clearinghouse Review: Journal of Poverty Law and Policy, 42,* 528–541.

Mirsky, L. (2003, May 20). SaferSanerSchools: Transforming school culture with restorative practices. *Restorative Practices E Forum,* pp. 1–7. Available from http://www.restorativepractices.org

Molsbee, S. (2008). Zeroing out zero tolerance: Eliminating zero tolerance policies in Texas schools. *Texas Tech Law Review, 40,* 325–363.

National Center for Education Statistics (NCES). (2006). *Contexts of elementary and secondary education: Tables.* Table 28-1. Retrieved from http://nces.ed.gov/programs/coe/2009/section4/table-sdi-1.asp

National Center for Education Statistics (NCES). (2007). *Percentage distribution of public elementary and secondary school enrollment, by locale and race/ethnicity.* Table 7-1. Retrieved from http://nces.ed.gov/pubs2007/minoritytrends/tables/table_7_1.asp

National Center for Education Statistics (NCES). (2010). *Status and trends in the education of racial and ethnic minorities.* Table 17b. Retrieved from http://nces.ed.gov/pubs2010/2010015/figures/figure_17.asp

National Middle School Association (NMSA). (2003). *This we believe: Successful schools for young adolescents.* Westerville, OH: Author.

Price, P. (2009). When is a police officer an officer of the law? The status of police officers in schools. *The Journal of Criminal Law & Criminology* (Northwestern), *99,* 541–570.

Reyes, A. H. (2006a). Criminalization of student discipline programs and adolescent behavior. *St. John's School of Law Journal of Legal Commentary, 21*(1), 73–110.

Reyes, A. H. (2006b). *Discipline, achievement, and race: Is zero tolerance the answer?* Lanham, MD: Rowman & Littlefield.

Siman, A. (2005). Challenging zero tolerance: Federal and state remedies for students of color. *Cornell Journal of Law and Public Policy, 14,* 327–365.

Skiba, R. J. (2001). Overrepresentation of Black students in school suspension. In W. Ayers, B. Dohrn, & R. Ayers (Eds.), *Zero tolerance: Resisting the drive for punishment in our schools* (pp. 176–187). New York: The New Press.

Skiba, R. J. (2008). Are zero tolerance policies effective in the schools? An evidentiary review and recommendations. *American Psychological Association Zero Tolerance Task Force.* Retrieved from http://www.apa.org/news/press/releases/2006/08/zero-tolerance.aspx

Skiba, R. J., & Peterson, R. L. (2000). School discipline at a crossroad: From zero tolerance to early response. *Exceptional Children, 66*(3), 335–347.

Solari, F. P., & Balshaw, J. E. M. (2007). Outlawed and exiled: Zero tolerance and second generation race discrimination in public schools. *North Carolina Central Law Journal, 29,* 147–184.

U.S. Census Bureau. (2011). *Overview of race and Hispanic origin, 2010 Census Briefs.* Retrieved from http://www.census.gov/prod/cen2010/briefs/c2010br-02.pdf

U.S. Department of Justice, Federal Bureau of Investigation. (2010). *Crime in the United States, 2009.* Retrieved from http://www2.fbi.gov/ucr/cius2009/data/table_43.html

Wasser, J. M. (1999). Zeroing in on zero tolerance. *Journal of Law and Politics,* 747.

Zweifler, R., & DeBeers, J. (2002). The children left behind: How zero tolerance impacts our most vulnerable youth. *Michigan Journal of Race and Law, 8,* 191–220.

Court Cases and Statutes

Brown v. Board of Education, 347 U.S. 483 (1954).

Fuller v. Decatur Public School Board of Education, 78 F. Supp.2d 812 (C.D. Ill. 2000).

Goss v. Lopez, 419 U.S. 565 (1975).

Individuals with Disabilities Education Act, 20 U.S.C. §§ 1412 (a)(24), 1418 (d)(1)(A)(B).

Ingraham v. Wright, 430 U.S. 651 (1977).

Ratner v. Loudoun County Public Schools, 16 Fed. Appx. 140 (4th Cir. 2001).

Vann v. Stewart, 445 F. Supp.2d 882 (E.D. Tenn. 2006).

Should educators be liable for failing to stop bullying in classrooms?

POINT: Mary C. Bradley, *Indiana University Southeast*

COUNTERPOINT: Jesulon S. R. Gibbs, *University of South Carolina*

OVERVIEW

According to several sources, more than 75% of students have experienced bullying in schools. Statistics of this kind are troublesome considering that peer harassment and bullying can have long-term psychological effects on student victims. Although bullying affects all students, research confirms also that bullies often target students with disabilities as well as gay, lesbian, bisexual, and transgendered students. Moreover, recent student suicides that have been related to bullying in schools have been widespread in the media. As a result, debates surrounding what role educators should play in addressing bullying in schools abound. Several organizations have dedicated themselves to addressing the dangers of bullying. Such organizations include *Stop Bullying Now, The Safe Schools Coalition,* and *The International Bullying Prevention Association.*

School officials play a major role in providing safe educational environments that are free from peer harassment and bullying. In fact, as a result of the failure of educational officials and teachers to act, school boards have been sued as a result of bullying or harassment in classrooms. In these cases, parents have filed claims arguing that educators were negligent in failing to respond to harassment. Other parents have filed suits under Title IX of the Education Amendments of 1972, arguing that school officials were indifferent in addressing the harassment. Specifically, in 1999, the U.S. Supreme Court recognized in *Davis v. Monroe County Board of Education* that school boards can be liable for failing to prevent or discipline known acts of harassment. In this case, the Court found that school officials have clear responsibilities to respond to peer sexual harassment in public schools. Most of these suits, including *Davis,* have been based on Title IX.

In *Davis,* the Supreme Court articulated a standard of school board liability for peer sexual harassment. Specifically, the Court explained that the following factors must be present for school boards to be rendered liable for peer sexual harassment:

1. Appropriate school officials must have *actual knowledge* of the harassment.

2. Officials have to have control over the context (in school) where harassment occurred and the students who were involved.

3. School officials must have responded with *deliberate indifference* to the harassment (e.g., they did not do anything to stop the harassment or their response was *clearly unreasonable*).

4. The harassment must have been severe, pervasive, and objectively offensive.

5. The harassment must have had a negative impact on a student's education, such that it denied a child equal educational opportunities.

As a result of *Davis,* it seems that school officials have a duty to respond to known acts of harassment. In addition to a duty established under Title IX, more than 45 states have passed antibullying legislation. Bullying is related to teasing, taunting, hitting, and other threatening behavior that may or may not be sexual in nature. Unlike harassment, which is covered by federal law under Title IX (1972), bullying is governed by state law. Depending on the specifics of a state's law, teachers might also have a duty to act in cases of bullying. As a result, most school boards have adopted antibullying policies.

Although it is clear that teachers have a duty to stop bullying and harassment in their classrooms, some argue that this duty is above and beyond their call of duty. Teachers should not be expected to respond to bullying if they have had no formal training in this area. Also, some observers contend that teachers are there to teach the subject and not to teach manners or hygiene, or to respond to bullying. Although teachers play some part in these activities, some argue that not all responsibility should be placed on classroom teachers.

In other words, these people maintain that teachers need assistance from parents, school administrators, and school psychologists in addressing bullying in the classroom.

In the counterpoint essay, Jesulon S. R. Gibbs (University of South Carolina) seems to suggest that educators cannot bear the entire burden for bullying, and she notes that from a legal perspective, the standards for finding one liable for harassment are steep. She argues that school officials should be held liable for bullying only when "they negligently or intentionally allowed bullying to occur, or were deliberately indifferent to known accounts of bullying on school grounds." The counterpoint essay states also that "determining the occurrence of either [negligence or intentional] is not easy from a liability perspective." In the point essay, in contrast, Mary C. Bradley (Indiana University Southeast) takes a somewhat different approach, contending that safety should be the first priority for school personnel. She asserts that although it has often been assumed that the first priority of teachers is to teach, parents may expect schools to keep students safe and to protect them from harassment and bullying, and doing so may be a condition of effective teaching.

The point essay also suggests that there should be legal liability when educators fail to respond to harassment appropriately. Although the point essay does not explicitly state it, she seems to be arguing for a less stringent standard for liability than that imposed by *Davis*. Many antibullying advocates would agree with this approach.

This chapter examines the tensions surrounding whether educators should be liable for failing to stop peer harassment. In the point essay, Mary Bradley argues that educators must play a leading role in addressing classroom bullying. She stresses the importance of effective classroom management to help reduce the number of bullying incidents in the classroom. She recognizes also the role that school administrators and counselors can play in reducing bullying. In the counterpoint essay, Jesulon Gibbs explains that teachers are sometimes blamed for failing to stop classroom bullying when often their failure to respond is beyond their control. Gibbs stresses that families, friends, and the community must also do their part in addressing bullying. She notes that bullying often starts outside of the school and then manifests in the classroom.

Suzanne E. Eckes
Indiana University

POINT: Mary C. Bradley
Indiana University Southeast

S everal issues surrounding the education of America's youth stimulate great discussion while also raising important questions. Questions of effective instructional techniques, equal access to education for all children, and the impact of policies such as No Child Left Behind are just a few of the many issues that are discussed. With each issue come numerous perspectives and opinions. It is possible that in regard to educating America's youth, we have more questions than we do answers. Yet, regardless of the position one takes on these issues, it seems that all persons engaged in these debates have the best interest of children in mind. Some people engage in these topics or "pick a side of debate" only because they want the absolute best for *all* kids. They want children to have access to the best schools, the best teachers, the best instructional techniques, and the best of everything to be offered.

Some argue that promoting and ensuring the physical, emotional, and cognitive safety and well-being of all children is embedded within the ideology of "in the best interest of all children." Others might say that promoting and ensuring the safety and well-being of all students is a foundational principle that is assumed in nearly every debate of every topic surrounding children and education. Therefore, regardless of the issue being debated or the side from which a person is debating, everyone would always believe in promoting the safety and well-being of kids. It would seem this is such an "obvious," assumed belief; neither side debates the issue, simply because there is no debate. All persons want to promote and ensure the safety and well-being of children. This issue seems clear and perhaps is one of few issues regarding children and education that all persons can agree on.

However, when discussions begin on the issue of safety and well-being, more specifically, when discussions arise on the context of school bullying, the great debates begin once again. This debate is a question of responsibility and accountability; it is a question of who, if anyone, is responsible for stopping bullying behaviors in the classroom.

This point essay argues that educators are responsible for stopping bullying in their classrooms. There are several reasons why educators are responsible for and should be held accountable for ending this type of behavior; these reasons are highlighted throughout the debate. Dealing with and intervening in cases of school bullying is tied directly to student safety and well-being. As has been mentioned already, the importance of promoting and ensuring student safety, particularly in schools, is one of the few things educators seem to agree on; therefore effectively dealing with and impeding school bullying should be no different.

School bullying can have a direct impact on the physical, emotional, and cognitive experiences of all students. In light of this impact, some professionals believe bullying to be one of many factors that must be taken into consideration when developing plans for violence prevention to ensure safe schools. Educators must work actively to prevent bullying from occurring in their classrooms and throughout entire schools. Yet, when efforts to prevent the occurrence of bullying fall short, it can be hoped, and perhaps expected, that at the least, educators will intervene to stop these behaviors, especially in their classrooms.

To understand the perspective of this section and the position of this argument, it is necessary to specify two points. One, it is important to explain who are considered "educators." In this context, the term *educators* refers to all school professionals employed by and working for the school district, not just classroom teachers. Educators are also school counselors, assistant principals, principals, and even superintendents. These persons each share in the tasks of educating students and creating necessary school rules and policies, and they share the responsibility for the daily operation of a school or even a school district. The collective effort of all these professionals is necessary to teach effectively and impact students positively. The same is true for intervening with a difficult, complex issue such as school bullying. The assistance, cooperation, and authority of each of these persons are needed to deter and intervene effectively when bullying does occur.

The second point that must be specified is the specific context of this argument. This argument relates solely to school classrooms and student behaviors while in their classrooms. The argument is that educators should be responsible for stopping bullying behaviors as they occur in classrooms. This position does not speak to or address student behaviors throughout the entire school; this particular point is a significant component of this argument and must be clearly understood. Some studies suggest that bullying tends to happen in fairly "predictable" locations throughout the school. According to the National School Safety and Security Services (NSSSS), these locations include unsupervised areas such as hallways, lunchrooms, stairwells, and playgrounds. Classrooms are not where most bullying occurs, and significantly, classrooms are, or should always be, monitored by school personnel. Therefore, it is important to specify that this argument addresses only student behaviors in the classroom.

Unfortunately, some students are victims of horrific forms of bullying; some students are bullied on a daily basis. Students being bullied may spend more of their time and energy being afraid and wondering when they will be targeted again. They may become withdrawn and depressed, which clearly impacts their ability to concentrate and participate in their education (Quiroz, Arnette, & Stephens, 2006). In fact, some statistics suggest that up to 10% of high school students drop out of school as a direct result of being bullied (Greenbaum, Turner, & Stephens, 1988).

Students who bully may also suffer significant consequences. Some of these students have been victims of bullying themselves. Aggressive behaviors may have become their means of defending themselves, and the continued use of aggression can lead to more significant consequences during adulthood. Some bullying that goes unnoticed can turn into more violent behaviors such as stealing or other forms of criminal activity (Quiroz et al., 2006).

School professionals may not be able to rid their schools of all bullying. Educators cannot be in all places of the building at all times and cannot monitor students every minute of the day. However, one can hope that in the confines of classrooms, the combined effort of all school professionals will intervene effectively to end bullying in that classroom. Some would argue that parents send their kids to school every day assuming and perhaps expecting educators to keep their kids safe and protected from these types of behaviors. In fact, effective instruction may be a teacher's second priority only because their first priority is the safety and well-being of every student in the classroom. As noted in the counterpoint essay, educators can be held legally liable for negligence if they do not exercise reasonable care in responding to bullying in the classroom. Likewise, under Title IX, educators can be held liable when they are deliberately indifferent when responding to known acts of harassment in the classroom. These laws were necessary to send a signal to educators—that bullying is serious and that those who ignore it should be held liable.

Indeed, there are legal and ethical issues regarding why bullying must be stopped in the classroom. If bullying continues in classrooms, then students are not being protected and they may not be safe. By not controlling and putting a stop to these types of behaviors, educators are essentially accepting violence in their school. If bullying cannot be stopped in the classroom, students may ultimately have more control of the classroom than do the educators. But to keep the classroom "under control" and to maintain an environment conducive to learning, the collective effort of all school professionals is required.

CLASSROOM TEACHERS

When dealing with disruptive behaviors in their classrooms, teachers are "the first line of defense," so to speak. Teachers must be aware of what is happening in their classrooms and must respond to all incidents of bullying. Teachers can work to prevent bullying using good classroom management techniques to create a safe and comfortable environment. They should strive to create environments in which all students are engaged in the learning process, where they feel free to ask questions and especially to take educational risks. One can hope that by using strong classroom management techniques, teachers are working to build trusting, supportive relationships with all of their students.

Creating this type of environment is not always easy and does not happen overnight. Demonstrating effective classroom management techniques and strategies is essential for dealing with bullying in the classroom. Classroom management has a significant impact on students' relationships with each other and with their teacher. It also has an impact on students' ability, willingness, and desire to participate in their own learning. In handling bullying in classrooms, the importance of good relationships with teachers cannot be stressed enough. Insofar as teachers cannot see everything that happens in their room, they rely on students to tell them when they are being bullied or when they know of someone else being bullied.

Student reports of incidents of bullying are very important in effectively dealing with bullying in the classroom. Still, students do not always feel safe in telling a teacher or another adult in the school when they are being bullied. Students may not trust that the teacher or adult will believe their report. Students may also be afraid the teacher will respond in a way that embarrasses them or escalates the bullying. When this occurs, students are victimized even more and their experiences at school can become far worse. The importance of building strong, positive relationships with students cannot be stressed enough. Students need to believe they can trust their teacher or some adult in the building. Students need to know they can talk to their teacher. Students can be the eyes and ears of the school, and educators need the valuable information they have to handle things like bullying. Educators first need to prove they can be trusted and counted on so students are willing to talk with them.

SCHOOL COUNSELORS

School counselors can be instrumental in preventing and intervening in cases of school bullying. Insofar as school counselors are, or should be, student advocates, they have many roles and responsibilities within their schools. This approach provides counselors many avenues for prevention and intervention efforts. First, school counselors can intervene at the individual level. Their training prepares them specifically to work with students who are struggling academically or socially and who may need additional assistance. Therefore, school counselors can work individually with students who have been bullied, as well as with students who bully others. These school counselors can help bullied students to develop coping strategies to deal with this and better focus on other aspects of school such as academics and building healthy friendships. School counselors may be especially helpful when working with students who bully. School counselors can use individual therapy as well as group therapy to intervene with school bullies. They can talk to and collaborate with parents to understand more clearly why these students are acting out and how to help these students most effectively. Using the strengths and skills of the school counselor allows classroom teachers to spend more time and energy on instruction and helping kids academically.

A second way for school counselors to intervene is at a systemic level. School counselors can use guidance curriculum to help prevent bullying. Implementing curriculum to educate students about appropriate and inappropriate behaviors, as well as the rewards or consequences associated with these behaviors, can have a strong impact on the culture and climate of the school. Counselors can implement a curriculum that reaches all students, teachers, and staff and extends throughout the entire school year. This type of guidance curriculum allows for consistent and continual instruction for all students, and may have a stronger, longer lasting impact.

SCHOOL ADMINISTRATORS

Counselors and administrators can have a systemic impact on bullying in many additional ways. Counselors and school administrators such as principals or assistant principals can design school rules and policies specifically addressing bullying. To be the most effective, these rules and policies should be based on specific demographic and social factors impacting the school, teachers, and staff and student behavior. These policies can outline clearly how incidents of bullying are to be dealt with and how students will be disciplined for inappropriate behaviors. It is extremely important that all school professionals be made aware of these policies and discipline procedures. Even more important, all educators and school professionals must uphold and enforce these policies. As stated previously, it takes the collective effort and authority of all educators in the building to deter school bullying. Therefore, the strict and consistent enforcement of these policies, from all educators, must occur for these policies to be effective. All students must be held to the same standard, to the same policy, and must experience the same consequences. The adherence and enforcement of these policies cannot be left to interpretation or be decided on "case-by-case" bases. Students must be able to predict the consequences of their actions with 100% accuracy. Any rule and policy is only as effective as the consistency in which it is enforced.

School bullying can also be addressed specifically in student behavior codes; these codes can, and must, articulate the behavioral expectations of students clearly while on school property. Most schools in the nation already have disciplinary policies to address behavioral misconduct. As the NSSSS notes, clearly stated behavioral expectations and disciplinary strategies can help create a safer and more secure climate. The student behavior code, including behavioral expectations and disciplinary policies, must be given to all students and their parents.

ANTIBULLYING LEGISLATION

Perhaps the most poignant component of this argument is embedded in the law. As the watchdog organization Bully Police USA reports, to date, 45 states have passed antibullying legislation and two additional states seem to be close to passing legislation in the near future. The first antibullying legislation was passed in 1999 by the state of Georgia. Although the specifics of each law vary from state to state, there are some foundational principles on which they are grounded. Antibullying laws presume the state legislature believes a safe environment is necessary for students to learn and bullying can disrupt the environment and impede student learning. Antibullying laws suggest school boards and officials should take every precaution to protect students and all persons within the school building from bullying. In short, antibullying legislation mandates all public schools to establish very specific policies or programs for preventing and responding to bullying. With 45 states having already passed such legislation, most U.S. public schools have specific antibullying policies and programs in place. Moreover, if state legislation was not convincing enough, federal legislation on bullying has been introduced in an effort to ensure that all schools take every precaution for student safety. These laws not only suggest educators be held responsible but also clearly mandate all educators be held accountable for protecting students from bullying while in the classroom.

On a related note, it is not surprising that some states have also passed cyberbullying legislation. Through the use of the Internet, cell phones, and social networking sites, kids and teens everywhere have close to 24-hour access to each other. These multimedia communication technologies provide teens with a means of exchanging messages, uploading pictures and videos to an infinite number of people, all within just seconds. These communication technologies have become a means for bullying, harassing, and even extorting other teens. Classroom teachers will certainly need to address cyberbullying, as often what occurs outside of the classroom (e.g., via Facebook) is discussed in the classroom.

The consequences of cyberbullying have been severe and because of this, many states have passed legislation against cyberbullying. Some schools were quick to address this issue by implementing additional antibullying policies to target cyberbullying. Classroom teachers must monitor the use of technology in their classroom to ensure kids and teens are using such technologies for educational purposes only.

COUNTERPOINT: Jesulon S. R. Gibbs
University of South Carolina

Bullying, unfortunately, is not a novel phenomenon in the daily encounters of school administrators. Taunting, teasing, and ostracizing are perennial student behaviors, but school administrators have long been trained to address such academically, socially, and psychologically debilitating behavior. However, there has been a heightened awareness of bullying in public schools since the school massacre in Columbine, Colorado, more than a decade ago. Investigators revealed that the two students responsible for the tragedy were bullied and decided to take matters into their own hands. Since then, a series of student suicides have shifted the understanding of the prevalence of bullying in schools. Conversations on bullying, such as this debate, exist not because bullying is a newly emerged facet of modern public education. Rather, educators, parents, courts, researchers, policymakers, and society are now much more sensitive to the potential affects and effects of bullying. As a result, a concerted effort has arisen to eliminate bullying, and pressure has been put on the classroom teacher to address bullying.

As attempts are made to pinpoint the causes of bullying and to fashion the best preventive measures, such as the classroom management and instructional techniques raised by Bradley in the point essay discussion, efforts are equally being made to determine responsibility. Experts want to explain why students bully and why interventions and/ or barriers are not in place to minimize such behavior. Unfortunately, fingers mostly point toward educators, while other major influences in a student's development are discounted. Although the actual act of bullying occurs at school, the major underlying causes of bullying often occur away from school. Students experience various emotional and psychological changes in stages that require efforts at school, and away from school. Yet, in modern times, with the rise of technology and communication devices designed to make communication as simple as a click of a button, students are abusing such tools while in the classroom without the knowledge of educators.

School safety, accountability, and responsibility are compelling concerns raised by Bradley as universal values held by educators. However, school officials should not be held liable for bullying unless they negligently or intentionally allowed bullying to occur, or were deliberately indifferent to known accounts of bullying on school grounds. Determining the occurrence of either is not easy from a liability perspective.

The position of the point essay to the contrary notwithstanding, this counterpoint essay argues for limits on school board liability for bullying in classrooms. First, the essay explains the applicable principles of tort law. Second, it reviews a seminal education law case on board liability for student-to-student harassment that is at the heart of the analysis when reviewing bullying. Third, the counterpoint essay ends by presenting a theoretical framework for addressing bullying based on the "social-ecology" of bullying.

TORT LAW AS APPLIED TO BULLYING IN CLASSROOMS

In the point essay discussion, Bradley argues that teachers must hone their classroom management skills so that they can prevent the emergence of bullying. She also contends that state legislators are so committed to this idea that many legislatures have passed antibullying laws. Yet, even though 45 states have passed antibullying legislation mandating school officials to adopt an antibullying policy, such policies generally do not create a right to sue the district if the policy is not implemented properly. Therefore, school officials cannot be liable under these antibullying laws unless otherwise stated in state law. Instead, prior to the passage of actual antibullying legislation, bullying lawsuits were analyzed under tort law and/or harassment law. This legal scheme has not changed. As such, even with the significant increase in attention and effort toward the proper implementation of legislation mandated antibullying and antiharassment policies, most claims against school districts for bullying are brought as negligence and/or harassment claims. The required legal analysis for each follows.

First, a tort is a civil wrong for which a court assigns remedies by providing damages, such as money, for pain and suffering. Tort law is based on the notion that individuals should be held accountable when their actions result in harm to others. In school law, the tortious behavior of school officials is usually classified as negligence, an intentional tort, or defamation. Of the three tort classifications, negligence is the most relied on in civil suits against schools and, therefore, will be the focus of this section.

Negligence is an unintentional harm arising from the breach of one's duty to reasonably protect another from harm. The failure to perform one's duty, such as properly supervising students while at school, creates a breach that can amount to negligence. Four elements must be proven to establish a valid claim of negligence. They are duty of care, breach of duty of care, causation, and injury.

First, the *duty of care* element is established by showing that school officials were responsible for performing an established job function. Examples of the duty of care owed by educators toward students include, but are not limited to, adequate supervision, appropriate instruction, safe facilities, and the duty to warn of known or reasonably foreseeable dangers.

Second, a *breach of the duty of care* arises when school officials, such as teachers, fail to perform any of the aforementioned duties. For example, if students are taunted and/or teased in classroom settings, such actions amount to bullying and teachers know or should have known this behavior but failed to address it properly, they may have breached their duty to supervise and manage their classrooms. It is important to note that courts use a reasonable person standard when assessing foreseeability. A reasonable person is representative of a fictional individual who has the physical, social, emotional, intellectual, and professional competence and experience of the school official in question. However, intelligence, temperament, and memory are assumed to be normal even if a defendant does not have a normal level of either. Courts determine how a reasonable or average school official, similarly situated as the school official under review, would perform given the circumstances, regardless of how the individual actually performed. For example, continuing with the hypothetical taunting and teasing in classrooms, a court reviewing the incident would be concerned with whether a reasonably prudent teacher would have responded to the behavior as the supervising teacher did.

Third, to establish the element of *causation*, the negligent behavior must have been the proximate cause of an injury. Proximate cause is established by showing that a student's injury is a direct result of events caused by school officials. There must have been no intervening events breaking the chain of causation. For example, in the hypothetical based on taunting and teasing in a classroom, a school board is likely to be liable only if the physical, psychological, and/or emotional harm to the student was a result of the taunting and teasing, not some other intervening event such as a preexisting ailment.

Finally, to establish the *injury* element, the student must have suffered from an actual injury to his person or personal property. Negligence cannot be established based on what could have happened. Instead, an actual harm must have been manifested. Generally, claims of bullying are based on the financial costs associated with the physical, psychological, and/or emotional harm to the student who is bullied.

Practically, parents believe that if their children were bullied in school classrooms, then certainly it is only because teachers or some other school officials failed to monitor situations adequately. However, legally, in accordance with the aforementioned synopsis of tort liability, school district liability for bullying is weakened easily when the focus shifts to an actual duty, breach of duty, and causation. It is only when school officials fail to adhere to a reasonable standard of supervision and care that a legal claim of liability can be upheld. Even so, it is possible that teachers may ensure that their classrooms are properly supervised; yet, bullies find ways to taunt, tease, or assault fellow students without teachers' knowing of such behavior. Further, those who are bullied often do not voice their concerns immediately, if at all. Therefore, under such circumstances, it is hard to prove that teachers or school officials actually breached a duty of care because victims had notified them that they were being subjected to bullying.

TITLE IX AND BULLYING IN CLASSROOMS

In addition to seeking a tort-based remedy for bullying, parents seeking damages for acts of classroom peer harassment often claim that school administrators were deliberately indifferent toward known harassment, in violation of Title IX. Title IX is a federal statute that prohibits discrimination based on sex, including sexual harassment. The deliberate indifference standard that is now applied in cases of bullying evolved out of *Davis v. Monroe County Board of Education* (1999), the first Supreme Court case on student-to-student sexual harassment.

In *Davis,* a fifth-grade female student in Georgia had her grades drop, was generally unhappy, and contemplated suicide because of unwanted sexual advances by a male classmate who had a troubled history. The male student engaged in unwanted touching of the female plaintiff and other students while verbalizing sexual innuendos. The student and her parents notified the principal, teachers, and a coach of what was happening. Even so, none of the educators took reasonable actions against the male student beyond threats to do so in defense of his female victim.

The Supreme Court in *Davis* sought to balance the need to protect students against its concern that school boards not be too easily held liable for peer-to-peer sexual harassment. To this end, the Court established a stringent, four-part test to protect both sides of the student-board equation when determining school board liability under Title IX in cases of student-to-student harassment. First, the Court noted that damages are limited to circumstances wherein school systems that are recipients of federal financial aid exercise substantial control over both the harasser and the context in which the known harassment occurred. Second, the Court maintained that judges must evaluate whether school officials, who were in a position to remedy the situation, had actual knowledge of the harassment. Third, the Court indicated that boards can be liable if officials with actual knowledge demonstrated deliberate indifference to the known acts of harassment, meaning that they were informed about what was happening but failed to act or responded inadequately. Fourth, the Court specified that the harassment was so severe, pervasive, and objectively offensive that it prevented the student from benefiting from an educational opportunity. Although the male student was eventually found guilty of sexual battery through the criminal justice system, the Supreme Court remanded the case for subsequent consideration of whether the board was liable for violating Title IX in light of the harm that the female student suffered.

Davis is increasingly applied as precedent in bullying litigation. Yet as with the establishment of tort liability, it is often difficult for parents to establish that school officials knew or should have known about their child being harassed and that school officials did nothing to intervene because these issues revolve around factual determinations. Students who are the victims of bullying are often apprehensive about telling their parents or school officials about the negative behaviors toward them. As a result, school officials often do not know and do not have reason to suspect that a particular student is being bullied. Therefore, they should not and cannot be rendered liable under such circumstances.

THE "SOCIAL-ECOLOGICAL" VIEWPOINT ON BULLYING

Considering the intricate dynamics associated with the cause and elimination of bullying, school administrators should not be rendered liable for the multiple influences resulting in bullying in the classroom setting, unless the elements of a tort or harassment claim can be satisfied. Bradley is correct when emphasizing the importance of classroom management and a commitment to systemic reform to address bullying at all facets of the school system. Student safety, accountability, and responsibility are all valid concerns raised by Bradley. However, the justice system only acknowledges these factors in terms of proving how a teacher and/or other school official failed to perform an established duty or intentionally caused harm to a student for liability purposes.

Unfortunately, teachers, school administrators, and the public education system as a whole are often the scapegoats for community-wide ills manifesting in student behavior at school, such as bullying. The old adage "it takes a village to raise a child" still has merit. Much research has been devoted to determining the correlation between student behavior measured against school, home, and community demographics. Such research garners support because it is well accepted that students are a product of their multiple environments, not just their school culture. In fact, a significant amount of credible research shows that parental involvement is the single most important factor in a student's academic, social, and psychological growth. Even the best resources and opportunities offered at schools do not outweigh the impact of a student's home and community influence. Research has shown consistently that bullies tend to suffer from emotional disturbance, abuse, rejection, aggression, disability, and/or the lack of family support. In addition, bullies are often the victims of bullying, and are thus mimicking their experiences.

Dorothy L. Espelage and Susan M. Swearer (2004) captured the multidimensional root cause of bullying in the classroom when explaining it from a social-ecological perspective. These researchers explained that bullying is manifested or subdued based on the interplay between the web of relationships among students, families, friends, school, and surrounding community. The social-ecological concept promotes approaching bullying by including members of each group that interact to dictate student behavior. Given the interrelatedness of school, home, and community, it is most appropriate when explaining the causes of bullying to assign liability with all contributors in mind, not just the teachers and other school officials—even when classroom management and instructional techniques are taken into account.

CONCLUSION

In sum, even though bullying has been the root cause of too many student tragedies over the past decade, liability usually cannot be attributed to school boards for behavior in classrooms without satisfying the elements of state torts claims act or state and/or federal antiharassment statutes such as Title IX. Antibullying and antiharassment are certainly valid educational policy agenda items. Even so, school boards and individual officials should not be liable for bullying in classrooms unless it can be proven that teachers or school officials acted unreasonably outside of the scope of their duty or ignored existing legal precedent and board policies.

FURTHER READINGS AND RESOURCES

Bully Police USA: http://www.bullypolice.org

Espelage, D. L., & Swearer, S. M. (Eds.). (2004). *Bullying in American schools: A social-ecological perspective on prevention and intervention.* Mahwah, NJ: Lawrence Erlbaum.

Gibbs, J. (2010). *Student speech on the internet: The role of First Amendment protections.* El Paso, TX: LFB Scholarly Publishing.

Greenbaum, S., Turner, B., & Stephens, R. D. (1988). *Set straight on bullies.* Malibu, CA: National School Safety Center.

Hinduja, S., & Patchin, J. W. (2009). *Bullying beyond the schoolyard: Preventing and responding to cyberbullying.* Thousand Oaks, CA: Corwin.

Kowalski, R., Limber, S., & Agaston, P. W. (2008). *Cyber bullying: Bullying in the digital age.* Malden, MA: Blackwell.

McGrath, M. J. (2007). *School bullying: Tools for avoiding harm and liability.* Thousand Oaks, CA: Corwin.

National School Safety and Security Services. (n.d.). *Bullying and anti-bullying legislation.* Retrieved May 6, 2011, from http://www.schoolsecurity.org/trends/bullying .html

Quiroz, H. C., Arnette, J. L., & Stephens, R. D. (2006). *Bullying in schools: Fighting the bullying battle.* Retrieved August 10, 2010, from http://www.schoolsafety.us/ pubfiles/bullying_fact_sheets.pdf

Zins, J., Elias, M. J., & Maher, C. A. (Eds.). (2007). *Bullying, victimization, and peer harassment: A handbook of prevention and intervention.* New York: Haworth Press.

COURT CASES AND STATUTES

Davis v. Monroe County Board of Education, 526 U.S. 629 (1999), *on remand,* 206 F.3d 1377 (11th Cir. 2000).

Title IX of the Education Amendments of 1972, 20 U.S.C.A. § 1681.

Should educators have legal obligations with respect to the prevention of student suicide?

POINT: Nathan Burroughs, *Indiana University*

COUNTERPOINT: Richard Fossey, *University of North Texas*

OVERVIEW

When addressing the issue of adolescent suicide, experts grapple with the question of whose responsibility it is to stop these tragedies before they happen. Among those most well positioned to assist in suicide prevention are parents, friends, primary care physicians, mental health professionals, and teachers. Many argue that teachers may be in the best position among these groups because of their knowledge of and daily contact with students. Teachers, through their normal daily routines, can easily observe and report students who are contemplating suicide. Teachers also have quick access to school counselors or psychologists in educational settings. As the point essay suggests:

> [G]iven the prevalence of student suicide, indirectly addressing the causes of suicide would be unlikely to reduce suicide rates. However, there should be a high burden of proof for holding educators legally responsible for a student's death. Rather, schools should be required to implement comprehensive suicide prevention strategies.

Engaging teachers as the gatekeepers in the fight to prevent adolescent suicide is complicated. Teachers are already charged with various tasks from teaching content to managing overcrowded classrooms. As a result, teachers cannot carry the heavy burden of preventing all tragedies. In fact, courts have not found school personnel liable for student suicide if the educators behaved in a reasonable manner. As the counterpoint essay argues:

> [S]chool leaders should respond reasonably to indications that a student is contemplating suicide based on moral and professional obligations. They need not worry unduly about being sued for damages if a student suicide occurs. In the overwhelming number of cases, courts have simply concluded that schools should not be held responsible for these tragedies.

Nevertheless, some states have created a legal duty for teachers regarding suicide prevention. For example, Idaho has implemented administrative rules including suicide prevention. Under these rules, all school boards in the state must adopt a districtwide policy addressing the prevention of student suicide. Under this rule, teachers with direct evidence about the suicidal tendencies of students have the duty to warn their parents. Similar rules are being debated in other states, a development that may be related to the increasing number of cases involving the issue of school board liability in failing to prevent student suicide.

Indeed, before any individual or group can assume a duty to protect adolescents from suicide, it is reasonable to believe that the responsible parties should be knowledgeable on the subject. Yet, research in Australia, where adolescent suicide rates are alarmingly high, indicates that both teachers and primary care physicians have gaping holes in their knowledge of the demographics and statistics, risk factors, precipitating factors, warning signs, and prevention and treatment of suicide in adolescents (Scouller & Smith, 2002). A related study in the United States polled high school health teachers about student suicide:

> This study found that most high school health teachers believed it is their role to recognize students at risk for suicide. . . . Nevertheless, only 9% of high school health teachers in the present study believed that they could recognize a student at risk for suicide. (King, Price, Telljohann, & Wahl, 1999)

If teachers, physicians, or any other single group are expected to assume a duty to protect students, there is a great need for additional training and education before they can be held responsible for identifying and assisting students who are at risk.

Despite their lack of knowledge and self-efficacy when it comes to student suicide, more than 70% of the health teachers in Keith A. King et al.'s (1999) study believed that one of the most important things that they could do as individuals and the school system could do as a whole would be to prevent student suicides. This way of thinking would be compatible with the educational institution's application of in loco parentis, a common law doctrine that may be made statutory, under which school officials are responsible for acting as parents while children are in their care.

In one study of teachers' knowledge and opinions of student suicide, 56 of 122 respondents, or almost 46%, said that they *did nothing* when they had concerns that a student was suicidal (Westefeld, Jenks Kettmann, Lovmo, & Hey, 2007). This lack of action may be born out of fear, indecision, or lack of knowledge. Even so, this is nonetheless concerning. Unlike with child abuse or neglect, there is no mandatory reporting law for teachers or school officials to inform authorities when they believe a child is in danger of committing suicide. Despite the lack of legal mandate, it seems that the teachers in King et al.'s (1999) study still may feel obligated to take on the role of interceding to help students not take their own lives. With the greater levels of responsibility that come with mandatory reporting, there are also greater levels of legal protection. Insofar as teachers lack this protection, it may leave some hesitant to proceed in uncertain situations.

This chapter examines the tensions surrounding the role of educators in preventing student suicide. In the point essay, Nathan Burroughs (Indiana University) argues that school boards and their personnel have a duty to prevent suicide. More specifically, he contends that schools should "have a duty to implement suicide prevention strategies." The counterpoint essay by Richard Fossey (University of North Texas) examines legal developments on the topic, acknowledging the tragedy of student suicide but explaining why school personnel should not have a legal duty to prevent students from committing suicide. He highlights cases demonstrating that courts rarely find school boards liable for failing to prevent student suicide.

Suzanne E. Eckes
Sarah B. Burke
Indiana University

POINT: Nathan Burroughs
Indiana University

This point essay argues that school boards and educators should assume a duty to prevent student suicides. Philosophical objections to intervening to prevent suicide are not applicable in the case of minors in the care of school officials. Although the counterpoint essay notes that courts have generally refused to find school boards and/or personnel liable for failing to prevent student suicide, rendering educators morally but not legally accountable for preventing suicide would be an inadequate response. Specifically, given the prevalence of student suicide, directly addressing the causes of suicide is necessary to help reduce suicide rates. However, there should be a high burden of proof for holding educators legally responsible for a student's death. Rather, school boards and educators should be required to implement comprehensive suicide prevention strategies.

THE PREVALENCE OF ADOLESCENT SUICIDE

For me, the question of whether school boards and educators should assume responsibility to prevent suicide is not a theoretical one. As a high school student, I suffered from bouts of depression, and like many of my peers, I entertained thoughts of suicide. Although I never attempted suicide, I cannot say with certainty that I might not have done so had I not been referred to counseling. It is only because people that I knew at school—my peers, teachers, and counselors—took an active role in monitoring my psychological well-being that I was able to get the help I needed.

I was one of the lucky ones. Statistics from the Centers for Disease Control and Prevention (CDC, 2010b) tell the story: Suicide is the third leading cause of death among 15- to 19-year-olds. Twelve percent of all adolescent deaths each year are suicides. Yet, this number only includes those who actually end their lives, the "completers." For every completed suicide, there are 100 to 200 suicide attempts. In a survey conducted in 2007, 15% of students seriously considered ending their own lives, what psychologists call suicide "ideation." Of those, just under half (7%) attempted to kill themselves.

If more than one in seven adolescents is at some risk of suicide, it is clearly incumbent on leaders in American social institutions to take the problem seriously. Research suggests that a broad community-based effort is the most effective means of reducing suicidal behavior, whether completions, attempts, or ideations, but educators have a special role to play. Although social service providers, churches, and other community actors should be involved, and parents must be given the resources they require to protect their children's well-being, only schools possess the necessary combination of resources, expertise, and frequent contact with students to pursue an effective strategy. From a practical point of view, enlisting the help of educators is our best means of preventing adolescent suicides.

THE MORAL DUTY TO PREVENT SUICIDE

Clearly, the problem of suicide lies within the scope of responsibility for educators, but should suicide prevention be considered a duty for schools? It depends on what one means by "duty." If "duty" refers to a moral obligation to prevent suicide, then the case seems relatively uncontroversial. Under nearly all religious and ethical doctrines, human beings are encouraged to prevent the suffering of others when they can do so without excessive cost to themselves. Further, even those thinkers who might argue for a right to commit suicide generally concede that others may intervene in an attempt to stop them, at least by persuasion; coercing people from committing suicide is a trickier matter. Although the permissibility of suicide is contested by moral philosophers (Cholbi, 2009), these debates have little bearing on adolescent suicides. Even if suicide is an acceptable response to a life that has become unlivable, and even if it is illegitimate to coerce others in efforts to save their lives against their will, as minors juveniles do not have the complete set of rights adhering to adults. The liberty of minors is clearly circumscribed in schools, where students have limited personal privacy and freedom of movement if it is a carefully considered response to a given situation and with all of the consequences of the act taken into account.

One could argue that, as minors, children are never fully rational, but I do not need to make such a strong argument to defend the appropriateness of intervention. The reality is that many suicides are the product not of rational consideration, in response, say, to a debilitating illness but are the result of mental illness or temporary despair. Many completed adolescent suicides also seem to be impulsive; they are in response to specific events and take place soon after those events (Miller & Glinski, 2000; Shaffer, Garland, Gould, Fisher, & Trauman, 1988). Rational decisions require educators and others to consider the future, whereas suicide in response to ephemera, however painful, is concerned solely with the present. Victims believe that their suffering will never end, when from an outside point of view, others can usually see that it will end. Therefore, even those who take the position that suicide is morally permissible and that intervention to prevent suicide is a violation of personal autonomy should accept that their stance has no application in the case of most adolescent suicides.

This point essay also contends that educators in schools have an especially strong responsibility to try to prevent suicidal behavior by their students. First, there is the question of schools' temporary guardianship of their students. Society in general and parents in particular entrust children to educational institutions for a substantial part of their lives. Often students spend more of their waking hours interacting with their teachers and peers than with their own families. As a consequence, educators assume many of the moral obligations that legal guardians bear toward those who have been placed in their care, including physical safety. Second, the stated mission of school to educate their students requires a strong ethic of care. Education includes academic and intellectual development, but educators have always taken greater responsibilities, including fostering physical, social, and emotional maturity. The survival of their students is a self-evident concern for educators; it is impossible to educate the dead. Beyond this, suicidality is a form of mental and emotional disturbance that not only should be of concern for its own sake, but also it can negatively affect a student's academic performance. Third, school officials themselves bear a responsibility for mitigating the risk of suicide to the extent that they contribute to the phenomenon. Mistreatment by peers, a perception of academic or social failure, and other risk factors take place in the schools, and as a consequence, it is the schools' duty to counteract them.

School officials do have the duty to try to prevent suicide among their students, and there is reason to believe that they have the capacity to do so. To hold school boards and educators responsible for the prevention of suicide implies that it is within their power to fulfill that obligation. Research on suicide prevention suggests that they do have such power. A range of signs indicate that students may be at risk for suicide, and these signs can be identified by educators, such as eating habits, social withdrawal, changes in personal appearance, substance abuse, complaints of specific physical ailments, loss of interest in previously valued activities, boredom, intolerance of praise, and so on (Ayyash-Abdo, 2002). Educators can screen for these warning signs in an effort to identify at-risk students (Prevention Division of the American Association of Suicidology, 1999). Successful school-based programs can also reduce suicidality by improving student coping abilities and providing access to counseling and support (Ayyash-Abdo, 2002; McLean, Maxwell, Platt, Harris, & Jepson, 2008; Shaffer et al., 1988).

THE LEGAL DUTY TO PREVENT SUICIDE

If educators have a moral duty to try to prevent suicidal behaviors among their students, should this obligation also be a legal duty? Moral duties do not automatically entail legal ones. Married couples are morally required to remain faithful to one another, but our society long ago stopped prosecuting errant spouses for adultery. Similarly, one could argue that although educators have an ethical obligation to prevent suicide, they do not have a legal one. Moreover, to date, as noted in the counterpoint essay, courts have been hesitant to lay the blame for suicides at the doorstep of educators.

Aside from the specific legal issues with holding educators accountable for student suicides, there are practical and philosophical objections as well. Although educators can reduce the risks of student suicide, it is not within their power to prevent them outright. It seems questionable therefore to render individual teachers accountable for something over which they have limited power. Exposing school systems and individual educators to litigation for failing to identify suicides could also be counterproductive since there would be an incentive to report every suspicious behavior associated with suicidality to prevent legal fallout. By attempting to treat everyone, regardless of whether they are suicidal or not, schools would not only strain their resources, but they also might miss acutely at-risk students among the flood of suspected cases.

At the same time, to say that there are problems with applying a standard of legal duty is not to admit that there should not be one at all. Let us examine an extreme example by way of illustration. Suppose that a teacher received a note from a student. In the note, the student describes her acute emotional distress and that she is considering suicide. The teacher, perhaps because of a previously poor relationship with the student, does not take the note seriously, throwing it in the trash. The student, believing herself abandoned by the teacher she trusted, then goes through with the suicide. It certainly seems as if the teacher has committed an act of gross negligence. Our intuition is that he should be held not only morally blameworthy but also criminally liable. If we believe that a teacher should face legal sanctions in such a case, then we are opening the door to a school's legal duty to try to prevent student suicides.

The question then becomes where to draw the line. We are rightfully leery of holding educators responsible for the lives of their students, and there should probably be a high burden of proof for an individual teacher or a school as a whole to be held responsible for a student's death. Yet, given the prevalence of adolescent suicide, it seems that educators should be legally responsible if they do not make a good-faith effort to mitigate the risks of suicide. The standard should not be "educators have a duty to prevent student suicides" but "educators have a duty to implement suicide prevention strategies." Ideally, state governments should mandate that school boards adopt programs that can reduce the risks of suicide, provide them with the resources to carry them out, and hold them accountable for implementing them. As the introduction to this chapter indicated, some states have passed administrative rules focused on suicide prevention.

In the absence of legal mandates, reliance only on the moral obligation of educators to prevent student suicides is an inadequate response to student suicide. The prevalence of adolescent suicidal behaviors requires a more direct approach, and schools are the best-equipped institutions to implement such responses. There is ample precedent for legal requirements that school officials address the problem of adolescent suicide. When institutional failure to meet moral responsibilities is sufficiently widespread and results in significant social harms, states have, in the past, resorted to the force of law to change their behavior. For example, private companies have always had an ethical responsibility to limit their pollution emissions and build safe products. The failure of company officials to act properly in a consistent fashion resulted in the adoption of laws subjecting these industries to regulations and legal sanctions. The alarming rate of adolescent suicide presents a similar case with respect to schools. However, in the absence of legal mandates, in an era of budget cuts and increased school accountability, we cannot expect that school officials will use their scarce resources in efforts to prevent student suicides.

THE NEED FOR A SYSTEMATIC APPROACH TO REDUCING ADOLESCENT SUICIDE

A serious effort to reduce the incidence of suicide requires a comprehensive, focused strategy. Unfortunately, currently the temptation is to adopt a reactive, piecemeal approach to suicide. Many school systems and officials are likely to respond to a suicide scare with a single-day seminar for the entire student body (Ayyash-Abdo, 2002), but more systematic approaches are generally lacking. According to the School Health Policies and Practices Study carried out by the CDC, states and school boards provide an average of only 1.4 hours of suicide awareness instruction in high school health classes. Two-thirds of states offer some form of professional development for health teachers and most have funding for mental health staff, but less than half of school districts (46%) offer suicide prevention services. Although health teachers and school counselors may have some expertise at identifying at-risk children, they lack the necessary day-to-day exposure to students.

Students considering suicide are far more likely to tell their peers than adults, but these peers generally adopt a "code of silence" and tell no one (Bloch, 1999). The corps of teachers as a whole probably has enough access to students to identify potential suicides, but the failure to share information about students across classrooms and the inadequate training in recognizing the warning signs of suicidality limits their effectiveness. Also of concern is the lack of training for substitute teachers in identifying students with mental illness. Research demonstrates that "gatekeeper" professional development, including not just teachers but support staff, is crucial if at-risk students are to be identified and helped (Prevention Division of the American Association of Suicidology, 1999).

Any effort to address suicide prevention must also be exclusively focused on suicide. It would be a mistake to rely on treatment for other social ills such as bullying or sexual harassment as a substitute for a suicide prevention strategy. Suicides come from a multiplicity of causes, stemming from psychological disorders, family problems, substance abuse, and social pressure (Ayyash-Abdo, 2002). Employing an indirect strategy for reducing suicidal behavior would neglect a host of other risk factors. It is also vital to acknowledge that suicide is not a simple phenomenon. Completion, attempting, and ideation all have very distinct characters (Bloch, 1999). Although students at the greatest risk of completing a suicide attempt should have the highest priority, the mental health of those who attempt suicide as a cry for help or those who only consider it must also be treated. Focusing simply on those who display signals of acute suicidality would neglect the emotional health (and academic development) of many other students.

CONCLUSION

The failure to treat suicide with the seriousness it deserves may stem from a broader unwillingness to view mental health as an integral part of education. For many years, suicide was viewed as a shameful, aberrant behavior undertaken by the deranged and desperate. Regrettably, for a large proportion of adolescents the transition to adulthood is an exceptionally difficult one. Students often lack the emotional resources and experience to recognize that this transition is temporary—that what seem unsolvable crises today will be revealed as much more manageable problems tomorrow—and fall into despair. Even if they do not reach the point of actually attempting suicide, the pressures of adolescence are sufficient to make many young people question whether life is worth living. That students feel this way is not a failure of these children, but their situation has encouraged them to feel this way, a situation that can be changed for the better. If it were just a handful of students who struggled to maintain their emotional equilibrium, then the problem might not require legal mandates. However, that such feelings are so widespread requires more than waving our hands at the problem. One-day seminars and an hour in health class are not an adequate response to adolescent suicide. Schools should be required by law to do more.

Author's Note: I would like to thank Dr. Danielle Whittaker, Michael Holstead, and Dr. Emily Rouge for their assistance in preparing this essay.

COUNTERPOINT: Richard Fossey
University of North Texas

This counterpoint essay argues that school boards and educators should not assume a legal duty to attempt to prevent students from committing suicide. Although courts have issued more than 20 opinions in cases involving student deaths by suicide, they have found in favor of defendant school boards and their employees in most of these suits. Thus, school boards should not divert scarce human and financial resources to suicide prevention out of fear of liability.

Of course, educators should do what they can to prevent students from ending their own lives, but they should approach this responsibility from a sense of moral and professional obligation, not from fear of a lawsuit. Protecting students from bullying and sexual harassment in the school environment, which school authorities have a legal obligation to do, will go a long way toward diminishing the number of suicides by young people. The point essay incorrectly places the burden on teachers and school districts in preventing student suicide. Most courts have correctly held that educators should not assume a legal duty unless it can be proven that the educator behaved in an outrageous manner and caused the student to commit suicide. To require a legal duty to prevent a student's suicide, when in most cases the suicide is not related to educators' actions, is too tenuous.

A BRIEF REVIEW OF PUBLISHED LITIGATION ON STUDENT SUICIDE

The first suit against a school board based on a student's suicide was filed at least 25 years ago. However, the first court to recognize a cause of action against a school board for a student's suicide was *Eisel v. Board of Education of Montgomery County,* decided by Maryland's highest court in 1991. Here, the father of Nicole Eisel sued his school board for negligently failing to prevent his daughter from committing suicide. According to the father, Nicole expressed a desire to kill herself in front of other students, who then conveyed her threat to school counselors. The counselors reportedly confronted Nicole about her self-destructive statements, but she denied making them. Nicole later died from a gunshot wound, an apparent victim of a "murder-suicide pact" (p. 448).

A trial court dismissed the suit, ruling that school officials had no legal responsibility to prevent Nicole from committing suicide. However, on appeal, Maryland's highest court reversed:

> The court identified six factors for determining whether [Nicole's father] had a viable cause of action: (1) foreseeability of harm, (2) public policy of preventing future harm, (3) closeness of the connection between the defendants' conduct and the injury, (4) moral blame, (5) burden on the defendant, and (6) insurability. (Fossey & Zirkel, 2004, p. 408)

Based on these factors, weighed in light of the plaintiff's allegations, the court decided that Nicole's father had presented a valid cause of action against the school board for his daughter's death. In the court's opinion, "counselors have a duty to use reasonable means to attempt to prevent a suicide when they are on notice of a child or adolescent student's suicidal intent" (*Eisel*, 1991, p. 456). As commentators noted, the Maryland court did not make clear whether the duty to prevent a student from committing suicide extended only to counselors. Neither did the court clarify what steps school officials should take when they are on notice that students might commit suicide beyond warning their parents (Fossey & Zirkel, 2004, p. 410).

Interestingly, although *Eisel* was a landmark case regarding liability for a high school student's suicide, it did not result in a damages award against the school board. At the conclusion of the trial, the jury determined that school authorities had not been negligent in the way they responded to the threat that Nicole might kill herself (Fossey & Zirkel, 2004, p. 410).

In the years since *Eisel*, more than 20 cases addressed claims against school boards arising from student suicides (Fossey & Zirkel, 2004, 2010; Zirkel & Fossey, 2005). Only one published appellate court opinion upheld a damages award against a school board based on the way its employees responded to a student's suicide threat. Even so, the court pointed out that the board was responsible for only one third of the damages (*Wyke v. Polk County School Board*, 1997).

In addition, the Tenth Circuit reasoned that parents of a 16-year-old special-education student presented a valid cause of action against a school principal in New Mexico and a school counselor for violating their son's constitutional right to substantive due process after the young man shot himself in the family home on the same day he was suspended from school (*Armijo v. Wagon Mound Public Schools*, 1998). The Tenth Circuit allowed the parents' constitutional claim to proceed under a danger-creation theory, whereby they could argue that the actions of principal and counselor put the student at a substantial risk of immediate harm.

Specifically, the parents claimed that even though the principal and counselor knew that their son was suicidal, they nevertheless left him at home alone with access to firearms and without notifying his parents.

In most published court decisions, however, courts have refused to impose liability on school boards and/or their employees for the suicide deaths of students. Although a review of all of the student-suicide cases is beyond the scope of this counterpoint essay, a brief review of key case law illustrates the theories courts have relied on to dismiss student-suicide cases against school districts and which support this counterpoint essay's argument that school defendants should not be accountable for such tragic losses. This review of litigation clearly shows that *Eisel* did not increase schools' exposure to liability for the suicide deaths of students, regardless of whether such claims proceeded under common law negligence or the allegation that school officials violated the constitutional rights of the student-suicide victims (Fossey & Zirkel, 2004).

Governmental Immunity

School boards, and often their employees, typically enjoy governmental immunity from litigation as courts have dismissed student-suicide cases on the ground of immunity. For example, in *Fowler v. Szostek* (1995), the parents of Brandi Nelson, a 13-year-old student in the Cypress-Fairbanks Independent School District, sued school authorities after their daughter committed suicide in her home with a firearm. Brandi took her own life after administrators suspended her from school in light of accusations she had sold marijuana to other students. Brandi's mother had begged officials to postpone the suspension until after the Christmas holidays because an immediate suspension would have been devastating for Brandi. After school authorities refused this request, the student took her own life.

A trial court in Texas dismissed the parents' suit and an appellate court affirmed. The court ruled that school employees owed no duty to Brandi after she left the school campus and that school administrators enjoyed statutory immunity for their discretionary actions.

Governmental immunity provides a robust defense to tort claims in many jurisdictions. In this regard, *Fowler* is one of a variety of cases in which courts dismissed claims against school boards and their employees following student suicides. It seems probable that some jurisdictions have experienced no published litigation involving student suicide because plaintiffs' attorneys realized that such claims would be fruitless based on the strong governmental immunity protection that school districts and their employees enjoy in many states.

Educational Malpractice

As discussed in a separate entry in this series, educational malpractice is a cause of action alleging that educators negligently failed to educate the students in their charge. However, virtually all courts have rejected this cause of action in their jurisdictions for a variety of practical and policy reasons. In at least two cases, courts agreed that since student-suicide cases were, in reality, claims for educational malpractice, their cases could be dismissed on the ground that educational malpractice was not recognized in the jurisdictions where the suits were brought.

In *Nalepa v. Plymouth-Canton Community School District* (1994), for instance, a second-grade student in Michigan hanged himself after viewing a movie at school that depicted a young person who had become so depressed that he twice tried to kill himself, including once by hanging. The child's parents sued, arguing that educators should not have shown the movie to their child, but an intermediate appellate court rejected their claim on two grounds. First, the court reasoned, school employees were acting within the scope of their authority when they showed the movie because state law authorized school boards to address students' mental health issues. The court thus maintained that the defendants enjoyed governmental immunity from suit under Michigan law. Second, the court pointed out that the parents were really bringing an educational malpractice claim against the school board in arguing that educators had been negligent when they showed a movie depicting suicide to second-grade students. Insofar as educational malpractice was not recognized in Michigan, the court ruled that this justified the dismissal of the parents' suit.

In *Scott v. Montgomery County Board of Education* (1997), the Fourth Circuit, applying Maryland law, rejected a student-suicide claim against a school board, at least partly because it was grounded in educational malpractice, a cause of action that the state's highest court refused to recognize. In addition, the Fourth Circuit pointed out that the suicide victim had been subject to multiple psychological stresses, concluding that arguing that the actions of the board and school officials contributed to the student's death was mere conjecture.

No Tort Liability for Another's Suicide

An array of courts have ruled that persons simply cannot be liable for another's suicide unless the defendant engaged in some outrageous act that caused the decedent to commit suicide without taking thought of the consequences. For example, in *Corales v. Bennett* (2009), Anthony Soltero, a 14-year-old middle-school student in California, walked out of school with other students to participate in a civil rights demonstration. When the student returned to school, the vice principal called him and three other student truants to his office. One student who attended this meeting said that the vice principal referred to the students as "dumb, dumb, and dumber" and threatened them with the possibility of police involvement, a $250 fine, and juvenile hall detention (p. 560). The vice principal also reportedly told them that they would all lose one school privilege, such as a school dance or a trip to Disneyland.

Apparently, the suicidal student was upset by the meeting with the vice principal because he had been in trouble at school before and was on probation for carrying a knife to school. Anthony's mother testified that a truancy conviction could have meant that he would spend 3 years in jail. Nevertheless, the student went back to class after his meeting with the vice principal and returned home at the end of the school day. Later in the day, the student talked by telephone with his mother about the truancy incident, but he said nothing that made her worry about his safety. About an hour after this telephone conversation, Anthony's mother returned home to find that he had shot himself. He died later that evening, leaving a suicide note.

Anthony's parents sued, but a federal trial court dismissed the suit. On appeal, the Ninth Circuit affirmed, dismissing both constitutional claims and state-law tort claims. As to the parents' negligence claim, the Ninth Circuit ruled that a defendant cannot be liable for another's suicide under California law "where the negligent wrong only causes a mental condition in which the injured person is able to realize the nature of the act of suicide and has the power to control it if he so desires" (*Corales v. Bennett*, 2009, p. 572). In such circumstances, the court explained that suicide "becomes an independent intervening force and the wrongdoer cannot be held liable for the death" (p. 572, internal citation omitted). In the Ninth Circuit's view, Anthony had an opportunity to appreciate the nature of his actions before he made the decision to commit suicide. The court pointed out that Anthony returned to class after his meeting with the vice principal, talked with his mother on the telephone, and wrote a detailed suicide note before he shot himself. The court observed that since Anthony had the opportunity to appreciate the nature of his own actions, school authorities could not be liable for his decision to take his own life.

The Supreme Court of New Hampshire reached a similar result in *Mixell v. School Administrative Unit No. 33* (2009). In this case, the mother of a seventh-grade student sued a school board and two of its employees after her son Joshua committed suicide by hanging. Approximately 2 months before he took his own life, Joshua told a teacher's aide that he "wanted to blow his brains out"

(p. 1053). The aide reported Joshua's statement to a counselor who had him sign a "contract for safety." The counselor called Joshua's mother and told her what her son had said, but the counselor reassured the mother that he was "okay now" and reportedly did not tell her about the safety contract (p. 1053). Two months later, the student was suspended from school for some minor disciplinary infractions and committed suicide by hanging that evening.

After a trial court dismissed the mother's suit, the Supreme Court of New Hampshire affirmed in its favor. As a general rule, the court stated, suicide is considered a deliberate, intentional, and intervening act, for which a third party cannot be held liable in negligence. The court noted two exceptions. First, an individual (or institution) can be liable for another person's suicide if the defendant (or its employees) intentionally engages in outrageous conduct that causes the decedent to have an "uncontrollable impulse to commit suicide" or prevents the decedent from realizing the nature of his suicidal act (p. 1054). Second, a defendant may be liable for an individual's suicide if the defendant was in a special relationship with the suicide victim and breaches a specific duty of care—usually a duty imposed through a custodial relationship like a prison or hospital setting.

In the opinion of the Supreme Court of New Hampshire, since neither exception applied to the facts of the case before it, the school board and its employees were not liable for Joshua's decision to take his life. According to the court, nothing that school officials had done rose to a level of outrageous behavior that would make them legally responsible for Joshua's death. In addition, the court was of the view that Joshua was not in a custodial relationship with school authorities that would have imposed a special duty of care on them to provide for his physical safety.

SCHOOLS HAVE A MORAL RESPONSIBILITY TO PREVENT STUDENT SUICIDE, NOT A LEGAL DUTY

In the years since the Maryland Supreme Court's decision in *Eisel*, most courts have ruled that school boards, and their employees, generally have no legal responsibility to prevent students from committing suicide. These courts entered judgments in favor of school boards on a variety of grounds: governmental immunity; the conclusion that the plaintiffs' claims amount to educational malpractice, a much disfavored cause of action; or that defendants cannot be liable for the suicides of others as a matter of law absent some outrageous conduct.

Of course, professional educators have a legal and moral duty to try to prevent a student from committing suicide if they know the student is a suicide threat. At a minimum, school authorities should alert parents if a student exhibits any suicidal behavior.

In addition, school officials have a legal responsibility to protect students from bullying and sexual harassment since strict attention to this legal duty will probably help reduce the number of student suicides. For example, in a 2010 case involving the suicide death of a first-year college student, a federal trial court in New York ruled that the student's mother stated a cause of action for violation of Title IX (20 U.S.C. § 1681) based on allegations that administrators at the private college acted with "deliberate indifference" to the student's report of being gang raped in a college residence hall (Fossey, 2010; *McGrath v. Dominican College*, 2009). Also, in a highly publicized case involving the suicide of a Massachusetts high school girl, questions were raised with regard to whether school authorities took appropriate action to protect her from pervasive and vicious bullying by fellow students (Eckholm & Zezima, 2010). Thus, school boards, and their employees, might be liable for not meeting legal obligations to protect students from sexual harassment or bullying if educators failed to come to the victims' aid and they committed suicide.

In short, school leaders should respond reasonably to indications that students are contemplating suicide based on moral and professional obligations. School boards and educators need not worry unduly about being sued for damages if a student suicide occurs. In the overwhelming number of cases, courts have simply concluded that school boards and educators should not be responsible for these tragedies. Although the point essay makes several compelling arguments about the important role school personnel can play in suicide prevention, educators simply cannot be expected to anticipate and be liable for this type of school tragedy.

Further Readings and Resources

Ayyash-Abdo, H. (2002). Adolescent suicide: An ecological approach. *Psychology in Schools, 39*, 459–475.

Bloch, D. S. (1999). Adolescent suicide as a public health threat. *Journal of Child and Adolescent Psychiatric Nursing, 13*, 26–38.

Centers for Disease Control and Prevention. (2010a). *School health policies and practices.* Atlanta, GA: U.S. Department of Health and Human Services.

Centers for Disease Control and Prevention. (2010b). *Suicide prevention.* Retrieved July 1, 2010, from http://www.cdc.gov/violenceprevention/suicide

Cholbi, M. (2008, July 29). Suicide. In E. N. Zalta (Ed.), *The Stanford encyclopedia of philosophy* (Fall 2009 ed.). Retrieved July 1, 2010, from http://plato.stanford.edu/entries/suicide

Eckholm, E., & Zezima, K. (2010, April 2). Questions for schools on bullying and suicide. *The New York Times,* Section A, p. 1.

Fossey, R. (2010, April 5). *McGrath v. Dominican College:* Deliberate indifference to gang rape in a college residence hall may violate Title IX. *Teachers College Record.* ID Number: 15942. Available from http://www.tcrecord.org

Fossey, R., & Zirkel, P. A. (2004). Liability for a student suicide in the wake of *Eisel. Texas Wesleyan Law Review, 10,* 403–439.

Fossey, R., & Zirkel, P. A. (2010, January 11). Student suicide and the law: The courts are reluctant to hold school districts and their employees liable. *Teachers College Record.* ID Number: 15893. Available from http://www.tcrecord.org

Hartmeister, F., & Fix-Turkowski, V. (2005). Getting even with schoolyard bullies: Legislative responses to campus provocateurs. *West's Education Law Reporter, 195,* 1–29.

King, K. A., Price, J. H., Telljohann, S. K., & Wahl, J. (1999). High school health teachers' perceived self-efficacy in identifying students at risk for suicide. *The Journal of School Health, 69*(5), 202–207.

McLean, J., Maxwell, M., Platt, S., Harris, F., & Jepson, R. (2008). *Risk and protective factors for suicide and suicidal behavior: A literature review.* Retrieved June 17, 2011, from http://www.scotland.gov.uk/Publications/2008/11/28141444/0

Miller, A., & Glinski, J. (2000). Youth suicidal behavior: Assessment and intervention. *Journal of Clinical Psychology, 56,* 1131–1152.

Prevention Division of the American Association of Suicidology. (1999). *Guidelines for school based suicide prevention programs.* Retrieved June 17, 2011, from http://www.sprc.org/library/aasguide_school.pdf

Scouller, K. M., & Smith, D. I. (2002). Prevention of youth suicide: How well informed are the potential gatekeepers of adolescents in distress? *Suicide and Life-Threatening Behavior, 32,* 67–79.

Shaffer, D., Garland, A., Gould, M., Fisher, P., & Trauman, P. (1988). Preventing teenage suicide: A critical review. *Journal of the American Academy of Child and Adolescent Psychiatry, 27,* 675–687.

Westefeld, J. S., Jenks Kettmann, J. D., Lovmo, C., & Hey, C. (2007). High school suicide: Knowledge and opinions of teachers. *Journal of Loss and Trauma, 12,* 31–42.

Zirkel, P. A., & Fossey, R. (2005). Liability for student suicide. *West's Education Law Reporter, 197,* 489–497.

Court Cases and Statutes

Armijo v. Wagon Mound Public Schools, 159 F.3d 1253 (10th Cir. 1998).

Corales v. Bennett, 567 F.3d 554 (9th Cir. 2009).

Eisel v. Board of Education of Montgomery County, 324 Md. 376, 597 A.2d 447 (1991).

Fowler v. Szostek, 905 S.W.2d 336 (C.A. Tx., 1st Dist. 1995).

McGrath v. Dominican College, 672 F. Supp. 2d 477 (S.D.N.Y. 2009).

Mixell v. School Administrative Unit No. 33, 972 A.2d 1050 (N.H. 2009).

Nalepa v. Plymouth-Canton Community School District, 525 N.W.2d 897 (Mich. Ct. App. 1994).

Scott v. Montgomery County Board of Education, 1997 WL 457521 (4th Cir. 1997).

Title IX of the Education Amendments of 1972, 20 U.S.C. § 1681.

Wyke v. Polk County School Board, 129 F.3d 560 (11th. Cir. 1997).

6

Must teachers report all suspicions of child abuse and neglect?

POINT: Susan C. Bon, *George Mason University*

COUNTERPOINT: Stephanie D. McCall, *Teachers College, Columbia University*

OVERVIEW

Sadly, one of the best kept dirty secrets in many communities in the United States continues to be child abuse and neglect. Child abuse and neglect combine to inflict immeasurable harm on children since such mistreatment, typically at the hands of loved ones, impacts their emotional, academic, social, and personal growth typically at a time when they are in school trying to develop normally like their peers.

Amazingly, as of 1963, no states had enacted child abuse reporting laws. However, Dr. C. Henry Kempe's seminal 1963 article, the first publication to use the term "battered child syndrome," created a medical profile of child abuse that served as the harbinger for a torrent of legislative activity at the state level. Also in 1963, the Children's Bureau of the National Center on Child Abuse and Neglect prepared the first model statute mandating the reporting of child abuse. Still, this model law limited the duty to physicians who were obliged to report suspected cases or face possible criminal sanctions.

As of 1967, all states had child abuse reporting laws in effect patterned after the model federal law. Further, by the early 1970s, most states had expanded the mandatory list of reporters of suspected child abuse and neglect to include teachers and other educators (Toth Johns, 2004). Good faith child abuse and neglect reporting is now a mandatory duty in all jurisdictions for educators and an array of professionals who interact with school children regularly.

The U.S. Congress enacted the first federal law on point, the Child Abuse Prevention and Treatment Act of 1974 (CAPTA), most recently reauthorized as the Keeping Children and Families Safe Act of 2003. CAPTA suggested standardized procedures for child abuse reporting and investigating while providing federal funds to ensure compliance with its provisions. As part of the 1988 reauthorization of CAPTA, Congress created the National Center on Child Abuse and Neglect, as well as an advisory board, task force, and national clearinghouse of information. CAPTA continues to offer grant programs designed to ensure that federal funds are available for research and to develop programs focused on the prevention and treatment of child abuse and neglect.

In Chapter 3 of its most recent report, based on data from 2008, the U.S. Department of Health and Human Services, Children's Bureau report of 2009 estimated that 772,000 or 20.9% of the more than 3.7 million children who were subjects of child abuse investigations or assessments were victims of "maltreatment." Although the victimization rate of 10.3 per 1,000 children in the population was similar to the previous year's rate, the report indicated that this was the lowest that it has been in the previous five years. Sadly, though, Chapter 4 of the report estimated that there were 1,740 childhood fatalities in 2008 resulting from abuse, and of those, 79.8% were younger than age 4.

Child abuse reporting laws have assumed center stage when coupled with high-profile cases such as occurred in New York City in 1987 when attorney Joel Steinberg murdered his unlawfully adopted 6-year-old daughter, Lisa; he also physically and emotionally abused his live-in companion, Hedda Nussbaum (Weithorn, 2001). What made this case even more tragic was that an array of the child's teachers, neighbors, and doctors observed her battered state but failed to report her condition. Horrific circumstances such as these can strengthen the support for mandatory reporting. However, even if educators mistakenly report child abuse and/or neglect, they are shielded from legal liability if they can demonstrate that they acted in good faith. School boards should provide annual sessions at which teachers and other staff are updated on how to recognize the signs of abuse and neglect so that they can fulfill their statutory duties. (Not all state laws make it mandatory.)

Because educators fear liability if they fail to report suspected cases of abuse and neglect, there may be concern that they will make erroneous good faith reports that actually harm families. For example, they may incorrectly assume that there has been abuse of children with disabilities who are awkward or bruise easily; and even with less vulnerable children, they may mistakenly suspect abuse when there are apparently unexplained bruises. On these occasions, parents are anecdotally forced to face a veritable gauntlet of dirty looks and probing questions from educators who are asking, actually demanding, that they explain how or why it is that their children have been injured. Thus, it is important to find a balance—educators must fulfill the responsibility to engage in good faith reporting while not overstepping the boundaries that protect familial privacy.

Against this backdrop, the two essays in this chapter examine the status of teachers as mandated reporters of child abuse and neglect. In the point essay, Susan C. Bon (George Mason University) focuses on the reality that insofar as teachers are in regular contact with students, they are in a key position to observe whether the children in their care are being abused or neglected. In light of the far-reaching harms that children who are abused and neglected experience, combined with their daily contact with teachers, Bon maintains that educators should report all cases of suspected harm to their students. Conversely, in the counterpoint essay, Stephanie D. McCall (Teachers College, Columbia University) raises some red flags about the challenges associated with mandatory reporting laws but clearly does not call for teachers to be silent. Rather, in light of concerns that McCall voices, such as whether teachers really understand what is involved in reporting, she concludes that perhaps it is best that teachers not be required to report all suspected cases of abuse and neglect even as society looks to do even more to protect children from abuse and neglect.

As you read these debates, ask yourself three questions. First, should educators be responsible for reporting all good faith cases of suspected abuse? Put another way, since teachers are mandated reporters, but are not investigators, to what extent should they look into suspected cases of abuse and neglect before filing reports? Second, given their potential liability if they fail to file reports, should teachers accept seemingly legitimate explanations from parents about how their children may have been bruised or other signs of possible abuse? Third, should school boards be permitted to establish policies directing teachers to report suspected cases of child abuse or neglect to administrators or counselors, rather than to state agencies as they are ordinarily required to do, who are then charged with the ultimate duty to decide whether reports should be filed?

Charles J. Russo
University of Dayton

POINT: Susan C. Bon
George Mason University

Child abuse and neglect constitute a social epidemic that jeopardizes the welfare and safety of children while negatively impacting their chances to learn, grow, and pursue the joys and opportunities of life. Child abuse is generally defined as an action taken against a child that includes physical, sexual, or emotional maltreatment. Neglect, however, is defined as the failure to act on behalf of a child and may result in physical or emotional neglect, such as medical neglect, lack of proper supervision, educational neglect, or the lack of affection necessary to promote psychological and social development. Because parents have a fundamental right to raise their children, ideally they are the primary protectors of their children as well. Yet, statistics reveal that approximately 80% of the perpetrators of abuse and neglect are parents. Given this alarming fact, children must rely on the caring intervention of outsiders, especially professionals such as teachers, who have a direct and ongoing presence in their daily lives.

The short- and long-term effects of abuse and neglect can be devastating to children and families. Children who suffer from abuse and neglect show immediate signs of distress, including high rates of anxiety, eating disorders, suicidal thoughts, behavioral problems in school, low test scores, and poor relationships with peers. The long-term effects of abuse and neglect may not be immediately apparent, but they are found to impact abused children as they become adults. These long-term effects of abuse and neglect include poor adult health, unstable personal relationships, economic hardship, and a high risk of engaging in violent offenses. Children who are neglected by their parents are also more likely to have criminal records as adults.

The negative impacts of abuse are slightly different when children are sexually abused; and for males especially, childhood sexual abuse is significantly related to later sexual offenses against children, such as child molestation. Children who are sexually abused also have higher rates of drug and alcohol abuse. Overall, the negative effects of child abuse and neglect are long-lasting and significantly affect not only the future generations of children but all members of society who may come into contact with an adult who was abused or neglected as a child. Child abuse and neglect are especially insidious crimes in society because of the overwhelming likelihood that future generations of children will suffer as the cycle of abuse continues.

Federal and state efforts to end child abuse are contingent on the collective efforts of individuals who are regularly responsible in their professional roles for the care, nurture, protection, and education of children. Some may dispute whether teachers should be included in the group of professionals charged with such an important role in the battle against child abuse. The source of disagreement over the inclusion of teachers as mandatory reporters often emerges from educators who express frustration because they believe they are ill-equipped and insufficiently trained to undertake such an important role. Teachers may also argue that their primary focus is on educating the child, and thus other professionals, such as school psychologists, guidance counselors, or others outside of school professionals, are better situated and trained to report child abuse and neglect. Although there may be merit to these concerns, the victimization of children who suffer abuse and neglect has such severe and long-lasting effects, it can only be eradicated through the collaborative and focused efforts of multiple professional groups, including school employees, educators, child care providers, mental health personnel, medical personnel, law enforcement, legal professionals, and social services personnel. Thus, this point essay argues that teachers should report all cases of suspected child abuse and neglect.

TEACHERS AS REPORTERS

Teachers provide an important front line of defense for children who suffer from abuse and neglect. In light of their daily interactions with children, teachers are in a unique position to recognize abuse and neglect as they intervene on behalf of abused or neglected children. Although teachers are primarily responsible for educating and engaging their students in the learning process, teaching is an inherently moral endeavor. Education is and has long been viewed as a key to future success in life. Not only do teachers work with children, who are vulnerable members of society, but they also provide them with the knowledge and skills to help them develop and prepare for adulthood.

Given the importance of education and its role as a critical foundation for full engagement in American society, there truly is a moral imperative to provide all children with equal educational opportunities. Compulsory attendance laws established the critical importance of education and mandated school attendance for all children. Consequently, teachers have regular interactions with children and are likely to be one of the first adults to notice whether a child's physical or emotional well-being is at risk. The vigilant and attentive efforts of educators are important to the well-being of children who are victims of abuse and neglect.

As noted, children often suffer both short- and long-term effects from the serious physical and emotional harms of abuse and neglect. When children are abused or neglected, they experience significant barriers to learning. Child abuse and neglect not only inflict harmful physical and emotional pain on children, but also they impose considerable limitations on the educational achievement of children because of these barriers to learning. These barriers to learning are exhibited as behavioral problems such as extreme withdrawal or aggression, unusual shyness, wariness of physical contact, and harsh treatment of other children. Abused children are also likely to experience higher rates of truancy, depression, and excessive crying.

Teachers are an important part of the ongoing efforts to end child abuse and may be a child's only hope of ending the maltreatment. Children often hide their injuries, making it all the more difficult to detect child abuse, especially for individuals who have infrequent contact with the children. This, in part, is why teachers and school officials, who interact on an almost daily basis with children, are so important to child abuse prevention efforts.

Teachers are responsible for enhancing the educational opportunities of children and are often provided with specific training so they can help students overcome academic, physical, and even emotional barriers to learning. This training might include the use of positive behavioral supports, response to intervention methods, or other such specialized training that will provide educators with the necessary skills and knowledge to fulfill the mandates of the Individuals with Disabilities Education Act and to ensure the unique needs of students with disabilities are addressed. Teachers should likewise be trained to identify and report suspected child abuse and neglect because the educational opportunities of students are also impeded significantly as a result of the trauma and residual effects of abuse and neglect.

IDENTIFYING AND PREVENTING CHILD ABUSE

Preventing and ending child abuse and neglect is viewed as a community responsibility. Mandatory reporting laws reflect the notion that prevention of child abuse and neglect is most likely to be achieved through the shared responsibility of multiple professional groups, including school employees, educators, child care providers, mental health personnel, medical personnel, law enforcement and other legal professionals, and social services personnel. Over the past 5 decades, state and federal efforts to end child abuse have increased. Child Protective Services (CPS) agencies have established two stages for responding to child abuse and neglect allegations. The first is the receipt of a referral from a professional or another person in the community. Without this initial referral, a CPS agency is unlikely to be aware of a child's plight and, as a result, the abuse or neglect may continue. Once the initial notification has been made to CPS staff alleging abuse or neglect of one or more children, the second stage of response to child abuse involves trained CPS employees who are responsible for conducting full investigations into the alleged abuse and neglect.

As indicated earlier, child abuse may be physical and emotional. Accordingly, teachers should be careful to notice physical signs of abuse such as unexplained or repeated bruising to the face, throat, upper arms, thighs, bottom, or back. When the pattern or shape of bruises is unusual, such as pinch or strap marks, this may signify abuse rather than typical childhood injuries. Unexplained cigarettes burns or rope burns may also be evidence of child abuse. Teachers should further be aware of unexplained repeated injuries, including lacerations, welts, scars, rib fractures, joint fractures, loss of hair, or bald patches.

Abused children frequently attempt to hide their injuries or make up unbelievable explanations. Although some victims may disclose sexual abuse, since not all children do, educators should be alert to the unique indicators of sexual abuse. For example, children who suffer from sexual abuse are likely to have poor peer relationships, sudden changes in behavior and grades, promiscuity or seductive behavior, age-inappropriate expressions of affection, and self-injury. Children younger than 6 years of age are at a higher risk of physical abuse, but the majority of reported sexual abuse cases involve adult or teenage males and underage females younger than 18.

Not only should teachers be aware of physical indicators of abuse, but they should also recognize that children who are abused are likely to exhibit behavioral problems. These problems may appear even when no physical evidence is observed. In addition, teachers may be inclined to think that aggressive or defiant behaviors occur simply because the child is deliberately being difficult or is just a "bad kid." Although these behaviors are not always indicators of abuse and neglect, teachers should consider the possibility that disruptive children are crying out for help or trying to draw attention to their abuse or neglect. Finally, when children exhibit a number of behavioral problems, they are less likely to be actively engaged in learning.

Abuse in schools is another source of child abuse that teachers are in an especially unique position to observe and discover. Child abuse in schools may include excessive physical discipline, such as severe bruising, physical injuries to sensitive locations, inconsistent and arbitrary punishment designed to instill fear, and unreasonable or inappropriate physical discipline given the child's age. When physical force is used by teachers with the purpose of instilling fear or out of anger and a loss of control, educators may have committed child abuse. Sexual abuse in schools may be an infrequent occurrence, but as a form of child abuse, it must be reported when a teacher has reason to believe that another teacher or school employee is sexually abusing a child.

Teachers should remember that any person who has contact with children could be a potential abuser. For example, parent, stepparent, babysitter, relatives, even school employees, such as teachers or coaches are possible abusers of children. The ultimate focus of teachers must be on the safety and welfare of the child when abuse or neglect is suspected. Trained professionals from a CPS agency are responsible for conducting thorough investigations of suspected abuse and neglect in a manner that is sensitive to the possibility of a false or unsubstantiated charge of abuse or neglect.

MANDATORY REPORTERS

As the statistics and supporting evidence suggests, teachers are an important part of children's educational pursuits and of children's overall well-being. Even if teachers fail to accept the moral and ethical foundation of their role as educators working with children, they are nonetheless bound by the legal mandates making them mandatory reporters of any and all suspected child abuse and neglect.

According to the child abuse reporting guidelines in the 50 states and U.S. territories, teachers and school employees are identified as mandatory reporters. A school employee typically includes teachers, principals, administrators, school nurses, school social workers, speech pathologists, and guidance counselors, who work in public and private schools, whether day or residential. Ohio law, for example, mandates reporting if a teacher [or other mandatory reporter] has reason to believe abuse or neglect is occurring and physical proof is not required. According to the Ohio statute, if a child is younger than 18 or 21 years of age, or if the child is mentally retarded, developmentally delayed, or physically impaired, a teacher is obligated to report any and all suspicion of child abuse.

Although the statutory requirements vary across the states, the federal Child Abuse Prevention and Treatment Act (CAPTA) establishes minimum standards for defining child abuse and neglect. According to CAPTA, child abuse and neglect includes a recent act or failure to act on the part of a parent or caretaker that results in death, serious physical or emotional harm, or sexual abuse or exploitation; or an act or failure to act that presents an imminent risk of serious harm. Generally, state statutes indicate that reports must be made when mandatory reporters know or have reason to suspect that a child is or has been subject to abuse and neglect.

Some teachers express concern about their role as mandatory reporters because they fear that parents will discover their identity, which would then negatively impact the important relationship between parents and their children's teachers. All of the state statutes maintain the confidentiality of abuse and neglect records and protect the reporter's identity. In states where reporting is mandatory and individuals are liable for failure to report, anonymous reports are typically permitted, but not encouraged if it would be difficult to document otherwise that the educator complied with the mandatory reporting law. Given the confidentiality standard mandatory reporting statutes, it would only be in rare circumstance and in a limited number of states where specific circumstances might lead to release of a reporter's identity, including for example, the knowingly filing of a false report.

Teachers may hesitate to report because they worry that their suspicions are not verified or because they fear that a child is making up the claims of abuse. Ultimately, it is the responsibility of a CPS agency to investigate and verify child abuse charges. False reports by children are infrequent, especially among younger children who rarely make up sexual abuse claims. Some teachers may also worry about incurring liability when they report child abuse because they believe that civil or criminal charges will be brought by the parents. Pursuant to many of the state mandatory reporting requirements, good faith reporters are protected from civil and criminal charges. Finally, given the mandatory nature of state reporting laws and the potential liability associated with failure to report, teachers may not assert that they simply do not want to get involved in personal family matters, such as child abuse and neglect.

CHILD ABUSE REPORTING AND THE COURTS

In *P.H. v. School District of Kansas City* (2001), a teacher was found guilty of four counts of statutory sodomy for sexually abusing a male high school student during a 2-year time period. According to the student, the teacher engaged in oral sex with him outside of school and during school hours by frequently removing him from classes. Other teachers complained to the principal because the student was frequently absent or tardy and his grades began to drop. The principal warned the teacher to discontinue his actions before removing him from the classroom and initiating actions to revoke his teaching license.

At no time during the 2 years of abuse was an official complaint about child sexual abuse made by the student or any adult on his behalf. Yet, when the investigation of the teacher was discovered, a colleague expressed relief that he was finally caught, referring to the sexual abuse charges. In this situation and others like it, the child's rights were not protected by adults who likely suspected the abuse but failed to speak out and protect the student. The sexual misconduct was finally discovered by the student's mother who alerted the principal. At this point, the principal reported the sexual abuse allegations to the Family Services Division, which investigated and petitioned for the revocation of the abuser's teaching license. The student then initiated a Title IX sexual harassment case, which was unsuccessful because the Eighth Circuit determined that school officials lacked actual knowledge of the abuse and did not respond with deliberate indifference. This case demonstrates how difficult it is for a student to report when they are sexually abused, especially by a teacher, and emphasizes how important it is for teachers to report any and all suspicions of child abuse and neglect, including sexual abuse.

Other state Supreme Courts have addressed the meaning and application of their mandatory child abuse reporting statutes, generally finding that teachers can be liable for failing to act. Consequently, teachers and school boards, who do not report suspected abuse, could face civil actions and be rendered liable for monetary awards to students who are later harmed by an abuser. In fact, school employees, including teachers, are typically held accountable for their failure to report suspected child abuse as required by the state mandatory reporting statutes.

CONCLUSION

Child abuse and neglect threaten the present and future of children who suffer silently from the devastating effects of maltreatment. If the professionals who interact most frequently with children, especially teachers, fail to intervene on behalf of abused and neglected children, these children may continue to be defenseless victims suffering from the immediate pains of abuse and the long-term devastating effects throughout adulthood. Teachers must thus recognize the significant power and influence that they have over the lives of children, who daily sit in their classrooms and turn to their teachers for instruction, guidance, and support. Finally, teachers must be aware of the specific legal mandates to report child abuse as identified in their respective state statutes. Given their tremendous responsibility in schools, teachers are obligated both legally and morally to report any and all suspicion of child abuse and neglect to the appropriate authorities.

COUNTERPOINT: Stephanie D. McCall
Teachers College, Columbia University

As the point essay maintains, reporting child abuse and neglect is certainly an ethical and legal obligation for teachers and school personnel.

However, mandating that teachers, in particular, report any and all suspicions of child abuse and neglect does not further the intent of the law.

One of the law's intended outcomes is the prevention of future abuse of children. Yet, reporting on abuse to professionals outside of schools does little to encourage strategies for prevention that could occur inside of schools. For example, reporting does not positively influence the nature of teacher–student relationships or alter school curricula—either of which could be productive to students' understanding of child abuse as a social issue. Reporting also does not guarantee that school officials will structure environments in which students and teachers work together to combat silence about or increase opportunities for critical conversations about violence. Reporting is not the same as talking and learning about abuse with colleagues and students. Mandated reporting seems to suggest that teachers should pass off their concerns to professionals outside of their schools while remaining quiet about child abuse inside of their schools. The legal mandate to report abuse is, accordingly, a policy generated out of concern for accountability instead of an ethos of professional care for students.

School officials report incidences of child abuse more than any other agency whose professionals are legally required to report. The federal Child Abuse Prevention and Treatment Act of 1974, most recently reauthorized as the Keeping Children and Families Safe Act of 2003, now mandates that school and other professionals report child abuse or neglect when there is reasonable cause to suspect or believe that these have occurred. Yet, there are more unreported cases in public schools than in any other social service agency. One explanation for this could be connected to compulsory education requirements but could also be explained by the many overlapping social processes that occur in school.

To better understand the challenges of statutorily mandated reporting, this counterpoint essay explores some central assumptions embedded in the duty to report related to social processes of teaching. The unaccounted-for complexity of these social processes can provide some explanation for the ways in which the mandate to report child abuse and neglect limits intended outcomes and complicates the decisions of teachers to report suspected abuse and neglect, meaning that perhaps they are not best suited to have to act in this capacity.

CARING FOR STUDENTS: TEACHER ROLES AND RESPONSIBILITIES

A central principle of the mandated reporting policy is the assumption that teachers are best positioned to report suspected child abuse and neglect.

In fact, as the point essay suggests, "teachers are in a unique position to recognize abuse," but the issue is much more complex. Insofar as teachers and school personnel generally have more contact and interaction with children than other social service professionals, teachers are assumed to know their students better and, in the case of suspected abuse, have knowledge of their students' lives outside of school. Even so, many obstacles, such as class size, the pace of the school day, and the time demands of high-stakes, standards-driven instruction, present challenges to observing students closely and having personal interactions with each one. Since teachers spend more time with children than other social service professionals does not mean that they fully understand the lives of their students and can interpret students' behaviors in relation to signs of abuse and neglect.

Two issues—the increased cultural and ethnic diversity of students and teacher conceptions of care—are particularly important when considering the position of teachers and their ability to identify abuse. First, the assumption that teachers are best positioned to report abuse is complicated by the rapidly increasing cultural and ethnic diversity of children who attend schools in the United States. This diversity presents an increased possibility that the cultural and ethnic backgrounds of both teachers and students are likely to differ. If norms of childhood experiences and family life are believed to be culturally embedded and culturally enacted, increasingly there will be gaps in the ability of teachers to understand the culturally specific experiences of each of their students in their social and familial lives. Although this does not mean that it is impossible for teachers to know and understand the lives of their students, the possibility exists that a given teacher may not understand the cultural nuances of each child's family. Teachers interpret student behaviors from their own experiences—both professional and personal—and cultural differences could lead to teachers misunderstanding or misinterpreting signs and symptoms of abuse.

Second, how educators care for and define what it means to care for children varies according to school climate and personal values. Teachers and other professionals are mandated to report based on assumptions of the role that schools and social agencies play in caring for children. However, for one teacher, caring may mean following the official school reporting protocol, while for another, caring may mean overlooking that protocol. There is a limited amount of research on teachers' decisions to report. Most of the research on teachers' decisions to report agrees that how teachers conceive of their desire or obligation to care for children is what often determines their response to the mandate to report. There is very little research on teachers who choose not to report suspected abuse and neglect. Teachers are hesitant to admit to researchers that they did not abide by a legally mandated responsibility to report a suspicion of abuse and neglect. These varying conceptions of care and how it should be enacted by teachers across diverse cultural landscapes in the United States are related to social processes that complicate the intended outcomes of mandated reporting by teachers.

GAPS IN THE KNOWLEDGE BASE

Current research points to empirical evidence of a knowledge gap in professionals' ability to identify and report child abuse and neglect. When trying to understand why teachers do not report, researchers are attempting to evaluate whether the failure to report is related to not understanding what to report and how to report or to teachers' hesitation to get involved. In mandating teachers to report and providing them with a minimum number of hours of education on how to identify child abuse as part of school district hiring practices, the assumption is that signs and symptoms of child abuse can be codified effectively and efficiently. Given that each state is responsible for providing its own definition of child maltreatment and abuse and that all teachers have their own experiences, there is much room for interpretation of abuse based on one's own theoretical perspectives and values in addition to the multitude of meanings that can be implied and understood in language.

Implications for the gaps in teacher knowledge relates to how they define and understand "reasonable cause." Specifically, there are variations in what actions, behaviors, signs, and symptoms count as "reasonable," which have been informed by each teacher's specific social location, background experiences, and opportunity to learn about child abuse in their particular state and school district. When considering the limitations of mandated reporting, the social context of knowledge construction cannot be ignored in assessing teachers' difficulty in detecting signs and symptoms and in attributing those to abuse. It is a fallacy that knowledge can be learned objectively, efficiently, and effectively enough to report abuse unless enough access to training is included in teacher education—in ways that make identifying and reporting abuse appropriate. In other words, objective standards regarding descriptions of abuse are possible and useful. It is similarly false to assume that the truth about abuse can be discovered if suspected and reported.

In recent discussions on the coordinated efforts to prevent child abuse and neglect, the strategies listed as prevention efforts do not include increased attention to the education of professionals. Moreover, although more knowledge could be beneficial for teachers through increased access to professional development related to child abuse, the complex dimensions of knowledge construction as a social process, particularly in this difficult area, in schools is difficult to avoid.

OVERREPORTING AND UNDERREPORTING

Research shows that both overreporting and underreporting present problems for child protection. For example, overreporting by teachers creates many false reports, or false negatives, which result in efforts to reduce false negatives that could likely lead to an increase in underreporting. There is little discussion of the impact of the false negatives in reporting and the consequences, but this conundrum is central to those who challenge the effectiveness of the mandate to report. Overreporting burdens the financial and human resources in agencies committed to the protection of children because of the legal obligation to investigate all of the reports. The resources used for investigation could be used instead for prevention of abuse and getting specific resources to families in need.

Further, the validity of mandated reporting calls into question the wisdom of requiring teachers to report any and all suspicions of child abuse and neglect. The Administration on Children and Families Report of 2003 shows that approximately two thirds of the reports are never substantiated. Teachers' reports are said to clog the system and may not get much attention by social service professionals because of the perceived lack of severity of the report. Research has demonstrated that Child Protective Services (CPS) agencies do not place much value on cases reported by school staff because CPS did not consider them serious enough. This research finding serves as a call to action to consider improvements in the way schools and social agencies can work together to improve the protection of children.

In addition to perceptions about reports of abuse made by teachers, there are the feelings that teachers have about reporting. Teachers have reported that they feel unprepared to intervene effectively on behalf of children by making reports because of limited understanding of what constitutes abuse. Another documented factor is teachers' fear of the consequences for the lives of children. The decisions of teachers not to report suspected abuse and neglect could be a response to a number of fears, including fear of public embarrassment, fear of further angering an abuser, and/or fear that families will be torn apart by authorities. There is a possibility that reporting, regardless of whether it is verifiable, could lead to unintended consequences for children and still not guarantee their protection from abusers or abusive situations. This point reiterates the ways in which the conceptions of teachers of caring can inform their responses to suspicion of abuse and neglect as well as their decisions whether to report. For one teacher, reporting is considered advocacy with an intent to end abuse; for another teacher, reporting can be considered intrusive in the way a report can create a new set of obstacles for a child.

CONCLUSION

This counterpoint essay presents some of the limitations and critiques at the center of the current debate on the mandate for teachers to report suspected child abuse and neglect. Even so, this counterpoint essay should not be read as an argument for silence, complicity, and noncompliance with the legal and ethical responsibilities of educators to report. A critical assessment of the policy mandating the reporting of child abuse and neglect is necessary to inspect more closely the promises and limitations of a requirement that is rarely interrogated for pitfalls, not to dismiss its significance in the aim at protecting children. The mandate likely goes without critical questioning because of legal consequences attached to it if a teacher does not report. It may thus be necessary to take an unpopular position on an issue in order to improve the functioning of the policy.

A significant highlight of the research on the mandate to report abuse is that compliance with the mandate by teachers is not guaranteed. Therefore, alongside the existence of this mandate, what else can be done to protect children and prevent future abuse? Much more discussion is needed on the ways the mandate to report can be leveraged in schools, communities, teacher education programs, and ongoing professional learning to support and increase critical conversations about the nature of abuse, the prevention of abuse, and the social processes that complicate the decision to report.

Currently, the emphasis on prevention is focused on teachers reporting abuse. Yet teacher access to knowledge and the challenges of codifying definitions and interpretations of signs and symptoms of abuse point to a realization that maybe the emphasis on prevention could be in other spaces inside *and* outside of school. For example, community centers and after-school programs are typically not bound by the pressures from mandated curriculum and standardized testing. These places could be a possible space for supporting critical conversations among children, parents, teachers, and all community members. The evidence on the problems with overreporting suggests that resources put into investigation could be shifted toward uses in alternative spaces for critical conversations about abuse as a social issue and building supportive social networks.

Reporting child abuse and neglect fulfills an obligation instituted by the law and professional standards of behavior in education as well as in many other professional sectors. However, educators should be encouraged to go beyond the legal mandate to report and begin constructing spaces for critical conversations about abuse, violence, neglect, and the silence that makes all complicit. Silence can operate to protect violence against children. Although it can be argued that reporting abuse is an attempt at breaking silence, it can also be argued that reporting abuse and neglect is a different response than talking and learning about abuse and neglect as a social issue.

Further Readings and Resources

Melton, G. (2005). Mandated reporting: A policy without reason. *Child Abuse & Neglect, 29,* 9–18.

Reiniger, A., Robinson, E., & McHugh, M. (1995). Mandated training of professionals: A means for improving reporting of suspected child abuse. *Child Abuse & Neglect, 19*(1), 63–69.

Tite, R. (1993). How teachers define and respond to child abuse: The distinction between theoretical and reportable cases. *Child Abuse & Neglect, 17,* 591–603.

Toth Johns, J. A. (2004). Mandated voices for the vulnerable: An examination of the constitutionality of Missouri's mandatory child abuse reporting statute. *University of Missouri-Kansas City Law Review, 72,* 1083–1096.

U.S. Department of Health and Human Services, Children's Bureau. (2003). *The role of educators in preventing and responding to child abuse and neglect.* Retrieved from http://www.childwelfare.gov/pubs/usermanuals/educator/educator.pdf

U.S. Department of Health and Human Services, Children's Bureau. (2008). *Mandatory reporters of child abuse and neglect: Summary of state laws.* Retrieved from http://www.childwelfare.gov/systemwide/laws_policies/statutes/manda.cfm

U.S. Department of Health and Human Services, Children's Bureau. (2009a). *Child maltreatment 2008.* Washington, DC: U.S. Government Printing Office. Retrieved July 2010 from http://www.acf.hhs.gov/programs/cb/pubs/cm08/index.htm

U.S. Department of Health and Human Services, Children's Bureau. (2009b). *Definitions of child abuse and neglect: Summary of state laws.* Retrieved from http://www.childwelfare.gov/systemwide/laws_policies/statutes/define.cfm

U.S. Department of Health and Human Services, Children's Bureau. (2009c). *State statutes search.* Retrieved from http://www.childwelfare.gov/systemwide/laws_policies/state

Weis, L., Marusza, J., & Fine, M. (1998). Out of the cupboards: Kids, domestic violence and schools. *British Journal of Sociology of Education, 19*(1), 53–73.

Weithorn, L. A. (2001). Protecting children from exposure to domestic violence: The use and abuse of child maltreatment. *Hastings Law Journal, 53*(1), 1–156.

Zellman, G. (1990a). Linking schools and social services: The case of child abuse reporting. *Education Evaluation and Policy Analysis, 12*(1), 41–55.

Zellman, G. (1990b). Report decision-making patterns among mandated child abuse reporters. *Child Abuse & Neglect, 14,* 325–336.

COURT CASES AND STATUTES

Child Abuse Prevention and Treatment Act of 1974, reauthorized as Keeping Children and Families Safe Act of 2003, 42 USC §§ 5101 *et seq.*

Individuals with Disabilities Education Act, Pub. L. 101–476, 104 Stat. 1142 (2004).

P.H. v. School District of Kansas City, 265 F.3d 653 (8th Cir. 2001).

7

Should corporal punishment in public schools be abolished?

POINT: Aimee Vergon Gibbs, *Dickinson Wright, PLLC, Detroit, Michigan*

COUNTERPOINT: Emily Richardson, *Indiana University*

OVERVIEW

The notion of "spare the rod and spoil the child," which traces its origins to a similar adage in the Bible in Proverbs 13:24 that calls for the use of corporal physical punishment to discipline misbehaving children, clearly reflects the thinking of adults since ancient times. As reflected in this adage, corporal punishment has, until recently, also been a staple of educators throughout the world, including in the United States. Yet, even though most nations have forbidden teachers and other school officials to use corporal punishment in disciplining misbehaving students, controversy over its use continues in the United States. In fact, corporal punishment is still legal in about 20 states, although the number of jurisdictions permitting educators to use it to discipline students continues to dwindle (Center for Effective Discipline, 2010).

Under the common law doctrine of in loco parentis, literally, "in place of the parents," American educators since the Colonial era have had the all but unilateral authority to impose reasonable corporal punishment on their students. To this end, absent explicit prohibitions that have rendered corporal punishment illegal in the majority of states, American educators still may employ the practice to discipline students even if their parents oppose their doing so, provided that it is allowed by local school board policy (*Baker v. Owen,* 1975a, 1975b).

In seeking to resolve the conflict between the duty of educators to maintain safe and orderly learning environments by imposing reasonable discipline on students and the rights of parents to direct the upbringing of their children, a shift is occurring with regard to the legal status of corporal punishment. More specifically, as reflected by the increasing amount of legislation prohibiting its use and the corresponding decrease in litigation challenging the imposition of corporal punishment, many school boards have abandoned the practice at least in part as a result of respect for parental wishes. At the same time, the imposition of unreasonable or unauthorized corporal punishment or behavior in violation of board policy or state law can lead to the dismissal of teachers (*Bott v. Board of Education, Deposit Central School District,* 1977).

Perhaps the oldest American case involving the use of corporal punishment was resolved in 1859. The case arose when a high school student, who was in the company of friends, saw one of his teachers outside of school and called him by name, "old Jack Seaver." After the teacher whipped the student in school the following day, the Supreme Court of Vermont upheld the educator's use of corporal punishment. According to the court, corporal punishment was a justifiable means of discipline insofar as the student's behavior had " a direct and immediate tendency to injure the school and [helped] bring the master's authority into contempt" (*Lander v. Seaver,* 1859, *5).

Yet, less than 20 years later, another case rejected the use of corporal punishment. In this incident, the Supreme Court of Iowa ruled that educators improperly used corporal punishment on a female student who was allegedly "insolent" after her father asked that she be excused from algebra class because of health concerns. Instead, the court ruled that the student should have been expelled rather than subjected to corporal punishment (*State v. Mizner,* 1878).

In its only case on the merits of the practice, *Ingraham v. Wright* (1977), the Supreme Court refused to invalidate corporal punishment as unconstitutional per se. The Court ruled that the Eighth Amendment's prohibition against cruel and unusual punishments was designed to protect those who were guilty of crimes and was thus inapplicable to paddling students in order to preserve discipline. In part of its analysis, the Court rejected an analogy between children and the use of physical punishment on inmates. Tracing its history in the United States and noting that most jurisdictions that addressed corporal punishment at that time permitted its use, and that professional and public opinion has long been divided over the use of practice, the Court refused to strike it down as unconstitutional in all circumstances.

Against this backdrop, the debates in this chapter consider divergent attitudes toward the use of corporal punishment in public schools. As reflected in the point essay, Aimee Vergon Gibbs (Dickinson Wright, PLLC, Detroit, Michigan) takes the position that corporal punishment should definitely be eliminated insofar as it is an archaic form of punishment. Among the arguments that Vergon Gibbs uses against corporal punishment is that it is counterintuitive to tell students not to use violence to resolve their differences with peers even as educators can discipline them by means of force. She also maintains not only that corporal punishment is an ineffective form of discipline but also that it may well result in unintended harmful consequences for students who both receive and witness this form of discipline.

Conversely, Emily Richardson's (Indiana University) counterpoint essay begins by examining the Supreme Court's reluctance to limit the use of corporal punishment in all circumstances before exploring the interplay among federal, state, and local control on education. In this way, she argues that the use of corporal punishment in schools should remain a state or local issue. Richardson believes that a total ban on the use of corporal punishment as a means of helping impose discipline is unhelpful for the missions of public schools. Here she asserts that such a ban would both deprive local educational leaders of the opportunity to respond to needs in their immediate areas and deny them of the means of selecting, and using, appropriate disciplinary techniques.

As you read these essays, ask yourself two questions. First, what do you think about the use of corporal punishment generally? Second, if you live in a state that still permits corporal punishment, ask yourself whether teachers should be able to discipline your child(ren) in this manner without your permission.

Charles J. Russo
University of Dayton

POINT: Aimee Vergon Gibbs
Dickinson Wright, PLLC, Detroit, Michigan

Corporal punishment should be abolished because it is an archaic, ineffective method of disciplining school children and causes a myriad of detrimental effects on students of all ages. This holds true regardless of whether students are the actual victims of corporal punishment or witnesses to this draconian form of school discipline. Although public policy endorsing corporal punishment has long been employed by parents and schools alike as a means to control children, it should not be perpetuated based solely on its historical origin, particularly when the positive outcomes of corporal punishment are insignificant and the negative consequences are substantial. Not only is corporal punishment an ineffective method of managing and improving student behavior and conduct, but it also sends a confusing message to students who are often being disciplined because they themselves engaged in some form of violent behavior. Prior to examining the many detrimental effects of corporal punishment on students, it is essential to specify what constitutes corporal punishment, define the scope of the problem, and review historical and current opposition to the use of corporal punishment in the nation's schools.

DEFINITION OF SCHOOL CORPORAL PUNISHMENT

The American Academy of Pediatrics defines corporal punishment as the intentional use of physical force to cause a child to experience pain, but not injury, in order to correct or control the child's behavior. Furthermore, the National Association of School Nurses defines corporal punishment as the intentional infliction of physical pain as a method of changing behavior. All descriptions of corporal punishment contain the element of intentional physical pain. Based on these definitions, it is counterintuitive to teach students not to hit or slap or inappropriately touch other students when the form of discipline the school employs is physical in nature. There are a range of physical actions that constitute corporal punishment, including hitting children with a belt, a ruler, or a paddle; and pinching, slapping, or spanking or striking a student across the buttocks, hands, or thighs. These types of punishment undertaken by school officials under the purview of discipline and the inherent definition of corporal punishment itself belies the physical and emotional harm that results from corporal punishment. In light of the substantial negative effects of this type of treatment, corporal punishment is not permitted in the military, mental institutions, juvenile correction facilities, and prisons. However, corporal punishment is still allowed in a number of states in the United States.

PREVALENCE OF CORPORAL PUNISHMENT IN SCHOOLS

As noted in the Overview, corporal punishment has been used as a disciplinary measure in the United States since the Colonial period. The concept of corporal punishment extends even farther back into history, however, and was originally widespread in Britain and other European countries as a form of discipline in the 19th and 20th centuries. Among the first countries to ban corporal punishment was Russia, later the former Soviet Union, which forbade its use in schools from the 1917 revolution onward as inconsistent with its ideology. Britain outlawed the practice in 1987, and most of continental Europe has banned school corporal punishment for decades. Other countries have followed suit and prohibit corporal punishment as a disciplinary practice, including Japan, South Africa, and New Zealand. More recently, in 2004, the Supreme Court of Canada officially outlawed the use of corporal punishment in the country's school in its decision in *Canadian Foundation for Children, Youth and the Law v. Canada* (2004). Today the United States is the only nation in the Western world that has not completely banned corporal punishment in its schools.

The clear trend in recent decades is toward abolishing school corporal punishment because of its inefficiency and the resulting harm to students. Most professional associations and academic experts advocate the banning of corporal punishment, including all accredited teachers' colleges in the United States, The American Academy of Child and Adolescent Psychiatry, The American School Counselor Association, The American Academy of Pediatrics, The American Civil Liberties Union, Human Rights Watch, and the National Association of Secondary School Principals. However, the United States has not enacted a nationwide ban of corporal punishment and many schools still permit corporal punishment as a method of discipline. Although Congress has not adopted federal legislation banning corporal punishment in American schools, the increasing desire to eliminate the harsh, unfair, and ineffective punishment is evident as more and more states implement state legislation prohibiting corporal punishment. To date, about 30 states have banned corporal punishment in their schools. In the remaining states, the prevalence of corporal punishment has declined consistently notwithstanding its legality.

Despite the clear downward trend in the use of corporal punishment, the incidents of corporal punishment occurring in American schools is still alarming because even one student hit, spank, slapped, or paddled by a school official is one too many. According to recent data from the U.S. Department of Education, Office for Civil Rights, 223,190 students nationwide were paddled at least once in the 2006–2007 school year. This is down dramatically from previous rates. Thus, even where state legislation has not yet been rewritten to prohibit corporal punishment officially in schools, education administrators and teachers have unofficially banned corporal punishment as a viable method of discipline by eliminating it from their schools on a practical level.

OPPOSITION TO CORPORAL PUNISHMENT IN THE COURTS

Although the courts have not uniformly acted to abolish corporal punishment in the nation's schools, there has been extensive litigation that has effectively narrowed the authority and scope of corporal punishment that is permitted in the schools. Since the second half of the 20th century, the historically broad common law authorization to use corporal punishment has come under a concerted attack in both the courts and the state legislative chambers. In the 1970s, two noteworthy cases were brought by parents against schools regarding the use of corporal punishment and alleging that such punishment violated the Constitution, particularly the Fourth, Eighth, and Fourteenth Amendments. The cases reached the Supreme Court, which ruled that corporal punishment does not implicate the Eighth Amendment's bar against cruel and unusual punishment, nor does it violate procedural due process constitutional protections (*Baker v. Owen*, 1975a, 1975b; *Ingraham v. Wright*, 1977). Although the Court rejected these challenges to corporal punishment, numerous cases have subsequently attacked its constitutionality on substantive due process grounds.

A variety of federal appellate courts, for instance, agreed that under appropriate circumstances, substantive due process violations may, as a matter of law, be demonstrated and actionable in Section 1983 claims. Typical of these cases is one in which a student in New Mexico was suspended upside down by one administrator while another struck her repeatedly on the front of her thighs with a wooden paddle until they bled (*Garcia v. Miera*, 1987, 1988).

In addition to these successful suits finding that corporal punishment violated students' substantive due process rights, policy review and revision of the practice at the state level also increased in the 1990s. Although the *Ingraham* court in 1977 held that corporal punishment did not constitute cruel and unusual punishment, the Justices pointed out that only New Jersey and Massachusetts prohibited corporal punishment of school children as a matter of state policy, implying that the threat of harm to children was *de minimis*. As discussed, though, the number of states that now recognize the ineffective and detrimental effects of corporal punishment leading them to prohibit it as a matter of policy has grown to at least 30. This state policy activity was fueled, in large part, by the growing social science evidence calling into question the effects of corporal punishment on students and schools.

INEFFECTIVE POLICY RESULTS AND NEGATIVE CONSEQUENCES

Not only is evidence lacking that corporal punishment is an effective method of disciplining students, but also there is substantial evidence that its use in schools has many harmful unintended consequences for the children subjected to such punishment, as well as for those who witness the form of discipline. These detrimental consequences flow from a variety of causes, but they have uniformly negative implications for children. These causes include the following:

1. *Corporal punishment is not an effective discipline tactic and sends children the contradictory message that physical violence is an acceptable method of handling conflict.*

Studies conducted about the effectiveness of corporal punishment often stem from parental corporal punishment. Even so, the findings of such studies can easily be extrapolated to school corporal punishment. These studies find that although corporal punishment may result in immediate compliance or stop the unwanted behavior momentarily, it does little in the way of promoting long-term appropriate behavior. One of the seminal studies examining the efficacy of corporal punishment on children discovered that corporal punishment actually decreases children's internalization of moral rules (Gershoff, 2008). In other words, where the objective of punishment is to decrease or eliminate certain negative conduct and prevent the child from engaging in the misconduct in the future, corporal punishment is not effective. This is particularly true when discipline is administered through corporal punishment without proper explanation regarding why the discipline is warranted, and the reasons and importance of behaving correctly.

At the same time, it is counterproductive to teach children not to engage in misconduct such as hitting, shoving, or pushing classmates, by having a school official hit the offending students. When physical contact is initiated by an authority figure, such as a teacher at school, it teaches children that violence is a way to solve problems. Research has demonstrated that this lesson is learned not only by the students who receive the corporal punishment but also by others who witness the incidents. We should not allow our teachers or other school officials to act by indirectly promoting physical intervention as an acceptable method of controlling individuals or situations. Not only does such drastic punishment create distrust and increased aggression in children, it also undermines parental support and community confidence in public schools and the judgment of school officials. There are many more effective ways of handling and resolving conflict than resorting to corporal punishment.

2. Academic achievement is negatively correlated with use of corporal punishment.

As can be expected, such harsh punishment is not only an ineffective method of altering students' behavior, but also it harms the future educational success of the student. Students who are subjected to, or witness, incidences of corporal punishment feel less safe in school. Moreover, the frequent use of corporal punishment against students establishes a negative threatening school environment. As a result of this inherently negative atmosphere, students' ability to perform academically is negatively impacted. The in-school behavior and chances for student academic success are significantly worsened by harsh physical punishment, in part, as a result of the student feeling marginalized and becoming disengaged from school.

In fact, in states where corporal punishment is used frequently, schools have demonstrated lower academic scores than their counterparts that prohibit corporal punishment. It has generally been shown that states that have abolished corporal punishment have higher ACT scores and higher graduation rates. This may in part be a result of the inability of students to attend school and concentrate on the objective of learning rather than on being fearful or distracted by the school's disciplinary measures.

According to the Center for Effective Discipline and the data from National Center for Education Statistics, 89% of students educated in states where corporal punishment is illegal scored above the national average on the ACT. This compares with only 36% of students in states where corporal punishment is used. Additionally, in states that do not use corporal punishment, 66% evidenced higher than national average graduation rates. Among states that use corporal punishment, however, 57% had graduation rates below the national average. Students have enough obstacles to academic success in today's world that are out of their control and should not be subject to physical discipline from the very ones who are charged with protecting and educating them.

3. Corporal punishment is disproportionately used against students with disabilities and students from minority and/or lower socioeconomic backgrounds.

In states still permitting the use of corporal punishment, it is not consistently implemented among different student populations. Poor children, minorities, and children with disabilities are hit more frequently in schools. For example, data from the U.S. Department of Education, Office for Civil Rights, indicate that of the 223,190 students subjected to corporal punishment during the 2006–2007 school year, 41,972 were students with disabilities. As such, students with disabilities made up 18.8% of all students who received physical punishment notwithstanding the fact that they comprise only 13.7% of the national student population. The frequency of corporal punishment used against students with disabilities, many of whose disabilities may actually preclude them from consistently conforming their behavior to school expectations, signals the often indiscriminate use of corporal punishment for already at-risk students.

4. *Corporal punishment has long-term negative implications for students' social, emotional, and mental well-being.*

For some time, research has shown that students who are subjected to corporal punishment feel humiliated, helpless, depressed, and angry as a result. In addition to these immediate negative reactions, corporal punishment has also routinely been associated with more long-term consequences such as higher levels of violence and aggression, decreased self-control, and a host of social, emotional, and mental problems. Many students who go through a degrading and painful experience of corporal punishment in school develop antisocial behavior and distrusting attitudes, which are reflected in the decreased mental health outcomes for these individuals. These students are also more likely to experience long-term depression and feel helpless to control situations as a direct result of being physically reprimanded by educational personnel in positions of authority. All of these negative emotions combined with anger and embarrassment over the incident can often lead to increased aggression and may result in criminal behavior. Data from the National Center for Education Statistics indicate that 8 of the top 10 states that most frequently use corporal punishment are also in the top 10 states with the highest incarceration rates. Corporal punishment is not only ineffective in correcting student misconduct, therefore, but it also has long-term negative consequences including increasing the very aggressive and violent behavior it attempts to control.

CONCLUSION

The failure of corporal punishment to decrease student misconduct, as well as the numerous unintended negative consequences that emanate from the use of physical discipline against children, renders this form of discipline an inefficient, ineffective, and often detrimental approach to controlling student behavior and promoting school safety. Furthermore, there are better alternatives to disciplining students in lieu of corporal punishment, including establishing clear codes of misconduct, enforcing the rules consistently with equivalent punishment, holding conferences about (mis)behavior, and requiring teacher/parent special conferences regarding misconduct and use of in-school suspensions or detentions.

COUNTERPOINT: Emily Richardson
Indiana University

As of 2011, approximately 30 states have individually made the use of corporal punishment, which is generally defined as the intentional infliction of pain in an effort to change behavior, at schools legally impermissible. Even in states that have not outlawed the practice, school boards have sometimes created policies prohibiting the use of corporal punishment for misbehaving students. In addition, the prevalence of corporal punishment in those states and localities that do allow its practice has decreased in recent years as individual school boards and local school policies have further specified how corporal punishment is to be applied and by whom it can be imposed. However, as reflected by a bill that was introduced in the House of Representatives in September 2011, the Ending Corporal Punishment in Schools Act, there may be a move toward a federal ban on corporal punishment in schools (H.R. 3027, 2010).

This counterpoint essay argues that a federal ban on corporal punishment is unnecessary and indeed may harm the educational independence of state and local governments as well as limit discipline options for school administrators. Even so, this essay does not argue that corporal punishment is appropriate for all discipline issues nor does it justify action that is statutorily defined as abuse. First, the essay addresses the Supreme Court's reluctance to limit corporal punishment. Second, this counterpoint essay explores the interplay among federal, state, and local control on education, arguing that corporal punishment should remain a state or local issue. Finally, this essay examines other reasons why a total ban of corporal punishment would be unhelpful for the missions of schools.

CORPORAL PUNISHMENT AND THE AMERICAN COURTS

Corporal punishment has a long tradition in the American educational settings. Common law has permitted the practice of corporal punishment under the theory of in loco parentis, or in place of the parents, which allows school officials to share traditional parental roles such as that of disciplinarian. The form of corporal punishment most prevalent in schools today is paddling, but other forms continue to be practiced. The most common reason given for continuing the practice of corporal punishment is the need to maintain an orderly school environment, which is safe and promotes learning. Although courts have struck down individual incidents of egregious corporal punishment, they have not agreed that its use as a whole is unconstitutional. This section describes the constitutional status of corporal punishment before arguing that the Supreme Court was correct in refusing to place a total ban on corporal punishment.

In *Ingraham v. Wright* (1977), the Supreme Court held that corporal punishment did not violate the Eighth Amendment's prohibition of cruel and unusual punishment. The Court found that the Eighth Amendment was not implicated in school settings; instead, the Justices explained that its application was limited to criminal settings. Reasoning that school settings were more open environments than those of prison or other detention locations, the Court ruled that the "state itself may impose such corporal punishment as is reasonably necessary 'for the proper education of the child and for the maintenance of group discipline'" (p. 662).

Also at issue in *Ingraham* was whether the Due Process Clause of the Fourteenth Amendment required procedures such as notice or a hearing before school officials imposed corporal punishment on students. The Due Process Clause requires that certain procedural rights be given when the government takes away life, liberty, or property. The Court observed that *Ingraham* implicated due process because students have a liberty interest in not being punished or restrained physically. However, the Supreme Court pointed out that the availability of private tort remedies for assault and battery provide adequate remedies for due process violations. The Court noted that these existing remedies provide a disincentive for bad behavior by school officials. In the interest of fairness, the Court additionally encouraged school officials to provide students with limited due process protections such as giving them notice of the charges and a chance to refute them before administering corporal punishment. Yet, the Court concluded that these processes were not required under the Due Process Clause.

Although *Ingraham* did not outlaw corporal punishment, it did spur state legislation which served the same purpose. In 1977, when *Ingraham* was decided, only New Jersey, Hawaii, and Massachusetts banned corporal punishment in public schools. Twenty years after *Ingraham*, 27 states had such bans, with many of the statutes being enacted in the early 1980s, a number that has now increased to about 30.

Some advocates of a ban on corporal punishment argue that the practice is unnecessarily cruel for use in schools; they may cite horrific examples of students' punishment with baseball bats, belts, extension cords, or choking. Others claim that corporal punishment is meted out for minor offenses. However, these severe examples of corporal punishment may already be illegal; they may not meet the current reasonableness test that is used by most courts. Like the limits placed on parental corporal punishment by state law, school officials are similarly restricted by what constitutes reasonable corporal punishment.

The substantive Due Process Clause of the Fourteenth Amendment forbids punishment that is abusive and excessive; such punishment may also be prohibited by state constitutional provisions and statutes. Even though the Supreme Court in *Ingraham* refused to rule on the issue of excessiveness, other courts have addressed this claim. The substantive Due Process Clause protects against some severe cases of government action that is unreasonable or arbitrary; the threshold for recovery is high, requiring the government actions to "shock the conscience" in order for students to recover.

In *Hall v. Tawney* (1980), the Fourth Circuit held that corporal punishment violates the substantive Due Process Clause if an injury was so severe that the punishment was so disproportionate to the offense; and the punishment was "so inspired by malice or sadism rather than a merely careless or unwise excess of zeal that it amounted to a brutal and inhuman abuse of official power" that the corporal punishment shocks the conscience (p. 613). This is commonly referred to as the "reasonableness test." Other federal circuit courts applied a similar standard. For example, the Eleventh Circuit in *Neal v. Fulton County Board of Education* (2000) concerned the case of a coach who struck a student with part of a weight apparatus, causing a serious eye injury. The court determined that students could recover damages from school officials who administered corporal punishment that is "intentional, obviously excessive, and creates a foreseeable risk of serious injury" (p. 1071).

Ingraham was not the first case to refuse to intervene in public education. Indeed, courts are often reluctant to interfere with the decision-making authority of public school officials. For instance, courts dislike making decisions concerning curricular issues, reasoning that school officials have more of the understanding necessary for making those types of judgments. Courts are additionally reluctant to intervene in school issues for fear that doing so is likely to spur additional litigation about subjects that are better left to educators.

THE LOCAL NATURE OF EDUCATION

Corporal punishment should not be banned federally because education is a function of state and local governments. To this end, insofar as education is not mentioned in the U.S. Constitution, it has been reserved for state control under the Tenth Amendment. State control is useful for at least two reasons. First, it allows states to experiment to seek the best result. Indeed, state experimentation has produced many successful policies, which spurs further adoption across state lines. One recent example of state experimentation is the charter school movement. Charter schools were first implemented in the early 1990s in Minnesota, and this type of school has since been adopted in many states.

A second reason for allowing states to experiment is that permitting officials the ability to use practices such as corporal punishment allows them to maintain closer fidelity to local customs. It is not surprising that some states and localities would like to continue its use, especially considering the role it has played in the history of American schooling. Corporal punishment has been a long-term fixture in schools, and some believe that its use is religiously mandated. In fact, those who continue to allow corporal punishment are mostly located in the southern states, an area of the country that is more overtly religious than other regions (Center for Effective Discipline, 2010). It is no surprise, then, that this preference for corporal punishment is reflected in schooling in these locales.

Even more than states, individual communities should be empowered to make decisions regarding education. In the event that states do not ban the use of corporal punishment in their schools, local communities are even better situated to judge whether corporal punishment is appropriate for their communities. Communities are local checks for schools and their customs, as schools are generally visible and open. Although outside control of schools is limited, schools do have some democratic processes. Since school boards are elected, parents are free to speak with educational officials about issues of concern and to join advocacy groups such as Parent Teacher Associations.

Like states, local school boards and their officials experiment when the state and federal governments have not already mandated specified policies. Communities are local checks for school systems, and members of that community may demand certain limitations on corporal punishment. Most schools that practice corporal punishment allow parents the choice to opt out of its use on their children. Also, even if school board policies allow the use of corporal punishment, they also permit many teachers to use alternative discipline systems. In this way, school boards do not often mandate the use of corporal punishment by individual teachers. Issuing such a mandate would not only be difficult to enforce, but it would also be counterproductive to the educational benefits that corporal punishment may have.

CORPORAL PUNISHMENT'S USEFULNESS IN THE EDUCATION SETTING

School discipline is an increasingly important issue. Classroom disorder is a direct detriment to student learning, and classroom management continues to be a challenge for many teachers, especially new teachers. Although classroom management is complicated, few would argue that punishment does not play a role in classroom management. Of course, positive incentives and reinforcement can also play a role. Assuming that corporal punishment is being administered appropriately, it can be a very useful tool for school officials.

Removing a form of punishment from school administrators means that their choices may be increasingly limited, and these remaining discipline choices may detract from student learning. For example, in a school where corporal punishment still exists, students might be paddled after stealing from classmates. Yet, once corporal punishment is no longer permissible, that same students might be punished by suspension or perhaps for a repeat offense, expulsion. Removal from schools, although sometimes appropriate, decreases learning time. Parents may complain about this loss of learning time and further complain that additional accommodations have to be made for supervision during their child's suspension. Additionally, students may view time out of school as a vacation. As with any type of psychological punishment, whether suspensions, detentions, timeouts, or the like, it is hard to predict the perceptions of students. To this end, some students may understand isolation as a punishment, whereas others may think of it as a break from their busy social schedules.

Corporal punishment may provide some solutions to some of these issues. After corporal punishment, students may immediately resume learning. At the same time, parents may not have to find alternative child care since corporal punishment does not have a vacation-like quality that suspensions or expulsions do when physical pain is more universally accepted punishment.

Furthermore, administering corporal punishment may be a more efficient practice in terms of administrator or teacher time expenditures. Managing classrooms and schools takes up a large amount of educator time, and certain types of school discipline, such as in-school suspensions or Saturday schools, further reduce that available educator time, both in managing the bureaucracy that supports these types of disciplinary measures and in supervising the actual punishment. Additionally, these types of school discipline do not inherently provide valuable educational opportunities and may not offer some of the other benefits of corporal punishment.

Other educational benefits are also associated with corporal punishment. Some argue that corporal punishment is a good tool for learning since it provides immediate feedback to students (Gershoff, 2002). In turn, this immediate feedback generally provides at least short-term compliance with school rules. In contrast, other forms of discipline may not provide the same sort of immediate feedback. For example, a high school may have detention every Friday afternoon. If students violate school rules on Tuesday that require detentions, the first real punishment would occur 3 days later. Additionally, if the same students break other school rules on Wednesday and receive other detentions, they would not receive their punishment until the following Friday. The delayed punishment may thus detract from the value of the punishment for many students.

Banning corporal punishment in schools may impact more practices than just paddling. Recall the definition of corporal punishment given above, the intentional infliction of pain in an effort to change behavior. Paddling is not the only form of punishment that fits within this definition; instead, many of the traditional punishments used by coaches in physical education and in sports also fit. Vockell (1991) provided a helpful sports-related example. He explained that a coach who, after failing to maintain his players' attention, requires the players to run "wind sprints" is administering a form of corporal punishment. Vockell argued that this exercise may be more uncomfortable than traditional corporal punishment given via a paddle but that, "[a]ssuming that the coach has valid goals in mind and that the players are able to handle the sprints, this infliction of physical pain is probably an appropriate form of punishment" (p. 280). It will likely have the intended effect of student players paying closer attention during practice. Insofar as this type of corporal punishment is an effective and common practice in gymnasiums throughout the United States, a ban on its use is unnecessary.

CONCLUSION

Although many, including the point essay, argue that now is the time to pass a national ban on corporal punishment, this widespread ban is not in the best interest of all schools. Instead of national interference, individual states and school boards should be allowed to promulgate their own policies. Corporal punishment may be unpopular in some localities, but in others, it is an accepted and successful disciplinary practice. Allowing those localities that accept corporal punishment to continue its use gives administrators additional choices in discipline that may be more effective for certain students. Corporal punishment is not educationally appropriate for all situations, and abuse is never appropriate nor is it permitted by law, but it is not the role of the federal government to ban its practice in all schools.

FURTHER READINGS AND RESOURCES

American Academy of Pediatrics. (2006). *Corporal punishment in schools.* Retrieved from http://aappolicy.aappublications.org/cgi/content/full/pediatrics;106/2/343

Arcus, D. (2002). School shooting fatalities and school corporal punishment: A look at the states. *Aggressive Behavior, 28,* 173–183.

Benatar, D. (1998). Corporal punishment. *Social Theory & Practice, 24*(2), 237–260.

Center for Effective Discipline. (2010). *U.S.: Corporal punishment and paddling statistics by state and race.* Retrieved August 9, 2011, from http://www.stophitting.com/index .php?page=statesbanning

Center for Effective Discipline. (n.d.). *Discipline at school (NCACPS).* Retrieved June 17, 2011, from http://www.stophitting.com/index.php?page=atschool-main

Fuller, J. (2010). Corporal punishment and child development. *Akron Law Review, 43,* 537–602.

Gershoff, E. T. (2002). Corporal punishment by parents and associated child behaviors and experiences: A meta-analytic and theoretical review. *Psychological Bulletin, 128*(4), 539–579.

Gershoff, E. T. (2008). *Report on physical punishment in the United States: What research tells us about its effects on children.* Columbus, OH: Center for Effective Discipline.

National Parent Teacher Association. (2010). *Position statement—Recommendation on corporal punishment.* Retrieved from http://www.pta.org/1749.htm

Punke, H. H. (1959, September). Corporal punishment in the public schools. *NASSP Bulletin, 43*(248), 118–138.

Robinson, D. H., Funk, D. C., Beth, A., & Bush, A. M. (2005). Changing beliefs about corporal punishment: Increasing knowledge about ineffectiveness to build more consistent moral and informational beliefs. *Journal of Behavioral Education, 14,* 117–139.

Society for Adolescent Medicine, Ad Hoc Corporal Punishment Committee. (2003). Corporal punishment in schools: Position paper of the Society for Adolescent Medicine. *Journal of Adolescent Health, 32,* 385–393.

Vockell, E. L. (1991). Corporal punishment: The pros and cons. *The Clearing House, 64*(4), 278–283.

Wasserman, L. M. (2011). Corporal punishment in K–12 public school settings: Reconsiderations of its constitutional dimensions thirty years after *Ingraham v. Wright. Tauro Law Review, 26,* 1029–1101.

COURT CASES AND STATUTES

Baker v. Owen, 395 F. Supp. 294 (M.D.N.C.1975a), *aff'd,* 423 U.S. 907 (1975b).

Bott v. Board of Education, Deposit Central School District, 392 N.Y.S.2d.2d 274 (N.Y. 1977).

Canadian Foundation for Children, Youth and the Law v. Canada, 1 S.C.R. 76 (2004).

Garcia v. Miera, 817 F.2d 650 (10th Cir. 1987) *cert. denied,* 485 U.S. 959 (1988).

Hall v. Tawney, 621 F.2d 607 (4th Cir. 1980).

Ingraham v. Wright, 430 U.S. 651 (1977).

Lander v. Seaver, 32 Vt. 114, *5 [online Westlaw designation at 1859 WL 5454] (1859).

Neal v. Fulton County Board of Education, 229 F.3d 1069 (11th Cir. 2000).

State v. Mizner, 50 Iowa 145 (1878).

U.S. Congress (111th), H.R. 5628, June 29, 2010.

Should there be a distinction between academic dishonesty and student conduct violations?

POINT: Phillip Blackman, *Pennsylvania State University*

COUNTERPOINT: Peter L. Moran, *Pennsylvania State University*

OVERVIEW

Plagiarism is "a kind of theft [whereby] one writer steals the ideas or even the exact words of another writer without giving credit where it is due" (Weidenborner & Caruso, 1982, p. 97). A charge of plagiarism, the failure to provide adequate attribution for borrowed ideas or words, can have a devastating impact on those found guilty of plagiarizing another's work. Much of the increased attention to plagiarism reflects the ready availability of specialized computer programs that can check for unattributed copying. The increasing requirement by instructors that students turn in both their written assignment and a software report of this database comparison has enhanced the likelihood that unattributed copying will be discovered. As one federal district court observed regarding one of these computer programs (Turnitin), the numbers are staggering; "Over 7,000 educational institutions worldwide use Turnitin, resulting in the daily submission of over 100,000 works to Turnitin" (*A.V. v. iParadigms,* 2008, p. 78). The same vulnerability that students experience in terms of discovery of plagiarism can apply as well to faculty. Just as a proved charge of plagiarism can result in a student's dismissal from a university (*McCawley v. Universidad Carlos Albizu, Inc.,* 2006), so also can a proved charge of plagiarism against a faculty member result in dismissal (*Agarwal v. Regents of University of Minnesota,* 1986) or denial of tenure (*Boateng v. Inter American University,* 1999).

The enforcement of academic penalties against plagiarism has resulted in an increasing number of lawsuits with a surprisingly wide range of legal claims. From the obvious challenges by students or faculty to the efforts of educational institutions to impose discipline on them for their plagiarism, plagiarism litigation has extended to damage claims by persons charged with plagiarism against those who have published allegations of plagiarism (*Slack v. Stream,* 2008), as well as damages and injunctive relief claims against the plagiarizers by those persons whose work has been plagiarized (*Dodd v. Ft. Smith Special School District Number 100,* 1987).

The threshold issue in plagiarism is constructing an appropriate and generally acceptable definition. Legal authorities agree that plagiarism involves "misappropriate[ion] [of] another's words as their own without acknowledging the contribution or source" (Bast & Samuels, 2008, pp. 778–784) but disagree as to whether plagiarism requires some degree of mental culpability (Johnson, 2008, pp. 73–74).

Thus, although plagiarism in its broadest definition is the unattributed copying of another's work, a finding that a person has in fact plagiarized may involve an examination of two kinds of analyses, one objective and the other subjective. An objective analysis considers only whether copying without appropriate attribution has occurred without regard to a person's intent to plagiarize. However, in terms of this objective analysis, plagiarism does not apply to "matters of general knowledge," although it will apply to undocumented use of "ideas and expressions" from another source (Winkler & McCuen, 1985). As a rule of thumb, "a piece of information that occurs in five or more sources may be considered general knowledge" (p. 40), but the line between general knowledge and attributable material is not always easy to determine and can vary from one academic discipline to another. A subjective analysis considers whether plagiarism can occur only when intent to plagiarize has occurred, or whether proof of negligence or carelessness is sufficient to support a charge of plagiarism.

Clarification of the meaning of plagiarism has led many educational institutions to include samples of acceptable and unacceptable uses. Although such examples can be useful in determining when appropriate attribution is required, they tend, in the absence of express language to the contrary, not to require proof of intent to plagiarize. The First Circuit, in upholding discharge of a faculty member, declared that the intent to plagiarize was not a necessary requirement for a finding of plagiarism since "one can plagiarize through negligence or recklessness without intent to deceive" (*Newman v. Burgin,* 1991). Similarly, in a leading student plagiarism case where a student's diploma was withheld for

1 year after graduation as a result of plagiarism, a New Jersey court observed that the university's new handbook provision requiring "deliberate use" for plagiarism did not mean that "the proscribed plagiarism must have been [done] with the intent to pass off the submitted work as the student's own" (*Napolitano v. Princeton University,* 1982, p. 270).

Against this backdrop of plagiarism, the debates in this chapter consider divergent attitudes toward the punishment for plagiarism. Phillip Blackman (Pennsylvania State University) in the point essay takes the position that plagiarism is fundamentally a question of ethics operating under the premise that many plagiarism incidents occur because students do not understand the educational institution's ethical expectations. This author contends that student plagiarism violations stem from parental and social pressures to succeed, laziness, poor time management, and inadequate research skills. Incidents of plagiarism will diminish where students are afforded appropriate counseling to address pressures on students to plagiarize made much easier today because of student intimacy with technology. Blackman connects plagiarism and the copyright act, reasoning that educational institutions should instruct their students in the copyright act as a way for disabusing students of the notion that information taken from the Internet is free and requires no attribution.

Peter L. Moran (Pennsylvania State University), in the counterpoint essay, asserts that with respect to plagiarism, the distinction between academic violations and student conduct is a false dichotomy. He cautions that academic dishonesty results from students' lack of respect for academic integrity because students do not perceive academic violations as having the same consequences as disciplinary violations. Moran argues for due process hearings with charges of plagiarism and advocates the implementation of an academic integrity framework.

Ralph D. Mawdsley
Cleveland State University

POINT: Phillip Blackman
Pennsylvania State University

Teachers and administrators in K–12 schools inevitably address instances of academic dishonesty since cheating and plagiarism are perpetual problems in education. Sadly, millennial students, those born between the years of 1982 and 2000, seem to be engaging in academic dishonesty more frequently than their predecessors (McCabe, 1999; McCabe & Trevino, 2005; McCabe, Trevino, & Butterfield, 2001).

Research indicates that a variety of factors has fostered the increase in academic dishonesty (Howe & Strauss, 2000; McCabe, 1999; McCabe et al., 2001). These factors include perceived pressures to succeed that are fueled by obsessive parents; artificially inflated levels of self-esteem coupled with exaggerated senses of entitlement; intimacy and proficiency with technology that leads to a dangerous reliance on such technology; and an ignorance of, ambivalence toward, or blatant disregard for U.S. copyright law (Madray, 2007; Rivera, 2008; Wilson, 2004). If one accepts these factors as the root cause for the increase in academic dishonesty, then all of the involved parties may benefit if teachers and schools employ educationally supportive adjudicative processes to address directly the novel forces leading millennials to commit academic dishonesty at higher rates than in the past and not treat them simply as matters that are dealt with as if they were simply disciplinary violations or infractions.

ACADEMIC VERSUS DISCIPLINARY VIOLATIONS

Prior to discussing the rationales that support this approach, one must understand the difference between academic dishonesty and student conduct violations. Academic dishonesty includes such offenses as plagiarism, cheating, unauthorized help on one's work, and other similar academic offenses. Conduct violations include such actions as underage drinking, assault, vandalism, theft, and other activities that are usually considered criminal offenses. Under this approach, supportive and educational adjudicative processes for academic dishonesty simply mean that academic violations would involve disciplinary procedures to help students grow academically and socially in addition to potentially providing appropriate punitive sanctions. Conduct violations, in contrast, should continue to be addressed with more traditional punitive measures.

Courts have not always defined clearly the distinction between conduct and academic violations. Nonetheless, a general trend to differentiate between student conduct violations and academic dishonesty now exists in the courts. However, many school officials use the same disciplinary procedures for both academic and conduct violations. This all-encompassing approach should be changed.

ADDRESSING ACADEMIC DISHONESTY

Teachers and administrators must guide students through their educational and personal growth by combating the forces that caused them to commit academic violations. This approach allows educators to use the student discipline process to help educate students about their academic and social responsibilities. Supportive educational environments also provide significant deference to educators. Further, adversarial adjudicative models based on criminal law procedures are a poor fit for educational institutions. Finally, these models fail to reflect the mores and ideals of an academic community. As such, school officials may be well served to use supportive and educational disciplinary processes for academic dishonesty. By doing so, schools officials and teachers will gain a greater understanding of why students cheat and the capacity to deal with the causes of academic dishonesty.

Many underlying issues that cause academic dishonesty are fundamentally a question of ethics. Some students enter and persist through school without clear guidance about what ethical responsibilities accompany their own education. School officials and teachers could help alleviate this problem by employing methods that help students gain the ethical compass necessary to succeed academically. For example, school policies could integrate their expectations for academic integrity into each class, employ honor codes, and/or create pervasive atmospheres of academic and social accountability. School officials would be able to foster positive educational and ethical environments once they recognize that many academic disciplinary violations arise from students' ethical confusion and not malice. Recognizing this, institutional policies and officials would then be able to address the specific factors that lead to academic dishonesty in educational contexts.

Supportive and educational adjudicative processes would help combat the unique forces that lead millennials to commit academic dishonesty. Institutional approaches can temper these forces by implementing various types of educational and counseling programs to address specifically each unique impetus for students' dishonesty. Parental and social pressures to succeed are psychological issues. Student reliance on technology likely results from laziness, poor time management, and/or a lack of research skills. Students' disregard for copyright law seems to stem from peer cultural norms and/or an ignorance of copyright law. Supportive educational adjudicative processes address these underlying issues in addition to penalizing justly the violation at hand. Further, education-ally supportive models would not only address these issues retroactively through the adjudicative process but also allow institutions to take steps proac-tively to attack problems by incorporating remedial measures into their curri-cula. Despite the fundamentally positive approach, one must accept that a supportive and educational adjudicative process must still carry appropriate punitive measures. However, first offenses warrant a review of why students cheated in an effort to identify and rectify the underlying reason(s) for their aca-demic dishonesty. Subsequent violations likely reveal students' disregard for aca-demic accountability, and thus, harsher punitive measures would be appropriate.

Employing supportive and educational adjudicative processes could help reduce student academic dishonesty that results from perceived pressures to succeed. Students' parents, peers, and own expectations can create intense pressures to succeed in school. Many students associate their future opportuni-ties and potential career success to their grades. These intense pressures and pervasive expectations can lead students to cheat. Institutions should thus provide counseling to students feeling the need to cheat so that they can suc-ceed academically. Since most schools already employ counselors, additional fiscal expenditures should not be required to accomplish this goal. Moreover, counselors and teachers should guide students to the academic and social resources that will help foster the student's self-confidence and academic achievement. This approach should help relieve the pressures that lead some students to cheat. Supportive resources can include both internal and external psychological support, time management skill development, and supportive mentor/mentee relationships with teachers. Ultimately, school officials should help students to address the psychological pressures that could lead to cheating in efforts to help them grow both emotionally and academically.

Supportive and educational adjudicative processes could help reduce stu-dent academic dishonesty stemming from a reliance on technology. Plagiarism and cheating often result from students' intimacy with technology. Many of today's students grew up with computers in their home, cell phones in their hands, and iPods in their ears. This pervasive interaction has led this genera-tion to have a connection and fluency with technology like no other generation before them. Today's students have also relied largely on the Internet for their information and media. Students access this information and these media with ease. In fact, many of today's youth expect the music and media they enjoy to be free. This easy access and sense of entitlement can create problems for stu-dents. Many students fail to provide appropriate time for completing their assignment because completing other tasks with technology is simple and fast. Other students simply lack the necessary research skills to cite the referenced work properly. Both of these problems can be addressed by means of supportive and educational disciplinary processes.

Once the root causes of violations are identified as (over) reliance on technology, institutional officials should provide remedial education on library-based research techniques, proper citation requirements, and time management skills. These types of programs will yield better students and a more productive educational environment. Institutions should also adopt supportive responses in effort to impart the foundational research and time management skills necessary for student success. Many students have never been exposed to "hard-copy" research and simply need some guidance and encouragement to embrace such research methods. Institutions can accomplish these goals by offering tutorial seminars/webinars and personal instruction in research skills and time management training. These types of hard and soft educational opportunities embrace various learning styles and the technology that today's students find so comforting.

Supportive and educational adjudicative processes could help reduce student academic dishonesty resulting from confusion related to copyright law. Many of today's students knowingly or unknowingly plagiarize because they disregard or are ignorant of copyright law. Today's students routinely download music, films, pictures, and other forms of media on a daily basis. Many of these students knowingly or unknowingly violate copyright law when downloading this material. Students have come to treat the Internet as a free resource for knowledge and media. This has led some students to rely on the Internet to not only supplement their work but also to pass on others' work as their own.

In an effort to combat this lack of knowledge, school officials should provide students with foundations in copyright law and compliance if they determined that students' academic dishonesty stemmed from ignorance of, ambivalence toward, or disdain for copyright law. At the same time, institutions should adopt supportive responses in efforts to educate students about the protections afforded to copyright owners and the value of intellectual property rights. School officials can accomplish this goal by offering tutorial seminars/webinars in copyright compliance and proper citation techniques, as well as extracurricular programming that heightens student awareness about copyright law compliance. School library staff would be essential to making this goal a reality. School policies could then easily justify stronger punitive sanctions for plagiarism once students are knowledgeable of their academic responsibilities and the value of intellectual property.

Supportive and educational adjudicative processes allow institutions to apply just punishments retroactively for academic violations while maintaining a positive and encouraging environment. School policies allow the teachers and administrators to educate their students by using the students' first academic dishonesty offenses as "teachable moments." Students could receive small punitive sanctions for first offenses while the main goal of discipline remained to correct the underlying cause of the violation. This allows institutions to apply just punishments, such as forcing students to rewrite plagiarized papers and awarding zeros on examinations retroactively, while implementing supportive solutions to help them grow both academically and socially. This approach will help build stronger relationships with students and their parents, making schools appear as partner in students' educational pursuits and not as adversaries.

Institutions should also implement proactive measures to combat academic dishonesty by identifying and understanding the underlying causes for such student violations. Once institutional officials identify and understand the root causes of academic dishonesty, they can implement strategies to combat those causes proactively. Using first-year classes to build students' research skills and teach proper citation techniques is one example. Another example is requiring students to attend copyright law and compliance seminars. These proactive measures would assure that the students are educated on their responsibilities for using the work of others and their liability for failing to credit such use. A proactive approach allows schools to impart the students' academic and social responsibilities to them early and often. This, in turn, can help teachers and administrators distinguish which students commit academic dishonesty from malice and those that are motivated by other innocuous motivations.

THE PROBLEM WITH PRESCRIPTIVE PUNITIVE MEASURES

Predetermined punitive responses to academic dishonesty can be unjust and ineffective, and they can breed animosity toward teachers and administrators. Acts of plagiarism can range from slight to extreme. For example, students could mistakenly use notes that they took from the Internet for a sentence or two in completed works. In contrast, students could pass off entire papers acquired from the Internet as their own work. These two acts of plagiarism are not the same in kind or quality and should not receive the same punishment. Nonetheless, many schools have prescribed punishments for any act of academic dishonesty. This results in unjust punishments for many students who made mistakes but did not act maliciously. Students who cheated because of unreasonable expectations, a dangerous reliance on technology, or an ignorance of copyright law should be given the chance to amend their mistakes.

This educational and supportive approach would help educate students and not simply punish them as a dogmatic punitive process would.

Further, strict punishments may not be effective in combating future acts of plagiarism. School officials fail to understand or help alleviate the forces that led students to cheat initially by simply prescribing fixed punishments, zero tolerance style, for academic violations. This leads students simply to accept the punishments without having to identify why they cheated. Punishments convey to students that their acts were wrong but do nothing to relieve the stress, confusion, or ignorance that led them to cheat. For instance, fixed punishments do not help students deal with the pressure they may feel from their parents in any way. In fact, strict punishment may lead to more stress in such situations because a student may forego the opportunity to convey to their parents the negative feelings that stem from underlying pressures to succeed for fear of additional repercussions. Students should have the opportunity to express their reasons for cheating in open and supportive environments so that the larger detrimental forces that led them to cheat can be addressed.

Strict punitive adjudicative processes may also breed animosity toward teachers and administrators. Students who feel that they are punished unfairly would likely hold disdain for those who subjected them to punishment. Prescriptive punishments could easily lead to unjust results that create this type of animosity. Individual teacher and/or school officials would likely find it difficult to engage students in their education once they lose respect for their educators. Conversely, teachers would have better opportunities to engage students in their own educations if teachers help them to grow from their mistakes. Students would seek help from supportive teachers who are helping them to address either the particular educational or the psychological difficulties that caused them to cheat in the first place. This approach would also likely yield trust and respect for teachers, administrators, and the educational process. This respect, in turn, would lead to higher rates of student persistence and a more supportive educational environment.

CONCLUSION

Students, teachers, and administrators would all benefit by using supportive and educational adjudicative processes for students' first academic dishonesty offense. Students would receive the necessary educational and psychological support to help them become positive and productive members of their academic community. Teachers and administrators would be free to educate and help mentor students through difficult circumstances in a supportive manner. The disciplinary process would not simply impose prescribed punitive measures without consideration for the particular circumstances of each violation. Thus, all parties would be well served to use supportive and educational adjudicative processes for academic dishonesty cases that do not treat offenses simply as matters of school discipline.

COUNTERPOINT: Peter L. Moran
Pennsylvania State University

The judicial distinction between academic and disciplinary violations creates a false dichotomy that trivializes the egregiousness of academic dishonesty by requiring a lower threshold of detection. Courts claim that disciplinary violations involve misconduct, which is subject to fact-finding procedures, while academic actions fall within the expertise of professional educators. However, plagiarism involves not only an academic violation but also an explicit behavior of misrepresenting another's works as one's own. Disciplinary actions afford students the right to hearings; academic decisions are often made on ill-defined ad hoc bases. Academic decisions often exist in a nebulous world; teachers are not necessarily sure what plagiarism is nor are students, who often lack the information literacy skills to document and evaluate the credibility of their sources. Therefore, the blanket protection offered to academic actions may prevent the development of clear definitions and guidelines for plagiarism. This all arises in a context wherein plagiarism and cheating levels are high among today's youth (McCabe, 2005). Since today's youth may have different views about plagiarism, institutions must proactively combat the issue of academic dishonesty and develop frameworks to equip students with information literacy skills.

Institutional frameworks relying on the main components of disciplinary procedures—detailed description of infractions, clear and consistent procedures, prescribed punitive measures, and transparent adjudicative processes—would establish academic integrity as a core component of institutional identity. In such a framework, institutional identity would educate students about sources and writing, explicitly defining the procedures for academic dishonesty violations, detailing the procedures for handling cases, and administering punishments. If educators treat academic violations too lightly by failing to punish the behavior, then students will understand neither the severity of their offenses nor the importance of academic integrity. Therefore, schools should adopt an institutional framework, which educates students about academic integrity but also harshly punishes academic violations.

ACADEMIC DECISIONS AND THE COURTS

Courts traditionally have been reluctant to interfere with the academic decisions of schools in the United States. Academic decisions concern issues such as curriculum, pedagogy, and academic dishonesty in the forms of cheating and plagiarism. In contrast, disciplinary decisions relate to conduct violations such as assault, theft, and other traditionally criminal conduct. Courts apply different standards of constitutional protections in cases that involve disciplinary action than in those that lead to academic sanctions. Students facing disciplinary conduct violations must be afforded due process protections under the Fourteenth Amendment to the United States Constitution (*Dixon v. Alabama State Board of Education,* 1961a, 1961b). The rationale for the distinction is that schools employ fact-finding procedures that mimic judicial procedures in disciplinary cases and, therefore, the heightened constitutional protections ensure fundamental fairness. Conversely, the courts claim that only educators possess the requisite expertise to make decisions concerning academic integrity. Therefore, courts generally defer to the academic decisions of educators with the upshot that academic institutions have not had to implement the same due process–protective procedures in plagiarism cases as they do when dealing with conduct violations. This lack of prescribed procedures and guidelines for dealing with academic actions, as opposed to disciplinary actions, likely contributes to the difficulties educators face in developing academic integrity among students.

THE INFORMATION LITERACY OF MILLENNIALS

In their efforts to combat plagiarism, educators face several challenges. The main theme of these challenges is "confusion." In today's information age, more and more academic research is conducted via the Internet. Millennial students, who were born between 1982 and 2000 (Strauss & Howe, 1991), are comfortable with technology and increasingly view the Internet as an academic resource. However, the comfort that students enjoy with the Internet has not necessarily translated to information literacy. In this regard, commentators have expressed their doubts about students' information literacy and ability to engage in critical evaluation as to the credibility of their sources (D'Esposito & Gardner, 1999; Jenson, 2004; Metzger, Flanagin, & Zwarun, 2003). Insofar as millennials are not developing the necessary skills to identify appropriate sources and evaluate their credibility, "few students arrive on college campuses with a thorough knowledge of the relationship between plagiarism and proper source attribution" (Wilhoit, 1994, p. 162).

At the same time, insofar as millennials have grown up in an era when people can illegally download copyrighted works with ease, they often have erroneous conceptions of plagiarism. Further, since new technology has offered students more opportunities to plagiarize the works of others, they may not view their actions as academic dishonesty or cheating. In such environments, since educators cannot possibly develop detection measures to keep pace with the rapidly changing technological landscapes, they must examine their overall approach to academic dishonesty.

THE EFFECTS OF THE FALSE DICHOTOMY

The solution for the plagiarism problem in K–12 education is for educators to take steps to dissolve the false dichotomy between academic and disciplinary decisions. The dichotomy is a judicial construction for purposes of due process analysis. Consequently, school officials should just *choose* to use the same hearing and fact-finding procedures in academic decisions as disciplinary decisions. The dichotomy is premised on the belief that academic decisions are based on the subjective evaluation of educators. However, this belief assumes that teachers and administrators have constructed concrete definitions of plagiarism. Teachers and administrators with varying levels of experience may not be overly familiar with acts of plagiarism, and they may apply standards that violate school policies. Additionally, the false dichotomy presupposes that fact-finding procedures are more appropriate for disciplinary decisions because they involve conduct, but plagiarism involves both an academic and disciplinary violation. Plagiarism is an academic theft that involves not only the appropriation of another's ideas but also the active misrepresentation of those ideas in schoolwork. As soon as students pass off the ideas of other persons as their own in papers or presentations, they engage in plagiaristic behavior.

The false dichotomy also likely contributes to students' lack of respect for academic integrity. Disciplinary decisions that have clear definitions of violations and employ consistent procedures and punishments, alert the educational community to their importance. Plagiarism may often result from unclear policies on academic dishonesty. The lack of consistent policies and procedures in many educational institutions may encourage students to engage in plagiaristic behavior because they are ignorant of the importance of academic honesty. When institutions have not formulated plagiarism policies and procedures, plagiarism has no visibility with the result that school officials implicitly endorse a "culture of copy." Students have reported that the risk of being caught and punished for cheating is not severe enough to deter academic misconduct (Hollinger & Lanza-Kaduce, 2009). A system with clear definitions of violations, consistent procedures, thorough detection measures, and prescribed punitive measures would notify students that plagiarism is not an acceptable practice in schools by addressing transgressions with appropriately harsh penalties.

Last, the false dichotomy deemphasizes the deplorable nature of plagiarism. If school officials reserve formalized hearings for disciplinary decisions, students can develop the impression that discipline is a core value of their institutions rather than academic integrity. Otherwise, why would school officials devote so much institutional energy to disciplinary conduct? If academic integrity is so important to institutions, then why have school officials not offered detailed descriptions of forbidden plagiaristic behavior? Why have officials not developed clear policies and procedures to detect and punish plagiarism? In essence, why have school officials not fostered educational environments that value academic integrity?

THE ACADEMIC INTEGRITY FRAMEWORK

Once the false dichotomy between disciplinary and academic violations is eliminated, an Academic Integrity Framework (AIF) is one possible institutional alternative to addressing academic dishonesty. The AIF is a strategy to foster academic integrity in high schools that highlights the benefits of discarding the false dichotomy between academic and disciplinary decisions. This multiyear initiative would combine programming with punitive measures for academic violations to produce an educational environment that values academic integrity.

The four key attributes of an institutional framework for academic integrity "are transparency, appropriateness, fairness, and consistency" (Park, 2004, p. 294). Since the AIF is intended for high school students who are still in the midst of academic development and may possess a dichotomous view of knowledge, the fairness attribute becomes a featured component. To address the fairness issue, the AIF contains a 4-year course aimed to establish information literacy and critical thinking skills. Since libraries increasingly transfer their content online and librarians are uniquely trained to manage academic resources, libraries could function as the educational environment for librarians to facilitate the development of identifying sources, evaluating their credibility, and using those sources to develop arguments. During the first year, the course could focus on one topic, such as "climate change," and students would learn how to identify sources to research the area. At this level, students would learn about the varying degrees of credibility between and among such sources as blogs, newspapers, books, videos, and the like. The aim of the first year is source familiarity.

During the second and third years of high school, students may learn how to use and credit sources in their papers on climate change. At this level, educators may focus the entire class on one side or perspective of an issue for the second year and then switch to the opposite side of the argument during the third year. In this instance, teachers call on students to rely on researching sources that stress the negative impacts of climate change during the second year and then switch during the third year to resources that emphasize the importance of minimizing the effects of climate change. By researching the issue from two different perspectives, students will learn that arguments can be made for either side of a debate, so to evaluate a position, they need to discern the credibility of supporting evidence.

The capstone experience may involve the completion of a writing assignment in which students communicate their own perspectives on climate change and support their claims with credible sources. By accompanying students through the process of researching and writing, educators demonstrate the difficulty and merit of building arguments to the students. Hopefully, students would develop a better appreciation for original ideas as well as information literacy skills.

Another attribute of an institutional framework is appropriateness. Since students would learn about research over a 4-year period, appropriate policies would be implemented each year, including prescribed punitive measures. A system of escalating penalties commensurate with students' experience would be developed to punish academic transgressions during all 4 years of high school. Each year, the expectations of students would increase because they would build on the information literacy skills from the year before, but even early in the curriculum, students would be expected to exhibit academic integrity. Once students learned the fundamentals of proper source attribution during their first year, any instance of plagiarism, in any course, would be subject to punishment.

Therefore, a first-time offense for plagiarism during the second year of high school would result in a failing grade for the assignment, while a second offense would result in a failing grade for the course. During the third and fourth years, first-time offenses would result in failing grades in the course, although subsequent offenses would initiate expulsion proceedings. During the first year, while students are still learning proper source attribution, first-time offenses would receive a warning, second-time offenses would result in failing grades for the assignment, and third-time offenses would lead to failing grades in the course. By identifying and correcting behaviors that violate academic norms with increasing penalties, this scheme will establish clear expectations of appropriate conduct at each level of AIF.

Consistency is another attribute of the framework, since without consistent policies, students will continue to cheat because they do not fear repercussions of their actions. Appropriate punishments will be developed to correspond with students' class year in the high school. Critics may decry the prescribed measures as draconian, but within the context of the AIF, they buttress the high value that the initiative places on academic integrity and accountability. Some may argue that prescribed punitive measures focus educators on discipline, rather than the root causes of plagiarism. To the contrary, consistent procedures and punishments actually address the confusion underlying students' misperceptions of plagiarism by increasing their accountability for plagiarism with each year of progress in the academic honesty curriculum. With each additional year of training, students are expected to understand and abide by the rules that they have learned and are punished for noncompliance. This clarifies the importance and severity of academic dishonesty in the same manner that harsh criminal penalties highlight the deplorable nature of crimes. The escalating penalties help internalize a respect for academic honesty. Insofar as students must learn to police themselves, prescribed punitive measures contemporaneously highlight improper behavior while establishing social norms of academic integrity.

Alleged plagiarizers will have the right to hearings. However, hearings are not likely to create animosity between educators and alleged plagiarizers because the AIF will cement academic integrity as a core value of the educational community. While teaching competencies to students provides them with the skill set for academic integrity, normative modes of behavior, instilled by the 4-year curriculum, will establish academic integrity as a core institutional value and encourage community members to uphold its fundamental principles.

The fourth attribute of an institutional framework is transparency. First, school officials must specify which types of actions qualify as plagiarism since this definition will serve as a guideline for both students and teachers. Second, school officials must list the policies, procedures, and punishments for adjudicating academic dishonesty violations. For example, Park (2004) listed graduated punishments for each violation, which range from resubmission of assignments to expulsion from school. Insofar as the prescribed punishments create clear expectations of behavior, students will know the ramifications of their actions if they decide to engage in acts of plagiarism. Third, the prescribed punishments should ease the burden placed on both teachers and administrators. Instead of the risk that some teachers and administrators will implement more punitive measures than others, a graduated sanction scale would ensure that the punishment for a transgression corresponds with the offender's progress through the academic integrity curriculum. Additionally, since academic integrity is likely be a core institutional value, plagiarism should be viewed as an offense against the educational community rather than an isolated grievance between individual teachers and students.

The AIF would also feature transparent, formalized, public hearings and sanctioned detection procedures. The public hearings would establish a documented record of the community's expectations of behavior and also inform teachers of the contours of plagiarism. Rather than demonizing court-like hearings as adversarial adjudicative proceedings, these forums should be viewed as an effective teaching tool for communicating the academic standards of the institution to the community. Additionally, sanctioned detection procedures offer teachers the proper tools for uncovering academic dishonesty. Teachers would have a clear idea of the definition of plagiarism, the procedures for detecting violations, the intricacies of formalized hearings, and the potential punitive measures. The hearings would also provide alleged plagiarizers with a recourse to defend themselves against the allegations. The AIF eases the uncertainty of reporting violations and handles the punishment of offenses in a transparent, documented forum. Similar to the Anglo-American common law tradition, the decisions from a particular school's hearings chronicle the community's evolving definitions, expectations, policies, procedures, and punishments regarding academic honesty.

CONCLUSION

The false dichotomy between academic and disciplinary violations minimizes the atrocious nature of plagiarism. Teachers and administrators must develop a thorough framework that nurtures the development of academic integrity but also holds students accountable for acts of academic dishonesty. Under this system, teachers, students, and administrators eliminate the false dichotomy, cultivate an appreciation for academic integrity, establish openly the norms of behavior, and promote academic integrity as a core institutional value.

FURTHER READINGS AND RESOURCES

Bast, C. M. ,& Samuels, L. B. (2008). Plagiarism and legal scholarship in the age of information sharing: The need for intellectual honesty. *Catholic University Law Review, 57,* 777, 778–784.

D'Esposito, J. E., & Gardner, R. M. (1999). University students' perceptions of the Internet: An exploratory study. *The Journal of Academic Librarianship, 25*(6), 456–461.

Hollinger, R., & Lanza-Kaduce, L. (2009). Academic dishonesty and the perceived effectiveness of countermeasures: An empirical survey of cheating at a major public university. *NASPA, 46*(4), 587.

Howe, N., & Strauss, W. (2000). *Millennials rising: The next great generation.* New York: Vintage.

Jenson, J. D. (2004). It's the information age, so where's the information? Why our students can't find it and what we can do to help. *College Teaching, 52*(3), 107–112.

Johnson, V. R. (2008). Corruption in education: A global legal challenge. *Santa Clara Law Review, 48*(1), 73–74.

Madray, A. (2007, June). Developing students' awareness of plagiarism: Crisis and opportunities. *Library Philosophy and Practice* [e-journal].

Mawdsley, R. (1994). *Academic misconduct: Cheating and plagiarism.* Dayton, OH: Education Law Association.

McCabe, D. L. (1999). Academic dishonesty among high school students. *Adolescence, 34*(136), 681–687.

McCabe, D. L. (2005). *Levels of cheating and plagiarism remain high: Honor codes and modified codes are shown to be effective in reducing academic misconduct.* Center for Academic Integrity, Duke University. Retrieved from http://www.academicintegrity.org/cai_research/index.php

McCabe, D. L., & Trevino, L. K. (2005). It takes a village: Academic dishonesty & educational opportunity. *Liberal Education, 91,* 26–31.

McCabe, D. L., Trevino, L. K., & Butterfield, K. D. (2001). Cheating in academic institutions: A decade of research. *Ethics and Behavior, 11*(3), 219–232.

Metzger, M. J., Flanagin, A. J., & Zwarun, L. (2003). College student web use, perceptions of information credibility, and verification behavior. *Computers & Education, 41,* 271–290.

Park, C. (2004). Rebels without a clause: Towards an institutional framework for dealing with plagiarism by students. *Journal of Further and Higher Education, 28*(3), 291–306.

Rivera, C. (2008, March 30). High tech cheats, low tech reasons. *Los Angeles Times.* Retrieved June 17, 2011, from http://articles.latimes.com/2008/mar/30/local/me-cheat30

Strauss, W., & Howe, N. (1991). *Generations: The history of American's future, 1584–2069.* New York: William Morrow.

Weidenborner, S., & Caruso, D. (1982). *Writing research papers: A guide to the process.* New York: St. Martin's Press.

Wilhoit, S. (1994). Helping students avoid plagiarism. *College Teaching, 42*(4), 161–165.

Wilson, M. (2004). Teaching, learning, and millennial students. *New Directions for Student Services, 106,* 59–71.

Winkler, A. C., & McCuen, J. R. (1985). *Writing the research paper: A handbook* (2nd ed.). San Diego, CA: Harcourt Brace Jovanovich.

Court Cases and Statutes

Agarwal v. Regents of University of Minnesota, 788 F.2d 504 (8th Cir. 1986).

A.V. v. iParadigms, Ltd. Liability Co., 544 F.Supp.2d 473, 478 (E.D.Va. 2008).

Boateng v. Inter American University, 190 F.R.D. 29 (D. Puerto Rico, 1999).

Dixon v. Alabama State Board of Education, 294 F.2d 150 (5th Cir. 1961a), cert. denied, 368 U.S. 930 (1961b).

Dodd v. Ft. Smith Special School District No. 100, 666 F.Supp. 1278 (W.D. Ark. 1987).

McCawley v. Universidad Carlos Albizu, Inc., 461 F.Supp.2d 1251 (S.D. Fla. 2006).

Napolitano v. Princeton University, 453 A.2d 263 (N.J. Super. Ct. App. Div. 1982).

Newman v. Burgin, 930 F.2d 955 (1st Cir. 1991).

Slack v. Stream, 2008 WL 162618 (Ala. 2008).

Should teachers incorporate extrinsic motivators in classroom management plans?

POINT: Robin L. Fankhauser, *Indiana University Southeast*
COUNTERPOINT: Erin B. Snell, *Charles R. Drew Charter School*

OVERVIEW

Teachers take on several different roles and responsibilities throughout the typical school day. Yet, perhaps the most important and likely the most demanding task that teachers face each day is trying to maintain safe and well-managed classrooms. Given that it is extremely difficult for teachers to instruct and for students to learn in chaotic and disorderly classrooms, it is difficult to overstate the importance of teachers' ability to create collaborative learning environments with strong senses of structure. In fact, many researchers concluded that teacher effectiveness in their classrooms is the most important factor within the control of educational leaders that impacts student academic achievement (Marzano, Marzano, & Pickering, 2003).

Good classroom management is multilayered and requires that skilled teachers carefully consider a variety of elements in setting up and carrying out classroom operations. Early on, teachers often work to state positively the expectations of collaborative learning environments and teach explicitly the procedures that are to be used in their classrooms. The physical space of classrooms can also be arranged so as to help maximize the ability of teachers to engage in active supervision while moving throughout their rooms. Although these general practices help students take comfort in the predictability of classroom operations, teachers also face the daily challenge of finding new ways to engage students with creative lesson planning. After all, students who are engaged in positive learning activities are far less likely to create disciplinary problems. Last, when discipline problems do arise, skilled teachers are likely to be firm yet positive in redirecting negative student behaviors as they use a hierarchy of preplanned intervention strategies (Crimmins, Farrell, Smith, & Bailey, 2007).

Even as teachers strive to employ a variety of specific strategies to assist them in their classroom management techniques, it is important to note that teaching is a job that, at its core, depends on the ability of individual teachers to build meaningful relationships with their students. To be successful in managing their classrooms, it is imperative for teachers to seek to understand their own personalities and motivations as well as the personalities and motivations of their students (Bradley, Pauley, & Pauley, 2006).

Some teachers and researchers urge that educators seek only to nurture students' intrinsic motivation to learn while others argue that extrinsic motivations can be individually tailored and utilized to fulfill students' psychological need to see the fruits of their labor (Bluestein, 2008). As noted in the point essay: "[T]eachers must consider how intrinsic and extrinsic motivators inspire students in public school classrooms to follow the rules." However, the counterpoint essay stresses that teacher must act cautiously when implementing extrinsic reward systems in their classrooms.

Specifically, the counterpoint essay contends that, "if a child already has a love for reading and you start giving him prizes for reading, the prize may actually decrease his natural motivation for reading." The counterpoint essay's approach is consistent with research in this area. For example, some scholars warn that extrinsic motivation may come at the expense of decreasing levels of intrinsic motivation in children. For example, if a student is offered a piece of candy every time she practices the piano, then the student may spend less time practicing the piano than a child who received no extrinsic reward (see Lepper, Greene, & Nisbett, 1973).

Despite the various philosophical approaches, most researchers agree that knowing each student well is the first important step that allows teachers to tap into each student's potential positive motivations. Correspondingly, teachers that know their students well can also be more prepared to investigate and understand the root causes of misbehavior when it arises (Gootman, 2008). Some aspects of successful classroom management might be more intuitive for some individuals. To this end, Marzano (2007) has emphasized that the existing educational research demonstrates that good classroom managers are not born but made. Indeed, according to this approach, teachers can learn to become good classroom managers, he maintains, in a relatively short amount of time if they are taught to use specific techniques and strategies. However, at the same time, it is important to note that no permanently fixed set of classroom management strategies will be successful in all contexts. Instead, teachers must realize that successful strategies may change over time as the norms of our school classrooms adapt to shifts in culture and to the changing demands of the 21st-century work environment (Bluestein, 2008).

The point essay and counterpoint essay address different approaches to classroom management. In the point essay, Robin L. Fankhauser (Indiana University Southeast) stresses that classroom management is essential to maintaining a safe environment where students can learn. She argues that extrinsic motivators may be one helpful approach to helping teachers maintain control of their classrooms. At the same time, Fankhauser cautions that extrinsic motivators must be carefully considered. In her counterpoint essay, Erin B. Snell (Charles R. Drew Charter School) also stresses the importance of classroom management but takes a somewhat different approach. She focuses on developing intrinsic motivators, in which the teacher should play the role of student motivator or "warm demander" in trying to establish control. Snell stresses the importance of relationship development in attempting to manage a classroom.

Suzanne E. Eckes
Stephen M. Harper
Indiana University

POINT: Robin L. Fankhauser
Indiana University Southeast

As principals search for teachers to hire, they look for applicants who can demonstrate effective teaching qualities. Not only do building level administrators consider candidates who are strong in their content knowledge and pedagogical skills, but principals look also for those candidates who have the ability to manage their classrooms to ensure that students learn in safe and orderly environments. In fact, teachers who are strong in content knowledge and can both plan and deliver quality instruction cannot be effective if students are not on task in safe classroom environments that are free from disruptions and distractions.

The design of an effective classroom management plan may include various components, but the two most basic elements are the rules and the consequences. The rules are designed around elements that the teacher believes are necessary to ensure safety, civility, and a classroom environment free of unnecessary distractions. The rules, therefore, may focus on desired behaviors to help students learn as well as desired behaviors that keep others from not being able to learn. Examples of rules that address both types of desired student behavior might include the following:

- Stay on task

- Do your best work

- Keep your hands and your feet to yourself

- Respect yourself and others

Once teachers identified the critical rules for their classrooms, they take the first step toward being effective on the first day by explaining the rules, modeling and providing examples of the desired behaviors, and practicing them with the students. Along with the rules, teachers must design, explain, model, and practice the consequences for following and not following the rules.

The students' motivation to follow the rules then drives what teachers should consider as consequences for following and not following the rules. The great debate ensues among teachers and other educators on what motivates students and whether the motivators should be intrinsic or extrinsic. The argument becomes even more complicated when one ponders whether the two types of motivation are polar opposites or are just different means by which we set the stage for students to be engaged in learning and in acting appropriately. Additional complications to the argument arise when one considers whether a student can be intrinsically as well as extrinsically motivated.

As an undergraduate education student ponders these issues, one should first consider the following examples. The examples demonstrate how motivation could be linked to an undergraduate education major's general education experiences in three courses taken during his first 2 years of college. Think about each example and whether intrinsic or extrinsic motivation served to drive the student's success. Three of the student's general education courses were English literature, geology, and psychology.

1. During the English literature course, the student determined what work had to be successfully completed to earn a "B," which was the grade necessary to renew his scholarship. The student carefully monitored the graded assignments and did not work beyond what was needed, including participating in class discussions.

2. While taking geology, the student went on an optional field trip to a cavern, participated energetically in class discussions, looked forward to every class meeting, and always did the homework assignments first before tackling any other course's homework. He did extra credit work even though he did not need additional points to receive an "A."

3. While taking psychology, the student had to study a great deal to earn a "B," which was a requirement for admission to the school of education. The student hired a tutor, met with his professor several times, and spent more time preparing for the course than any other course taken during his first 2 years in college.

Consider whether there were intrinsic or extrinsic motivators at play in each experience.

The student was extrinsically motivated in the English literature course. The student did not enjoy any literature and was taking the course as one of the 6 hours of literature that the university required. He needed the scholarship money to be renewed because without the funds, he would have had to find a job. The student did not want to work during the summer or while he was away at college.

The student was intrinsically motivated in the geology course. The student loved any science course, had taken only science courses as electives, and hoped to become a science teacher. He worked hard and derived pleasure from learning in this course.

The student seems to be extrinsically motivated in the psychology course, working for the grade. On subsequent investigation, however, one would understand that this student has a great passion to become a teacher. The student aspires to become a teacher for its intrinsic rewards and the gratification of helping others. He does not view teaching as a job to earn a salary but as a calling. For this student, what seems to be an extrinsic motivator is driven by an intrinsic one.

With a better understanding of how both intrinsic and extrinsic motivators are demonstrated in older learners, consider a third-grade student who rarely finishes work in class and often talks to others while the teacher is speaking. In an attempt to address the problem, the teacher structures a point system for the student whereby she earns points for following the classroom rules by completing work, staying on task, and being respectful. The student loses points for not following the same rules. The points are traded for stickers that the student likes to collect. This point system, which is an example of extrinsic motivation, has been successful as the student completes work and does not disrupt as long as she is earning points for stickers. However, this student exhibits different behaviors when the class begins to make dioramas based on their favorite books. She listens intently while the teacher describes the expectations for the project, approaches her work with enthusiasm, and asks to remain inside during recess to work on her diorama. The teacher forgets to give the student points for being on task and she does not even notice. As with the college student taking geology, the pleasure is derived from the learning and the work itself serves as an intrinsic motivator.

As demonstrated by both of these students, teachers must consider how intrinsic and extrinsic motivators inspire students in public school classrooms to follow the rules. Teachers must consider this as they design their consequences for following and not following the classroom rules—the classroom management system. A visit to three classrooms can help to demonstrate how teachers embed intrinsic motivators, extrinsic motivators, or both types of motivators in their classroom management plans. As one visits each classroom, assume that each has well-designed lesson plans, each differentiates instruction, and each has strong content knowledge. The classroom rules are posted and relate to having appropriate behavior, being on task, and completing assignments. The focus of each visit will be on how each teacher has consequences for following and not following the rules.

In the first classroom, most of the students are engaged in learning. The students here are listening to the teacher, responding to her questions, and following the posted rules. Several students are not engaged and the teacher manages their behavior by walking toward them, standing by them, touching them, glaring at them, or redirecting them verbally. You observe that several of the students do not remain engaged after she stops the intervention she is using.

When asked about her classroom management plan, she explains she believes in intrinsic motivation. She does not believe in using extrinsic motivators such as rewards for following the rules. The teacher designs her lessons to ensure that children will love learning. She acknowledges that some of the students were not engaged. She believes that is because they do not enjoy learning. The teacher states also that she designs her lessons to encourage them in the hope that they will become engaged or at least learn to follow the rules.

This teacher fails to understand that she is using extrinsic motivators as she stands by students, glares at them, touches them, or verbally redirects their behavior. However, the extrinsic motivators she uses are ineffective for all students. The students who may not want to be engaged but do not want to have their names called or have the teacher hovering over them will follow the rules. The students want to avoid this unpleasant experience. For the students who do not find her interventions to be unpleasant, the inappropriate behaviors will continue.

In the next classroom, you observe the same level of student engagement as you enter the room. You notice that poker chips are stacked on the right corner of each desk. As the teacher is talking and interacting with the class, you see him add a chip to stacks on the desks of engaged students. As students fail to follow one of the posted rules, you see him take a poker chip off the student's stack of chips. When a student has lost all of his or her chips, the teacher puts the student's name on the board. You remain in the classroom long enough to observe a student sent to the office for having her name on the board four times.

When asked about his classroom management plan, the teacher explains that he believes in extrinsic motivation through using rewards for appropriate behaviors. He believes that it reflects what is found in the world of work. The teacher uses the chip system as it allows students to earn tokens for following the classroom rules and lose chips for not following the rules. He has a class store with school supplies that students can purchase with the earned chips. One adjustment that the teacher had to make to the plan was the placing of students' names on the board when they had lost all of their chips. The items at the store were not serving as motivators for some students so he had to find another kind of extrinsic motivator—punishment—to use with some students. The teacher comments that some students never lose all of their chips while never having enough chips to buy anything either. The teacher also expresses frustration with trying to keep up with the chips, putting the names on the board, keeping up with the reward items, and teaching while implementing the management system.

The teacher has not used extrinsic motivators effectively. He did not determine what extrinsic motivators were needed for his students as he developed his classroom management system. Those students who never cashed in chips but were never sent to the office were not motivated by the items but were motivated to stay out of trouble. Those who were sent to the office were not motivated by the items and may not be motivated to stay out of the office if they were sent there often. Those who earned chips to purchase items may have been motivated by the items and others may have been motivated to do well to please the teacher or their families. For some of those students, intrinsic motivators are at work. Instructional time is lost as the teacher implements the system; the classroom management system is managing the teacher.

As you enter the third classroom, you again see poker chips on students' desks. The teacher adds a red chip to stacks on the desks of engaged students. As a student fails to follow one of the posted rules, you see her place a blue poker chip on the student's stack of chips. Most of the students are engaged and the placement of a blue chip tends to bring a student back on task. A paper taped to a table in the back of the room has the following list: extra computer time, no recess, homework pass, positive note home, negative note home, highlighter, pencil, and "contracted item." Each has a different point value assigned to it.

When asked about the classroom management plan, the teacher explains that she first establishes a plan using extrinsic motivators. During the first week of school, she teaches the rules and reinforces them with the red chips for following the rules and with the blue chips for not following the rules. After she has determined that the students understand the rules, she establishes a process for the chips to serve as extrinsic motivators. She asks students to tell her what motivates them to learn or to identify what would make them want to earn red chips. She also asks them to identify what negative consequences would make them avoid earning blue chips. She uses this information to create the list of positive and negative consequences, which are the extrinsic motivators, for earning red or blue chips. Students can then make choices about their behaviors to earn something pleasant or avoid something unpleasant. She acknowledges that some of her students love to learn or want to do well for their own sense of accomplishment. She understands that intrinsic motivation is at play with them. She encourages these students and recognizes they may not work to earn lots of red chips but she distributes them anyway as part of the classroom management system.

This teacher has differentiated the system after determining what extrinsic motivators serve her students. She understands how extrinsic motivators can serve to keep her students on track with the classroom rules. She recognizes that there are those who are intrinsically motivated. She knows that they do not need the chips. The system is in place, however, for the times that they do not find the learning interesting. She believes she may not know when intrinsic motivation is at play and if she addresses what students identify as extrinsic motivators the classroom management system will work.

In preparing to start the school year, teachers have important decisions to make. The design of one's classroom management system should be at the top. In addition to identifying the classroom rules and determining how to teach them, the teacher must develop the plan to include reinforcement of following and not following the rules. The most efficient means is to build in extrinsic motivators. The teacher must consider how to identify the extrinsic motivators that are appropriate to the students' age and maturity level, the availability of financial and school resources to support the rewards, and the school or district policies on use of extrinsic motivators such as recess, time, food, and privileges. The teacher must consider the ease of implementation. A complex system can confuse the students and cause the teacher to focus more on the classroom management plan than on following the lesson plan to be managed by it. Students learn best in classrooms with effective teachers who know and understand what to teach, how to teach it, and how to establish a classroom environment free from distraction, disruption, and problems with student disciplinary issues.

COUNTERPOINT: Erin B. Snell
Charles R. Drew Charter School

I magine a brand new middle school teacher who thinks that classroom management is just about discipline, developing rules and consequences, and making sure that students know who is in charge. When the teacher creates her first classroom management plan, she quickly comes up with rules inspired by her textbook, brainstorms point systems to encourage positive behaviors and discourage undesirable behaviors, and designs prizes to be given for homework completion. The new teacher assumes that her students may or may not be intrinsically motivated to learn, so she develops a series of external rewards and consequences designed to motivate all her students. The teacher thinks of classroom management as separate from her instruction. After a few months of teaching, she realizes that her students have earned many points but seem totally unmotivated to focus in class and unwilling to dive into challenging work. Her classroom management plan fails her because it is incomplete.

Educators now understand that effectively managing a classroom is much more than just establishing order, making assumptions about students' levels of intrinsic motivation, and using easy extrinsic motivators. Yes, establishing and maintaining order is critical, students will have varying levels of motivation, and extrinsic motivators can be useful tools, but the more important part of a classroom management plan is creating a positive learning environment and encouraging student self-motivation.

CREATING A LEARNING ENVIRONMENT
Overview

Establishing and maintaining order and discipline is what teachers might traditionally think of when discussing the term *classroom management*. Most individuals have probably observed classrooms where there is so much chaos that the students seem to shut down and little productive learning takes place. It is clear that lack of classroom discipline and order can certainly make learning impossible and make students feel unsafe, yet we also know that it is more productive to create a learning environment, a place where students come to learn and are successful in doing so through collaboration with their teacher and classmates, than just a classroom that is under control.

Learning Environments

As educators, we have learned that classrooms are more productive when they are managed through caring, respectful relationships rather than through external rewards, punishments, and other coercive methods. From Jere Brophy's overview of research on motivating students and Carolyn M. Evertson and Carol Simon Weinstein's *Handbook of Classroom Management,* we also know that when students feel that their teacher cares about them, they are more likely to learn.

Students may disengage from learning in classrooms when they feel scared, bitter, or have other negative feelings toward their teachers. As part of building positive relationships, teachers must establish and monitor behavior expectations, procedures, and classroom organizational systems. Ideally, they would do so with a foundation of care and a focus on meaningful learning. Evertson and Weinstein suggest that teachers act in the role of "warm demanders" who show that they care and make their expectations clear to students. Teachers must explicitly and proactively teach students about classroom expectations and how to meet those expectations. This will prevent many after-the-fact discipline interventions.

Also, as part of being "warm demanders," teachers should have high expectations for students learning and behavior and a clear vision of the purpose of their class. It is not conducive to optimal learning if the students are behaving well but the teacher does not have clear learning objectives. Good classroom management is useless and cannot happen without a good instructional plan. Teachers and students need to know to what they are striving toward.

By creating learning environments with strong teacher–students relationships, proactive teaching of expectations, and a clear focus on meaningful learning, teachers can encourage the positive social, emotional, and moral growth of their students. Through this strong foundation, teachers can help students build more effective relationships, better self-regulate their own behavior, and improve communication with their classmates, which will lead to an orderly class.

CLASSROOM MANAGEMENT PLANS THAT DEVELOP LEARNING ENVIRONMENTS

Creating a learning environment involves many factors, including teachers establishing caring relationships with students, teaching and reinforcing expectations, having and communicating a clear vision for the high-level learning that students will do, and helping students grow as social, emotional, and moral beings.

When developing classroom management plans, teachers should consider how they will develop caring relationships with their students. Building positive relationships can start with strategies such as warmly greeting students each day, taking time to interact with students individually even if just in passing in the hallway, and speaking in a respectful way. Teachers should model how they wish students to treat others.

Teaching and reinforcing classroom expectations, rules, and procedures are also essential parts of a classroom management plan. Teachers need to dedicate sufficient time at the beginning of the school year to teaching these explicitly. Teachers should continue developing relationships by explaining expectations, rules, and procedures in a way that shows that they are beneficial to the students and that is based on respect for one another. To the extent possible, students should also be given the opportunity to give input into the classroom expectations and rules. In an ongoing way throughout the year, the teacher should reteach, when necessary, and monitor how students are doing in terms of meeting expectations.

Planning to set a vision for classroom learning is mostly part of a teacher's instructional plan, but this is a place where instructional plans have to be closely tied to classroom management plans. As part of their classroom management plan, teachers should show the clear purpose of learning.

To assist students in their growth as social, emotional, and moral beings, classroom management plans can include lessons on how to teach students to interact effectively with each other. In preparation for group work, teachers can guide students through dealing with conflict effectively. Additionally, a teacher's modeling of respectful and fair interactions will help students learn how to interact with others.

ENCOURAGING STUDENT SELF-MOTIVATION
Overview

An effective classroom management plan that functions at this higher level needs to assist a teacher in establishing a learning environment, as discussed previously, and also promote student self-motivation. In an ideal world, all learning would stem from individuals' fascination and love of learning (or intrinsic motivation), but in our society individuals are required to learn and master topics that they may not find to be inherently interesting or enjoyable. Yes, we hope our teachers can make the material as interesting and engaging as possible to students, but we must also prepare students to be motivated to learn even when they are not inherently interested in a topic. If teachers do not tap into and help children develop their self-motivation, the students may shut down whenever they come across a subject that does not naturally inspire them. To promote student self-motivation, it is helpful to understand what is known about motivation, including intrinsic motivation, extrinsic motivation, and other factors known to influence motivation.

Intrinsic Motivation

Through their work on motivation, Edward Deci and Richard Ryan found that humans have a basic need to feel competent and have free choice and that these desires lead individuals to be motivated to carry out certain tasks and behaviors for their inherent value. These researchers conclude that when student learning in school stems from these intrinsic motivations such as their desire to do something because they find it to be inherently interesting or enjoyable, that their attention to the task will last longer and result in more ingenuity and meaningful learning. For example, if a student naturally loves studying and learning about airplanes and gets to choose to do a project on this topic, then this type of learning will be more powerful than learning spelling words in order to pass a test. This kind of learning is more lasting that learning motivated by extrinsic rewards, such as doing well on a spelling test to earn a prize or points, or to avoid getting in trouble. Intrinsic motivation can be extended when individuals are allowed to be self-directed and feel successful in their learning.

Extrinsic Motivation: The Good and the Bad

Research has shown that extrinsic rewards can actually undermine intrinsic motivation. In their overview of motivation research and theory, Deci, Koestner, and Ryan (1999) reported that virtually all types of tangible rewards seem to have negative effects on intrinsic motivation (pp. 658–659). Other researchers found that threats, deadlines, directives, and competition also reduce intrinsic motivation because students experience them as attempts to control their behavior. For instance, if a child already has a love for reading and the teacher starts giving him prizes for reading, the prize may actually decrease his natural motivation to read. If individuals feel that someone else is taking charge of their learning and that they are no longer independent, they may lose interest and motivation.

Extrinsic motivators are not inherently negative. Deci and Ryan found that even though many types of extrinsic motivators interfere with intrinsic motivation, extrinsic motivators that allow for personal autonomy, align with an individual's existing interests, and connect them with their social community may actually increase intrinsic motivation. For instance, if a student dislikes grammar practice but loves writing and wants to be an author, then his teacher may be able to increase his motivation for achieving on grammar tests by explaining how success on these assignments will facilitate his ease and power as a writer and will help him be a more educated member of the writing community. This external pressure may actually increase his intrinsic motivation or at least be an innocuous extrinsic motivator because it aligns with his existing interests and will help him become a more prepared member of a social community of which he wants to be a part. Student intrinsic motivation also increases or is maintained when students' receive positive feedback for their learning. Extrinsic motivators can be powerful when used correctly, but they should be employed with thoughtful care.

OTHER FACTORS THAT INFLUENCE MOTIVATION

In addition to extrinsic and intrinsic motivators, many factors are known to influence an individual's motivation, including the relevance of a topic to an individual's curiosity and interest, individual goals and goal orientations, and self-efficacy beliefs, as discussed in the chapter on learning and motivation in *Psychology of Learning for Instruction* by Marcy Driscoll. Motivation has been found to be influenced by an individual's level of interest and curiosity about a subject or topic. For example, if a student really loves art but is not so into science, then she may be more likely to be motivated to work hard in art class than in science class. Or if a student is surprised by a topic in biology he may be more likely to be motivated to learn about it. Similarly, students with different personality types, such as extroverts who love talking and group work or introverts who love problem solving, and students with different learning styles, such as visual or auditory learners, may be motivated by an instructor whose teaching styles taps into their personality or learning style interests.

Additionally, we know that setting achievable learning goals contributes to motivation and can lead to improved performance. A student who sets a learning goal of writing an effective five-paragraph essay may work harder and be more motivated to write than a student who has no writing goal. The beliefs that individuals have about their ability to perform tasks successfully also influence their motivation. If a student thinks that he is just not good at mathematics and has experienced failure with it in the past, then he may lack motivation to try hard in his algebra class.

USING WHAT IS KNOWN ABOUT MOTIVATION AS A BASIS FOR CLASSROOM MANAGEMENT

As this brief overview demonstrates, motivation is complex and individualized. An individual's level of motivation depends on many factors, such as feelings of efficacy or interest in a subject, and individual motivation can be influenced in a variety of ways, such as through praise or positive reinforcement for effort or using certain instructional strategies. Drawing from what is known about motivation, ideally, teachers would teach in ways that tap into student intrinsic motivation, use effective and avoid harmful extrinsic motivators, and employ other strategies that are known to influence motivation.

Researchers found many strategies for tapping into students' intrinsic motivations. We know that teachers should give students choice whenever possible and allow them to ask their own questions and pursue topics that are important to them. By way of illustration, if students are given a choice when conducting a research project or allowed to choose how they demonstrate their learning (whether through Microsoft PowerPoint, essay, or poster) many students will be more invested.

Marcy Driscoll suggests that teachers can tap into students' motivations by gaining and sustaining their attention by using new and varied approaches to instruction and stimulating curiosity with interesting problems or mysteries. This can be as simple as starting a lesson with a joke or using a new technology. Teachers can also encourage intrinsic motivation by making instruction relevant to students' lives, interests, and goals. Relevancy may be found by having the students work in groups, which taps into students' interest in interacting with each other or serving as leaders, or connecting with real-life concerns that students have. In a classroom management plan, a teacher could commit to giving students choice with assignments whenever possible, using attention getters as parts of lessons, frequently varying instructional strategies, and making the learning relevant to students' lives. To extend student motivation, teachers can also plan for helping students build their confidence with the subjects and skills that they are learning by being clear with expectations, revealing expectations in a layered approach so students are not overwhelmed, giving students challenges that they can be successful with, and giving appropriate levels of assistance to students.

Teachers must also avoid certain behaviors that minimize student motivation. Teachers should avoid being too controlling of students, which takes away their feelings of independence and, therefore, their intrinsic motivation, and should try to move away from solely relying on extrinsic rewards, such as prizes and points.

CONCLUSION

Classroom management is much more than just disciplining students. To be effective classroom managers, teachers need to think of themselves as student motivators and "warm demanders." By building strong relationships with students, modeling kindness and care, keeping the purpose of instruction forefront, and explicitly teaching behavioral expectations, teachers can develop learning environments that will serve as a foundation for motivating students to achieve at high levels. Motivating students is not always an easy task, but by tapping into the existing intrinsic motivations of students and continuing to help students increase their self-motivation, students can grow as learners and as people.

FURTHER READINGS AND RESOURCES

Bluestein, J. (2008). *The win-win classroom: A fresh and positive look at classroom management*. Thousand Oaks, CA: Corwin.

Bradley, D. F., Pauley, J. A., & Pauley, J. F. (2006). *Effective classroom management: Six keys to success*. Lanham, MD: Rowman & Littlefield.

Brophy, J. E. (2004). *Motivating students to learn* (2nd ed.). Mahwah, NJ: Lawrence Erlbaum.

Crimmins, D., Farrell, A., Smith, P., & Bailey, A. (2007). *Positive strategies for students with behavior problems.* Baltimore, MD: Paul H. Brookes.

Deci, E. L., Koestner, R., & Ryan, R. M. (1999). A meta-analytic review of experiments examining the effects of extrinsic rewards on intrinsic motivation. *Psychological Bulletin, 125*(6), 627–668.

Driscoll, M. P. (2005). *Psychology of learning for instruction* (3rd ed.). Boston: Pearson Education.

Evertson, C. M., & Weinstein, C. S. (Eds.). (2006). *Handbook of classroom management: Research, practice, and contemporary issues.* Mahwah, NJ: Lawrence Erlbaum.

Gootman, M. E. (2008). *The caring teacher's guide to discipline* (3rd ed.). Thousand Oaks, CA: Corwin.

Lepper, M., Greene, D., & Nisbett, R. (1973). Undermining children's intrinsic interest with extrinsic rewards: A test of the over justification hypothesis. *Journal of Personality and Social Psychology, 28*(1), 129–137.

Marzano, R. (2007). *The art and science of teaching: A comprehensive framework for effective instruction.* Alexandria, VA: Association for Supervision and Curriculum Development.

Marzano, R. J., Marzano, J. S., & Pickering, D. J. (2003). *Classroom management that works: Research-based strategies for every teacher.* Alexandria, VA: Association for Supervision and Curriculum Development.

Rigby, C. S., Deci, E. L., Patrick, B. C., & Ryan, R. M. (1992, September). Beyond the intrinsic-extrinsic dichotomy: Self-determination in motivation and learning. *Motivation and Emotion, 16*, 3. Retrieved from http://www.springerlink.com/content/h2n7205042428750

Ryan, R. M., & Deci, E. L. (2000, January). Intrinsic and extrinsic motivations: Classic definitions and new directions. *Contemporary Educational Psychology, 25*(1), 54–67.

Sprick, R. S., Baldwin, K., Booher, M., Gale, M., Garrison, M., Nieves, A., et al. (2009). *CHAMPs: A proactive and positive approach to classroom management* (2nd ed.). Eugene, OR: Pacific Northwest Publishing.

Vanderbilt University. (2009). *Motivating students.* Retrieved July 10, 2010, from http://www.vanderbilt.edu/cft/resources/teaching_resources/interactions/motivating.htm

Wong, H. K., & Wong, R. T. (2009). *The first days of school: How to be an effective teacher.* Mountain View, CA: Harry K. Wong Publications.

Should school resource officers function strictly as law enforcement officers?

POINT: M. David Alexander, *Virginia Tech*

COUNTERPOINT: Jennifer Sughrue, *Old Dominion University*

OVERVIEW

In the years since the Columbine, Colorado, shootings, law enforcement personnel have become an increasingly more common sight in schools around the country. These law enforcement agents or school resource officers (SROs) are on contracts from local departments of law enforcement to help ensure that schools are safe. Although their jobs are typically funded through state or federal resources, these SROs have unique legal and social positions fostering many controversies among civil liberties organizations, school boards, administrators, parents, and students themselves. More specifically, there has been debate regarding the role that SROs should play in public schools. In this chapter, the point essay argues that SROs should function strictly as police officers while the counterpoint essay embraces a more holistic model of school policing.

As noted by both the point and counterpoint essays, one potentially controversial issue for SROs surrounds, most basically, who they work *for*. Do they work as agents of police departments or of schools? Are they investigating criminal activities or violations of school rules? These basic issues also influence how interviews are conducted and how evidence is collected in the event of alleged violations of the rights of students. Clear regulations must obviously be laid out before SROs can begin working in schools (Wheeler & Pickrell, 2005). Some of these same basic issues are at the heart of the American Civil Liberty Union's (ACLU's) misgivings about SROs, as outlined in their work, "Policing in schools: Developing a governance document for school resource officers in K-12 schools" (Kim & Geronimo, 2009). In addition to establishing the ground rules of who SROs work for, the ACLU cited concerns protecting the rights of students; the ACLU asserted that the role of SROs must be transparent to school staff and families, and that the job of SROs is to create a better climate in schools by employing nonpunitive techniques when dealing with students. Indeed, both legal commentators and civil rights advocates have expressed concerns that the existing ambiguity with regard to the role of SROs has both led to student civil rights abuses and undermined procedural due process requirements.

The issue of student rights is a major concern not only for the ACLU and legal commentators but also for parents and students. Police and school officials operate under different standards when it comes to investigating misbehavior and interviewing, not to mention searching students. Although school officials use the standard of "individualized reasonable suspicion," police are held to the higher standard of "probable cause" when dealing with students. This discrepancy must be dealt with through state law or judicial action to clarify the disconnect that SROs face between their new employers and their training as police or safety officers (Maranzano, 2001).

More broadly speaking, there is a concern among many that the presence of SROs in schools will increase the criminalization of student misbehavior—classifying it as criminal misconduct rather than as issues that should be resolved with school discipline techniques. Matthew T. Theriot's (2009) investigation of this issue in one school district compared the arrest rates at 13 schools with SROs to 15 schools without the presence of SROs. The researcher concluded that the presence of SROs in schools correlated with more arrests for disorderly conduct but with fewer arrests for assault and weapons charges. Overall, Theriot's research found that the number of arrests remained equal between the two groups of schools.

This chapter examines the tensions surrounding the role of SROs. In the point essay, M. David Alexander (Virginia Tech) argues that SROs should function strictly as law enforcement officers so not to confuse or mislead students, parents, or staff about their role in schools. The point essay further maintains that SROs should be educated to operate in school environments filled with children who vary in their cognitive, emotional, and social development. He contends,

> While holding SROs to the same legal principles that govern the actions of other law enforcement officers will not quell all questions regarding the functionality of SROs in schools, it would bring some clarification to the areas of greatest concern, such as searches, seizures, and interrogations.

In contrast, Jennifer Sughrue (Old Dominion University) posits in the counterpoint essay that the most effective school resource officer programs are those that allow SROs to function in multiple roles rather than being restricted solely to law enforcement. She indicates that the presence of SROs increased exponentially in the 1990s when school shootings were present in the media. As a result, she points out, the role of the SRO has become a necessary form of community policing to assist school leaders in assessing school safety concerns. Consequently, the role of SROs has evolved to be much more than that of law enforcement. In this regard, the counterpoint essay observes,

> School resource officers are not in schools to create a prison-like environment but rather to help students make sound decisions and stay out of juvenile hall or even prison. They play a vital role in creating and maintaining a safe and secure learning environment for students and staff alike, which requires much more than simply enforcing the law.

To be certain, this is a debate that is likely to continue—especially as school leaders are given conflicting information about the role of SROs.

Suzanne E. Eckes
Sarah B. Burke
Indiana University

POINT: M. David Alexander
Virginia Tech

Having police in the schools is not new. Some school boards have had their own police departments for years. For instance, as early as 1948, the Los Angeles Unified School District established the Los Angeles School Police Department (LASPD, 2011). In 1957, Dade County Schools (DCS) in Florida created a security liaison with law enforcement and other government agencies who was directly responsible to the Superintendent of Public Instruction; by 1966, DCS had a fully staffed Security Services Department (Miami-Dade School Police Department, 2011). Around the same time, in 1967, Clark County School District, Nevada, established its own force and now has 161 sworn officers to cover the fifth largest school system in the nation. In those early years, the role of police in schools was clear—to investigate crimes and to protect students, staff, and school property. Police did not pretend to be anything other than law enforcement agents.

As noted in the counterpoint essay, many school-based law enforcement personnel are called school resource officers (SROs) and claim to follow a progressive approach to campus policing referred to as the triad model. This form of police engagement in schools encourages sworn officers to function in three capacities simultaneously: as law enforcement, informal counselors or mentors, and law-related educators (Office of Community Policing Services, also known as COPS, 2010). What is misleading about this approach is that, first and foremost, SROs are law enforcement officers; the other two roles are subordinate to or are used in support of that primary function. Speaking to SROs on any given occasion does not come with guarantees of privacy or immunity, and what is conveyed can be used to further law enforcement ends.

With more police in schools, an emphasis is placed on the role of SROs in appeasing school and community concerns about school safety and security, even absent clear evidence that schools are unsafe. Although there has been a recent bump in school crime related to drugs and weapons, years of federal government statistics indicated a decreasing rate of school crime even prior to the push to adopt SRO programs in schools. Both the decreasing crime rate prior to the widespread hiring of SROs and the more recent increase in school-based crime, even with the presence of police in schools, calls into question the efficacy of SROs in schools.

More alarming, though, is the emerging body of research literature on the unanticipated consequences of having law enforcement officers in schools. It is this research and the variety of case law involving SROs that is circulating through the federal courts, including up to the U.S. Supreme Court, that underpin the assertion that SROs should function solely as law enforcement officers.

The premise of this point essay is to argue that SROs should function strictly as law enforcement so not to confuse or mislead students, parents, or staff about their role and should be educated to operate in school environments filled with children who vary in their cognitive, emotional, and social development. Further, as civil rights advocates, many legal scholars, and other researchers correctly insist, it is time to clarify and standardize the legal principles under which SROs should operate when questioning students, searching students, and obtaining information and evidence from school personnel (Holland, 2006; Kagan, 2004; Thurau & Wald, 2009). The counterpoint essay argues that the most effective SRO programs in schools are those allowing SROs to function in multiple roles and to not be restricted solely to law enforcement. As demonstrated by the many arguments that follow the counterpoint essay's approach is flawed.

STRICTLY LAW ENFORCEMENT, PLEASE

There is no compelling evidence that schools are quantifiably more secure and less dangerous with the presence of SROs, even though there are surveys indicating that students generally "feel" safer. Yet, there is evidence of organizational and procedural troubles that are resulting in an increase in the criminalization of student behavior in schools (Theriot, 2009; Thurau & Wald, 2009; Youth United for Change & Advancement Project, 2011); in furthering the disparity in the application of discipline across racial groups (ACLU & ACLU of Connecticut, 2008; NYCLU & ACLU, 2007); and in conflicts among administrators, teachers, and SROs when roles and responsibilities are not clearly defined or delineated (Thurau & Wald, 2009). A mounting number of cases are drawing attention to the many shades of gray that color the questions of student and staff rights as well as the constitutional limits on the actions of police while on duty in schools.

The increased presence of police in schools has many researchers, civil rights groups, and even judges increasingly concerned about the rise in school-based arrests, especially about arrests of young children, and for incidents that are not normally considered criminal acts. A study of three districts in Connecticut (East Hartford, West Hartford, and Hartford), published by the ACLU, noted several alarming trends. First, very young children were being arrested. In Hartford, for example, during the 2 years for which data are available, 86 primary-grade students experienced school-based arrest. A majority of these were seventh- or eighth-graders, but 25 were in Grades 4 through 6, and 13 were in Grade 3 or below. Second, East Hartford had a school-based arrest rate equaling 17 arrests per 1,000 students in 2006–2007, a rate that was more than 30% higher than the previous school year (ACLU & ACLU of Connecticut, 2008, p. 26). In addition, students of color were arrested at a rate much higher than their representation in the student population. In 2006–2007, African American and Hispanic students together accounted for 69 percent of the student population in East Hartford, but they experienced 85 percent of school-based arrests. Likewise, the same year, in West Hartford, African American and Hispanic students accounted for 24 percent of the population, but they experienced 63 percent of arrests (p. 25).

Two other disconcerting statistics established that students of color were more likely to be arrested than White students committing the same offenses, and for offenses involving drugs, alcohol, or tobacco, they were "ten times more likely to be arrested than were similarly situated white students" (ACLU & ACLU of Connecticut, 2008, p. 26). Lastly, the ACLU complained that there were credible concerns about students with disabilities being arrested at disproportionately high rates, but state officials refused to release data to confirm or dispel those worries.

There is a general consensus among those who study what is termed the "school-to-prison pipeline" that an increased presence of police on school grounds is related to an increase in the criminalization of disciplinary offenses that used to be handled by teachers and administrators (ACLU & ACLU of Connecticut, 2008; Cobb, 2009; NYCLU & ACLU, 2007; Texas Appleseed, 2010; Thurau & Wald, 2009). For instance, in the past, what were once considered "mouthy" remarks by teenagers or verbal scuffles in the hallways were handled by the principal as a typical discipline problem and as a teachable moment. Now those kinds of behaviors have been criminalized by school policing programs as "disorderly conduct" for which students receive a citation and have to appear in court. As noted in the Texas Appleseed study of disciplinary procedures in Texas public schools:

> Disrupting class, using profanity, misbehaving on a school bus, student fights, and truancy once meant a trip to the principal's office. Today, such misbehavior results in a Class C misdemeanor ticket and a trip to court for thousands of Texas students and their families each year. (2010, p. 1)

Likewise, the Texas study expressed similar concerns to that of the ACLU's Connecticut study inasmuch as there is some evidence of an overrepresentation of minority students and students with disabilities in disciplinary reactions to infractions.

CONFUSION IN THE SCHOOL

One problem that has exacerbated the situation is the lack of clearly described roles and responsibilities. There is often ambiguity and tension created when it is not clear who is in charge and under what circumstances. Also, it is unclear to students and staff what the differences in responsibilities are between and among the many categories of school security, such as Safety Officer, Resource Officer, School Resource Officer, Peace Officer School, Police Officer, School Police Resource Officer, School Security Guard, School Security Personnel, and Safety School Resource Officer.

A policy brief published by the Charles Hamilton Houston Institute for Race and Justice (CHHIRJ) in Massachusetts concluded that both training and lack of clarity of role responsibilities were impacting the task of SROs, school administrators, and teachers, with the ultimate victim being the student:

> [School resource officers] did not receive training in mediation, basic deescalation techniques, or in detecting symptoms and behaviors of youths who have been exposed to violence, trauma, or abuse. They rarely had any formal knowledge of, or training in, adolescent psychology or development, how to secure the respect and cooperation of youths, or on the behavioral precautions and protections that need to be taken with youths on Individual Education Plans. (Wald & Thurau, 2010, p. 7)

As concerned as unprepared SROs are to school staff, SROs voiced their own frustrations about teachers and administrators' lack of understanding about the role of law enforcement in schools:

> [T]eachers and administrators asked them to intervene in situations that were clearly school discipline matters. They commonly expressed the view that, when school officials and teachers failed to establish orderly environments, they turned too quickly to law enforcement solutions. This seemed particularly true in school systems where many of the teachers were relatively inexperienced. (p. 8)

The incident addressed in the case of *Samuels v. Independent School District 279* (2003) is representative of the misunderstanding about the role of SROs in schools. A 9-year-old boy, R. J., was in a verbal altercation with another student in class, during which the teacher feared a physical fight would ensue. The teacher called for help, and the administrative assistant showed up. Although the boys had stopped arguing, the administrative assistant took R. J. to the office, where he asked the SRO to handcuff the boy; the SRO admitted to doing so when he thought R. J. was "about to go off" (p. 3). Yet, since the SRO immediately realized that the administrative assistance's primary purpose in wanting R. J. handcuffed was "to teach him a lesson about the possible consequences of getting into fights at school," the SRO instantly removed the cuffs (p. 4).

The court ruled that being handcuffed, if only for 30 to 40 seconds behind closed doors, was considered a seizure. Both the administrative assistant and the officer had *seized* R. J., as defined in Fourth Amendment jurisprudence. The court held the administrative assistant violated the student's Fourth Amendment rights and was not entitled to qualified immunity. The officer was entitled to qualified immunity since he removed the handcuffs immediately after determining the administrative assistant's purpose was to teach the student a lesson and did not involve a health or safety issue.

There is an immediate need for mandatory and specialized training for SROs. Some states have clear mandates for training, but many do not, and most police or sheriff's departments, particularly smaller divisions, do not provide such training. It is assumed that the training provided an officer for the general duties of law enforcement is sufficient for patrolling schools. In other instances, lack of funding restricts the ability of school districts or police forces to prepare their officers properly for working in schools.

Likewise, there is little formality in the creation of the working relationship between school administrators and SROs and an absence of supervision or oversight. Most administrators who are charged with running a safe and educationally enriched environment have no training with the day-to-day coordination with police officials in the schools. Some school administrators abrogate their duties and acquiesce to police officers when it comes to discipline.

In yet another twist, there have been instances in which the administrator comes into conflict with the SRO. For instance, a highly regarded veteran principal in New York City was arrested for obstruction of governmental administration and for resisting arrest when he blocked the front entrance of the high school as an SRO attempted to lead a 17-year-old honor student in handcuffs out the door. The principal requested the student be taken out the back door of the school, so to avoid unnecessarily embarrassing her in front of hundreds of students. The SRO refused to comply with the request and proceeded to arrest the principal. In dismissing the charges, the judge opined:

> Unfortunately, this incident highlights the tension between school administrators and the NYPD concerning a principal's authority in overseeing school premises. Further, this incident highlights the need to exercise sensitivity in effectuating student arrests, as well as transporting arrested students out of school premises, particularly where large groups of students may be in close proximity.

It is the court's hope that the Department of Education and the NYPD can reach a meeting of the minds regarding a principal's leadership role, as well as the principal's exercise of discretion regarding student disciplinary matters and protecting the emotional and physical well-being of his or her students. (*People v. Federman,* 2008, pp. 481–482)

Given the likelihood that police will maintain a presence in schools for the foreseeable future, it is urged that more states and communities follow the lead of states like Kentucky, which defines its SROs as officers with "specialized training to work with youth" (Definitions for chapter, 2010) and follow the recommendations set forth by a Texas Appleseed (2010) study on school discipline in Texas, which suggests that SROs should receive additional training on topics that are related to youth.

Likewise, other organizations strongly urge local school officials to develop clearly defined disciplinary policies that describe the kinds of violations and behaviors that would invoke police intervention and the consequences of such interventions, and then ensure these policies are communicated to all factions of the school community, including students, teachers, and parents.

CONCLUSION

This point essay asserts that there are genuine concerns about the coalescing roles and responsibilities of school administrators and law enforcement in matters related to school discipline. In some cases, the blurring of roles and responsibilities has been encouraged by jurisprudence that often characterizes SROs as members of the school staff rather than as sworn officers of the law; therefore, they are not confined by constitutional strictures placed on "outside" police.

Apprehension regarding the seemingly devolving civil and constitutional rights of students is substantially documented in research, in legal analyses, and in case law. This worry is further exacerbated by studies that illustrate an increasing trend in criminalizing student behavior and in school-based arrests. They also highlight how these trends are having a disparate impact on students of color and on students with disabilities, and they are creating a school-to-prison pipeline whose diameter is growing exponentially with each citation or arrest.

The triad model that is so widely touted only increases the "complexity of modern school-law-enforcement collaborations" (Holland, 2006, p. 43) and further obfuscates what staff, students, and parents understand about the proper functioning of law enforcement in schools.

For these reasons, this point essay argued that SROs should function solely as law enforcement officers and, as such, should be held to the same standards as other law enforcement personnel. Peter Price (2009) urged a similar "bright-line rule" that would help resolve the more common conflicts that occur in schools as a result of a persistent police presence:

> Fundamentally, the question in the background of all of these issues is whether the actors, be they school officials or school security officers, act as school employees or as police officers. These questions would be resolved with a bright-line rule establishing that police officers are police officers at all times, whether acting at the behest of the police department or the school, and whether they are SROs or outside police officers on campus for a specific crime. Therefore, officers and SROs would always have to follow standard police protocol for interrogations and searches. This rule has the benefit of clarity for all involved. (p. 567)

While holding SROs to the same legal principles that govern the actions of other law enforcement officers will not quell all questions regarding the functionality of SROs in schools, it would bring some clarification to the areas of greatest concern, such as searches, seizures, and interrogations. This approach, coupled with the requirement that all SROs receive specialized training in order to prepare them to perform their duties properly within the context of school environments, would do much to further the educational mission of the school. Clear demarcations of roles and responsibilities will improve trust among all stakeholders and diminish the unfortunate outcomes that prevail when conflicts arise from miscommunication or misunderstanding.

COUNTERPOINT: Jennifer Sughrue
Old Dominion University

The most effective school resource officer (SRO) programs are those allowing SROs to function in multiple roles rather than being restricted to law enforcement duties alone (Office of Community Policing Services [COPS], 2010). In fact, the U.S. Department of Justice (USDOJ), along with various state departments of education and juvenile justice as well as professional associations such as the National Association of School Resource Officers (NASRO) and the National Education Association (NEA), strongly advocate the triad model, in which SROs function as counselors and mentors, teachers, and law enforcement officers.

The triad model allows SROs to build positive relationships with students and to be viewed in roles other than those of strictly law enforcement (COPS, 2010; NASRO, 2010b; NEA, 2008). Moreover, building positive relationships and being positive role models are considered essential practices for effective SROs. Building trust is an important objective that gives SROs the credibility they need when required to mediate conflicts, to act on information of impending trouble, and/or to investigate when crimes or serious breaches of school safety rules occur.

Building trust also results in learning about the needs of students and communities so that preventive measures can be taken that may reduce safety or security threats. Further, it provides SROs the opportunity to be proactive instead of reactive on matters of school and community safety. Learning about student, staff, and community fears, whether real or perceived, aids SROs in assessing environmental and organizational factors that may contribute to lapses in safety and security. Such evaluations should lead to recommendations to help educational and community leaders to improve school climates, to diminish opportunities for outsiders to disrupt school activities, and to better use law enforcement resources in communities. The point essay argument, that SROs should function strictly as law enforcement, is misguided.

COMMUNITY POLICING PHILOSOPHY

Visibility, accessibility, and communication within schools and communities are reasons why SROs are a part of the federal COPS community policing team and why the federal government provides competitive grants in support of law enforcement officers in schools. Schools are one of COPS' identified community partners, and community partnerships are one of the three essential components creating the foundation for the COPS initiative (COPS, n.d.). The other two prongs are organizational transformation and problem solving, which should be functional in schools, as well, once partnerships have been established. As the Office of Community-Oriented Policing (n.d.) explained it,

> Community policing is a philosophy that promotes organizational strategies, which support the systematic use of partnerships and problem-solving techniques, to proactively address the immediate conditions that give rise to public safety issues such as crime, social disorder, and fear of crime. (p. 3)

COPS asserted that "collaborative partnerships between the law enforcement agency and the individuals and organizations they serve [are needed] to develop solutions to problems and increase trust in the police" (p. 3). COPS further acknowledges that law enforcement personnel cannot protect the public by themselves and need community partnerships in order to accomplish those two objectives.

Community policing has become increasingly widespread throughout the nation and is no longer restricted to high-crime areas and urban centers. The same can be said of the employment and utilization of SROs in schools. Estimates claim that "one-third of all sheriffs' offices and almost half of all municipal police departments assign nearly 17,000 sworn officers" in schools (COPS, 2010, p. 1). During President George W. Bush's terms, the number and value of federal grants through the Office of Community Policing Services, an agency of the USDOJ, were increased substantially and made available to assist school boards in developing cooperative agreements with local law enforcement and in sharing the cost of placing officers in schools.

THE EVOLVING SRO ROLE

As noted in the point essay, the presence of SROs in schools is not a recent trend; they have been in schools for more than 5 decades. Initially SROs functioned primarily as law enforcement officers and little more. The presence of SROs in schools increased exponentially in the 1990s when a rash of high-profile school shootings grabbed national headlines. Parents and students, burdened by fears of such violence and concerned about the existence of drugs in schools, commanded school boards to do something to improve school safety and security. Boards sought the assistance of law enforcement to rein in crime on school grounds and at school functions.

Since the 1990s, as has happened with traditional law enforcement officer roles in cities and counties all over the country, the role of SRO has evolved under the philosophy of community policing. It was also during the 1990s that law enforcement began to embrace the concept of community policing. Thus, it was only natural that the SROs become the liaisons among law enforcement, schools, and larger communities. The responsibilities of SROs expanded to include actively engaging in proactive endeavors that were focused more on anticipating and solving problems than on reacting to them once they turned serious and dangerous. From this emerged the triad model in which SROs would connect with school staff, students, and community members in a variety of ways that could be construed as positive, proactive, and supportive.

The point essay's contention that SROs should function only as police officers runs contrary to current accepted practice. The triad model has grown in popularity, and it places the SRO in the everyday lives of the students at school and provides multiple opportunities to interact on a constructive level. As teachers, SROs are able to work with entire student bodies over time and to provide expertise on curriculum content that may not find its way into other courses. Common topics that can be taught by the SRO are as follows:

- Policing as a career
- Criminal investigation
- Alcohol and drug awareness
- Gang and stranger awareness and resistance
- General crime prevention
- Conflict resolution
- Restorative justice
- Babysitting safety
- Bicycling, pedestrian, and motor vehicle safety
- Special crimes in which students are especially likely to be offenders or victims, such as vandalism, shoplifting, and sexual assault by acquaintances (COPS, 2010, p. 5)

As counselors and mentors, SROs are available to students to talk about problems, especially those related to drugs and/or violence they may be encountering in and out of school. SROs conduct both "open door" and formal counseling sessions (Center for the Prevention of School Violence [CPSV], 1998) and, in some instances, are paired with and mentor students with discipline problems (National Crime Prevention Council [NCPC], 1995). SROs invite all students to just drop by, and they let them know they are always available to them to talk one-on-one. SROs listen and do act in confidentiality to the extent that the situation and the law allow. Further, SROs are likely to be able to direct students and their families to other agencies and resources that can help them resolve law-related issues that are beyond the scope of the SROs' duties or skills (COPS, 2010; NEA, 2008). However, it is clear that SROs are not to usurp the responsibilities of regular school counselors nor are they there to participate in day-to-day school disciplinary matters. Those are for the professional education staff to handle. SROs are there to deal with student safety and security and with juvenile justice issues.

As SROs earn reputations of good listeners, problem solvers, liaisons to community resources, and as individuals who can be trusted, community members, parents in particular, seek out SROs to help address trouble in homes and communities. A former principal of a large alternative high school described how neighborhood residents came to campus specifically to seek the assistance of the SRO when a crime was committed or to report concerns of an impending problem (V. Wanza, personal communication, June 12, 2010). Knowing that an officer is in close proximity and is easily accessible is believed to spur a sense of safety in the school and in the neighborhood.

The percentage of time spent engaged in each of these three roles varies according to the needs of the school and community. For instance, a 1998 survey conducted by the CPSV at the annual NASRO convention reported that SROs spend approximately 50% of their time involved in law enforcement activities while the remaining two roles, counselor and teacher, consume 30% and 20% of their time, respectively.

A later survey, again conducted at the NASRO annual convention, revealed a shift in time spent on the triad of roles, with 46% of the time going toward counseling and mentoring activities, while only 41% of the time was devoted to law enforcement (National School Safety and Security Services [NSSSS], 2002). Among the 658 survey respondents, 91% reported that the majority of their time was spent engaged in preventative duties, with only 7% saying that most of their time was spent on law enforcement and investigations. More than 81% described their jobs as comprising the triad model.

The survey compiled the variety of tasks that SROs reported they performed on the job in schools. Table 10.1 displays the range of activities and the percent of SROs engaged in these activities. It is important that the SRO be active in all three roles in order to have access to and to build rapport with all the students in the school and to extend proactive policing into the community (NASRO, 2010b; NEA, 2008).

PREPARING SROs FOR SCHOOLS

As with all professional personnel in schools, proper training, supervision, and leadership are essential to competency and success. SROs are usually trained law enforcement officers but lack preparation for working with culturally, linguistically, and racially diverse students across a range of age groups. SROs are also not necessarily prepared to teach or to engage in the role of counselor/mentor. Likewise, SROs must learn the unique environment of schools in which a variety of people come and go every day, including parents, volunteers, and vendors. Schools are also places where children learn and play and where adolescents try to find themselves and fit in, whether for good or for bad. Some middle and high school campuses are open and some are closed, altering how SROs monitor the safety and security of buildings, students, and staff. As the NEA (n.d.)

Table 10.1

2002 Survey Results Describing the Tasks Performed by SROs in Schools

Tasks Performed by School Resource Officers	% of Officers
One-on-one counseling with students	93%
Calls for service to classroom	88%
Classroom instruction	87%
Crisis preparedness planning	83%
Security audits/assessments of school campuses	82%
Special safety programs/presentations	78%
Faculty/staff in-service presentations	75%
Truancy intervention	70%
Group counseling with students	69%
Supervising/coordinating nonathletic extracurriculars	60%
Field trip chaperon	57%
Parent organization presentations	57%
Coaching athletic programs	30%

Source: 2002 NASRO School Resource Officer Survey by Ken S. Trump, M.P.A. Cleveland, OH: NSSSS. Copyright 2002, NSSSS. Reprinted with permission.

explained it, "One thing is clear: school security professionals need to be fully trained and have a clear understanding of not only security techniques, but also the unique nature of the school populations they are working with" (n.p.).

Training

All professional organizations, public and private, and every government agency, federal and state, involved with SRO programs advocate strongly for a variety of training modules focusing on meeting the needs of schools and on working with children, teachers, and administrators. Some state legislatures have taken the extra step by requiring SROs to meet specified educational and certification criteria before stepping into schools.

A large number of governmental, nonprofit, and for-profit organizations offer professional affiliation and training to all categories of school SROs. For instance, NASRO, NEA, NCPC, and NSSSS are among the many that provide an ongoing calendar of workshops, courses, and services related to SRO preparation.

The NEA has an affiliate group, Education Support Professionals (ESP), which includes school security personnel. ESP urges continuous and rigorous training for SROs in light of the distinctive nature of schools and their charges, the children. ESP's website provides a rich panorama of the training topics from the syllabus of the School Security Officer Training Program, which was produced by the NSSSS, a private security company promoting school security through professional services for which local school boards or communities may contract. Among the themes are the following:

- Legal system operations and procedures (juvenile and adult)
- Abused and neglected children (including how to identify and report suspected abuse under state law and school board policy)
- Legal procedures for search and seizure
- Human relations and cultural diversity
- Overview of child psychology
- Self defense and verbal de-escalation skills
- Weapon possession and concealment techniques
- Handling fights, conflict situations, and weapon-related offenses
- Current school crime trends
- Recognizing and managing gangs
- Drug abuse, possession, and sales
- Intervening with angry parents
- Stress management
- Security's role in crisis preparedness (bombs, bomb threats, hostage situations)
- Special event security/monitoring and supervising crowds
- Media relations
- Police, parent, staff, and community relations (NEA, n.d., n.p.)

A visit to the NASRO website provides another example of the training courses that are available to both novice and experienced SROs. For example, the organization offers a *Basic SRO* program that

> emphasizes three main areas of instruction: functioning as a police officer in the school setting, working as a resource and problem solver, and the development of teaching skills. Attendees will be given a working knowledge of the School Resource Officer concept and how to establish a lasting partnership with their schools. (2010c, n.p.)

The Advanced School Resource Officer Course is designed to provide experienced SROs with information about programs on school safety and with additional skills "to identify and diffuse potentially dangerous situations on campus" (2010a, n.p.). Among other courses offered are School Law Update and SRO Supervisors and Management.

Supervision

The latter course, SRO Supervisors and Management, brings to the discussion the importance of direct supervision of SROs by senior law enforcement officials or by the responsible administrators of school security forces. Again, the literature from a variety of private, public, and government entities stresses the importance of supervision to maintain the level of service and competency expected from SROs and to strengthen the bonds among the officers, schools, and law enforcement agencies. Workshops and courses are designed to prepare SRO supervisors for the unique work that SROs perform in schools.

Regular contact with and observation and evaluation by a law enforcement supervisor is important for SROs who are members of law enforcement agencies, as opposed to those who are directly employed by schools. Such a process helps SROs remain connected to their fellow law enforcement colleagues and minimizes a sense of isolation that SROs have reported.

Leadership

Leadership is another important ingredient in the making of good SRO programs. How and how often building administrators interact with SROs determines the success of the collaboration while sending strong messages to students and staff. The CPSV (2002) indicated that its research concluded that the "SRO-administer relationship is of critical importance . . . [and] suggested that the two perspectives share a common vision defined by a concern for creating schools in which students are able to be safe and successful" (n.p.). Importantly, developing strong relationships between administrators and SROs means diminishing misunderstandings about the roles and priorities of SROs while clarifying the boundaries between the responsibilities of the SRO and of the school administration and teachers. How SROs are introduced to school personnel and communities is equally critical in setting positive tones about the presence of SROs and their duties whether around school or in surrounding neighborhoods.

Strong relationships between administrators and SROs also translate into more constructive conversations and plans for identifying safety and security issues while developing strategies and environmental adjustments to address the concerns. This is where the second and third prongs of the community policing philosophy—organizational transformation and problem solving—come into play. SROs and school administrators, with the input of other stakeholders, can combine their expertise to determine what needs to be done to minimize safety and security problems in the school and how to do it. These concerns could range from violence and drugs within and outside of schools, to crisis management, and guarding against intruders.

CONCLUSION

A multitude of misconceptions are embedded in the debate on SROs. Among them are that they create an unnecessary danger because they are armed, they do not know how to work with children, they are there to catch kids and put them in jail, they create an atmosphere of fear in the school, and they do not work for the school district and, therefore, do not respond to directives and requests from the school administrators. As this counterpoint essay has argued, these concerns can be addressed if SROs are afforded the proper foundation through training and if they successfully build strong relationships with administrators, students, staff, and communities.

Equally important, SROs must have the latitude to function in a variety of roles, but most commonly as law enforcement officer, as counselors/mentors, and as teachers. This diminishes the perception that SROS are on campus only to catch kids doing bad things and, therefore, lessens the fear that students and parents may have of law enforcement personnel.

SROs assist school administrators in assessing school safety and security needs as well as in developing plans to respond to these needs. SROs provide valuable assistance to communities by being visible in schools and by being available to students and parents who wish to seek their expert counsel on matters related to law enforcement and safety.

Although schools are still much safer than the streets, it is naïve to ignore the fact that drugs, weapons, gangs, and bullying are present. SROs are not in schools to create prison-like environments but to help students make sound decisions and stay out of juvenile halls or even prisons. SROs play a vital role in creating and maintaining safe and secure learning environments for students and staff alike, a task that requires much more than simply enforcing the law.

FURTHER READINGS AND RESOURCES

ACLU, & ACLU of Connecticut. (2008, November). *Hard lessons: School resource officer programs and school-based arrests in three Connecticut towns.* Retrieved from http://www.aclu.org/racial-justice/hard-lessons-school-resource-officer-programs-and-school-based-arrests-three-connecti

Center for the Prevention of School Violence (CPSV), North Carolina Department of Juvenile Justice and Delinquency Prevention. (1998, February). The school as "the beat": Law enforcement officers in schools. *Center.Link Research Bulletin, 1*(3). Retrieved July 2, 2010, from http://www.ncdjjdp.org/cpsv/pdf_files/Res_Bull_national.PDF

Center for the Prevention of School Violence (CPSV), North Carolina Department of Juvenile Justice and Delinquency Prevention. (2002, June). School resource officers and school administrators: "Talking and walking" together to make safer schools. *Center.Link Research Bulletin.* Retrieved July 2, 2010, from http://www.ncdjjdp.org/cpsv/pdf_files/research_bulletin_sro_6_02.pdf

Cobb, H. (2009). Separate and unequal: The disparate impact of school-based referrals to juvenile court. *Harvard Civil-Rights Liberties Law Review, 44*(2), 581–596.

Holland, P. (2006). Schooling Miranda: Policing interrogation in the twenty-first century schoolhouse. *Loyola Law Review, 52,* 39–113.

Kagan, J. (2004). Reappraising T.L.O.'s "special needs" doctrine in an era of school-law enforcement entanglement. *Journal of Law & Education, 33,* 291–325.

Kim, C., & Geronimo, I. (2009). *Policing in schools: Developing a governance document for school resource officers in K-12 schools.* New York: ACLU.

Los Angeles School Police Department: http://www.laspd.com

Maranzano, C. (2001). The legal implications of school resource officers in public schools. *NASSP Bulletin, 85*(621), 76.

Miami-Dade School Police Department, News Center. (2011). *History.* Retrieved from http://police.dadeschools.net/?page_id=234

National Association of School Resource Officers (NASRO). (2010a). *Advanced School Resource Officer Course.* Retrieved June 19, 2010, from http://www.nasro.org/mc/page.do?sitePageId=114181&orgId=naasro

National Association of School Resource Officers (NASRO). (2010b). *Basic school resource officer course.* Retrieved June 19, 2010, from http://mwics.com/nasro.mobi/downloads/oldNASRO/nasro.org/course_basic.html

National Association of School Resource Officers (NASRO). (2010c). *Basic SRO.* Retrieved June 19, 2010, from http://www.nasro.org/mc/page.do?sitePageId=114186&orgId=naasro

National Crime Prevention Council (NCPC). (1995). Strategy: School resource officers. *350 Tested Strategies to Prevent Crime: A Resource for Municipal Agencies and Community Groups.* Retrieved July 10, 2010, from http://www.ncpc.org/topics/school-safety/strategies/strategy-school-resource-officers/?searchterm="school resource officers"

National Education Association (NEA). (2008). *More than "campus cops": School resource officers are also role models for students and staff.* Retrieved June 20, 2010, from http://www.nea.org/home/15729.htm

National Education Association (NEA). (n.d.). *Getting educated: Security services professionals.* Retrieved June 20, 2010, from http://www.nea.org/home/18628.htm

National School Safety and Security Services (NSSSS). (2002). *2002 National School Resource Officer Survey: Final report on the 2nd annual national survey of school-based police officers.* Cleveland, OH: Author.

New York Civil Liberties Union (NYCLU), & American Civil Liberties Union (ACLU). (2007, March). *Criminalizing the classroom: The over-policing of New York City schools.* Retrieved from http://www.nyclu.org/pdfs/criminalizing_the_classroom_report.pdf

Office of Community Oriented Policing Services (COPS), U.S. Department of Justice. (2010). *Assigning police officer to schools.* Problem-Oriented Guides for Police, Response Guides Series No. 10. Retrieved June 19, 2010, from http://www.cops.usdoj.gov/files/RIC/Publications/e041028272-assign-officers-to-schools.pdf

Office of Community Oriented Policing Services (COPS), U.S. Department of Justice. (n.d.). *Community policing defined.* Retrieved July 10, 2010, from http://www.cops.usdoj.gov/files/RIC/Publications/e030917193-CP-Defined.pdf

Price, P. (2009, Spring). When is a police officer an officer of the law: The status of police officers in schools. *Journal of Criminal Law & Criminology, 99,* 541–570.

Texas Appleseed. (2010, December). *Texas' school-to-prison pipeline: Ticketing, arrest, & use of force in schools. How the myth of the "blackboard jungle" reshaped school disciplinary policy.* Retrieved from http://www.texasappleseed.net/images/stories/reports/Ticketing_Booklet_web.pdf

Theriot, M. T. (2009, May–June). School resource officers and the criminalization of student behavior. *Journal of Criminal Justice, 37*(3), 280–287.

Thurau, L. H., & Wald, J. (2009). Controlling partners: When law enforcement meets discipline in public schools. *New York Law School Law Review, 54,* 977–1020.

Wald, J., & Thurau, L. (2010, March). *First, do no harm: How educators and police can work together more effectively to preserve school safety and protect vulnerable students.* A CHHIRJ research brief. Charles Hamilton Houston Institute for Race and Justice, Harvard Law School. Retrieved from http://charleshamiltonhouston.org/Publications/Item.aspx?id=100025

Wheeler, T., II, & Pickrell, T. (2005). Schools and the police. *American School Board Journal, 192*(12), 18–21.

Youth United for Change & Advancement Project. (2011, January). *Zero tolerance in Philadelphia: Denying educational opportunities and creating a pathway to prison.* Retrieved from http://www.njjn.org/resource_1707.html

Court Cases and Statutes

Definitions for chapter, Ky. Rev. Stat. Ann. § 158.441 (2010).

People v. Federman, 852 N.Y.S.2d 748 (NY Crim Ct of NYC 2008).

Samuels v. Independent School District 279, 2003 WL 23109698 (D. Minn. 2003).

Are state and federal teacher protection acts needed to protect teachers from litigation concerning student discipline?

POINT: Amy Steketee, *Baker and Daniels LLP,*
South Bend, Indiana

COUNTERPOINT: Janet R. Decker, *University of Cincinnati*

OVERVIEW

When teachers breach their duty to supervise their students, they may be liable for any ensuing injuries. When addressing whether teachers are liable, courts often consider whether they behaved as reasonably prudent teachers would have in those or similar situations and whether the injuries that others or they sustained were foreseeable. Generally, if teachers behave as reasonably prudent teachers would in those situations or the injuries were not foreseeable, they will not be rendered liable. Despite this fact, teachers continue to worry about litigation when they use reasonable force in disciplining students.

The No Child Left Behind Act includes a section called the "Paul D. Coverdell Teacher Protection Act of 2001" (2010, TPA). The intention behind this part of the larger act is to protect teachers in the event that they injure students while attempting to discipline misbehaving children. To be precise, under this provision, educators are immune from litigation if students are injured while school employees attempt to "control, discipline, expel, or suspend a student or maintain order or control in the classroom or school

(20 U.S.C. § 6736(a)(2))." After the TPA was enacted, other states adopted similar laws to protect teachers from liability when they may have injured students during disciplinary matters.

The National Education Association (NEA) cautioned teachers that the TPA "is so narrowly drawn and rife with exceptions, that—in practical terms—it affords school employees almost no real protection from lawsuits. Equally important, it provides no funding to help school employees pay for defending against even meritless lawsuits" (NEA-NM, n.d.). In other words, the TPA does not protect teachers from criminal charges, nor does it protect them from litigation resulting from negligence or other injuries incurred outside of disciplinary contexts. The NEA provides the following examples of student injuries that could trigger legal action because they fall outside of the TPA's narrow scope:

- Injuries caused by playground accidents
- Injuries incurred during a chemistry lab experiment
- Harm caused while being beaten up by other students
- Injuries incurred in shop class
- Assault during a field trip
- Sexual harassment by peers

There are also two important exceptions to the TPA. First, employees cannot claim immunity if they violated any federal, state, or local laws in injuring students. As such, students, typically through their parents and attorneys, need only claim that teachers violated their federal constitutional rights to proceed with viable causes of action. Second, courts only allow the use of "reasonable force": if staff members can be shown to have used "excessive force," they are not to be immune from prosecution (NEA-NM, n.d.).

As noted, in addition to the TPA, some states have passed their own teacher protection legislation. For example, in 2009, Indiana passed its own act that provides limited immunity to educators in discipline cases and allows them to be represented in court by the Indiana Attorney General's Office. The legislation was created in response to the perception that teachers were reluctant to "discipline students . . . for fear of being sued" (*Insurance Journal,* August 2009).

There is skepticism about the effectiveness of the Indiana law as well as other state laws. First of all, some question the assumption that teachers are failing to discipline students as a result of their fear of litigation. When asked about the new law, Monroe County Consolidated School Corporation Superintendent Tim Hyland reflected that it targets only a "very small group" of teachers. Education professor Suzanne E. Eckes suggests that such laws are unnecessary insofar as teachers were already protected when disciplining students as long as their conduct was consistent with what reasonable teachers would have done (Robison, 2009). Others have suggested that the law may backfire, leading teachers to think that they have been given broad immunity, while in reality the protections are narrow.

Advocates of these statutes contend that these laws will make it easier to defend teachers from frivolous litigation. More specifically, they maintain that judges will be more likely to dismiss cases now that these laws are in place. The laws may also prevent school boards from settling cases before suits are filed in order to avoid legal battles and give teachers a better sense of protection. Additionally, these laws highlight many of the challenges teachers experience in their classrooms when trying to discipline misbehaving students.

This chapter examines the tensions surrounding teacher protection laws. In the point essay, Amy Steketee (Baker and Daniels LLP, South Bend, Indiana) argues that school boards benefit from state and federal teacher protection laws. She contends that

> regardless of whether these acts actually produce a measurable deterrent effect in terms of discouraging plaintiffs from bringing litigation, there is little doubt that they have drawn considerable public attention to the challenges school officials face in administering discipline to students.

In her counterpoint essay, Janet R. Decker (University of Cincinnati) explains why she does not think that such laws are necessary. She argues that

> state laws often provide school districts with a defense of qualified immunity; plus, the current law that is in place in every state makes it very difficult for a plaintiff to prevail when suing a teacher for negligence. The Coverdell Act is a politically motivated federal act that is narrowly construed and ultimately unnecessary because it provides a false sense of protection. Teachers already have protection through state law and often garnish legal support from unions or private liability insurance.

Indeed, this controversy is likely to continue as more states consider adopting teacher protection acts of their own in order to help educators maintain schools as safe and orderly learning environments.

Suzanne E. Eckes
Indiana University

POINT: Amy Steketee
Baker and Daniels LLP, South Bend, Indiana

Since the enactment of the Paul D. Coverdell Teacher Protection Act in 2001, numerous states have followed the lead of the federal government in adopting similar legislation designed to protect teachers from liability when students are injured as educators attempt to discipline the children in their care or otherwise maintain order in and around schools. This federal act has been criticized in the counterpoint essay and by others as too narrow and as providing what they describe as illusory protections for teachers; however, it has served an important purpose in bringing to light some of the challenges teachers face in enforcing discipline and in maintaining order in increasingly volatile school environments. Contrary to the counterpoint essay's position, this point essay sets out some of the reasons why state and federal teacher protection legislation is important not only for protecting school staff and boards from litigation but also for empowering educational officials to take strong approaches in promoting orderly and safe school environments.

THE PREVALENCE OF CRIME AND VIOLENCE IN SCHOOLS REQUIRES GREATER SUPPORT FOR SCHOOL STAFF

Clearly, schools should be safe havens where students can learn. Yet, it is increasingly common for daily news programs to contain reports of student crime and violence—and sometimes extreme violence—in our schools. According to a U.S. Department of Education report, during the 2007–2008 school year, 85% of public school officials reported that one or more incidents of crime had taken place in their schools, which amounts to an estimated 2 million crimes (Robers, Zhang, & Truman, 2010). During that same academic year, 75% of schools reported one or more violent incidents of crime such as rape, assault, and/or robbery. In 2009, 8% of students in Grades 9 through 12 reported having been threatened or injured by means of weapons such as guns, knives, and/or clubs on school property. Although students are most likely to be the victims of crimes committed at school, teachers and other staff are also not immune. In fact, approximately 7% of teachers were threatened with injuries by students from their schools during the 2007–2008 school year. This percentage is even higher among teachers in urban settings and for those in secondary schools.

The prevalence of such crime and violence has an inevitable impact on educational programming and, in particular, on classroom environments in schools. According to this same U.S. Department of Education study, in 2007–2008, 34% of teachers agreed or strongly agreed that student misbehavior interfered with their teaching. Again, this figure was even higher for teachers of secondary school students. In another study coordinated by Public Agenda (2004), 77% of teachers surveyed reported that their teaching would be more effective if they were able to spend less time dealing with disruptive students. In addition, teachers in this survey reported that in addition to dealing with disciplinary issues in their classrooms, they are frequently reminded by their students that they may be sued. More specifically, 78% of teachers in this study reported that students regularly remind them of their rights and that their parents may sue. Further, 49% of these teachers reported having been accused of unfairly disciplining children and 52% report that behavior problems are often exacerbated because they perceive teachers to be "soft" on discipline because teachers "can't count on parents or schools to support them."

The prevalence of crime and violence in schools, coupled with teachers' perceptions of a lack of parental and administrative support and the likelihood of being sued, would have the logical effect of deterring educational officials from taking a strong position in enforcing disciplinary policies, let alone in administering restraints—even assuming proper training, districtwide policies on restraints, and appropriate circumstances warranting restraint or intervening in student scuffles. Teacher protection acts aim to heighten the awareness of these issues, to elicit greater support for school officials in cultivating and maintaining orderly environments, and to deter parents from bringing or threatening litigation against teachers.

DEFENDING EVEN WEAK NEGLIGENCE LAWSUITS IS COSTLY AND DISTRACTING FOR SCHOOLS AND TEACHERS

When students are injured at school, including when they are hurt in the course of the enforcement of school disciplinary policies, they seek legal recourse, typically through their parents, by bringing claims for negligence. It is not uncommon for students to pursue other claims as well, such as for intentional tort, constitutional and other federal claims, or if applicable, under the 2004 reauthorization of the Individuals with Disabilities in Education Act. However, since these claims are not covered by either the federal Teacher Protection Act or typical state teacher protection laws, they are beyond the scope of this essay. Moreover, there has been significant recent attention given to litigation arising out of the administration of restraints and the use of seclusion rooms at schools (General Accounting Office, 2009).

In the event that plaintiffs file negligence suits against school boards, their claims are typically handed over immediately to their insurance carriers for assignment to insurance counsel. Once counsel is assigned, board attorneys typically conduct internal interviews while gathering and reviewing documents in order to assess the strength of the claims and their viability of the defenses. This is typically done immediately after suits are filed and prior to submitting answers to the complaints. Even in a single plaintiff negligence case, this process typically requires significant amounts of attorney and staff time. Very often, school boards and insurers may attempt to settle suits at this point for nuisance values in order to avoid further distractions and expenses.

If the parties fail to reach settlements or if school boards and insurers choose not to reach settlement agreements, then cases typically enter the discovery phase, during which the parties exchange requests for documents and information while preparing for interrogatories and depositions. Depending on the claims in the cases as well on the number of plaintiffs and other witnesses, the discovery phase of claims can require more than a hundred hours of attorney time. Defendants can thus easily incur several tens of thousands of dollars in simply seeing suits through the discovery phase. In addition to the legal expenses, the distraction that the suits cause is often even more costly for school systems. Litigation requires school officials to be diverted from their regular responsibilities in order to gather documents, meet with attorneys, coordinate interviews, prepare for and participate in depositions and/or interrogatories, and review pleadings. Litigation is mentally and emotionally taxing for school officials and often results in workplace tension, loss of morale, and diminished productivity.

Following the discovery phase of negligence suits, defendant school boards often have their first opportunity to attempt to dispose of the claims before proceeding to trial. School board defendants often attempt to obtain dismissals by persuading courts that there are no factual disputes meriting review by juries or other fact-finders and that as a matter of law plaintiffs are unable to prove any of their claims.

Negligence and other tort-type cases, though, are particularly difficult for defendants to dispose of prior to trial. To do so, school boards must be able to show that there are no disputes as to any material facts in the allegations. In negligence cases, liability typically turns on whether the actions of defendants were reasonable, whether their behavior amounted to breach or breaches of duty owed to the plaintiff(s), or whether their actions were the proximate cause of injuries to the plaintiff(s). Since these inquiries are steeped in facts, they are not conducive to resolution by a judge as matters of law. In other words, since negligence claims are so grounded in the unique facts of their situations, they are among the least likely types of cases to be dismissed prior to trial.

Assuming that cases proceed, trials are rife with uncertainty. Rather than risk adverse judgments and the accompanying negative publicity, many school boards often opt to settle these types of suits. Although settlements avoid the uncertainty of trials as a means of resolving disputes, this approach is not without its own costs. Even though the terms of settlements are often confidential, the fact that litigation settles "out of court" is not confidential. When word spreads that school boards have settled claims, there is a common, albeit often mistaken, misperception that they and/or specified individuals were culpable in some way for the injuries that may have occurred. This misperception has the effect of undermining the credibility of the administration of school systems as well as the authority of educators who may have been involved in the case.

TEACHER PROTECTION ACTS: A SHIELD FOR TEACHERS

The Paul D. Coverdell Teacher Protection Act, passed as part of the No Child Left Behind Act of 2001, is a federal statute that aims to protect teachers from being sued as a result of their efforts to undertake "reasonable actions to maintain order, discipline, and an appropriate educational environment" (20 U.S.C. § 6732). Pursuant to its provisions, the act exempts teachers from liability for harm caused by their acts or omissions as long as they were acting within the scope of their employment; their actions were carried out in accordance with federal, state, and local laws in furtherance of efforts to maintain order; they were properly licensed (if required); and their conduct was not willful, criminal, or constituted gross negligence, reckless misconduct, or a conscious, flagrant indifference to the rights or safety of the student (20 U.S.C. § 6736(a)). Although some have argued that these limitations effectively swallow any protection afforded by the statute, the act is not simply superfluous. Put another way, one of the most significant effects of this statute is that it has prompted states to enact similar legislation if they have not already done so, some of which provides even broader legal protections for teachers.

In Indiana, for example, the General Assembly in 2009 passed Indiana's Teacher Protection Act. Under this law, if school officials are sued for disciplining students, they are entitled to immunity as long as their actions were reasonable under school policy. The law also provides that the Indiana Attorney General's Office will defend school officials at no cost to them or to their boards as long as the suits arose out of actions that the educators believed in good faith to be within the scope of their duties in enforcing school discipline policies (Ind. Code § 4-6-2-1.5(b)).

TEACHER PROTECTION ACTS MAY BE HELPFUL IN DISMISSING NEGLIGENCE CLAIMS PRIOR TO TRIAL AND AVOIDING COSTLY SETTLEMENTS

As noted earlier, teacher protection legislation provides teachers with immunity in specified circumstances. Teachers who are named as defendants in negligence suits arising out of the administration of student discipline can assert immunity as an affirmative defense under the applicable provisions of teacher protection acts. The application of the immunity defense is an issue that can be resolved by judges as a matter of law, rather than by juries as a matter of fact. Teachers who invoke an immunity defense are provided with an important vehicle for disposing of claims prior to trial and, very often, even before completion of the discovery phase of the litigation. By disposing of claims earlier in the life of cases, teachers and school boards are able to avoid some of the costs, economic and noneconomic, associated with defending suits and preparing for trial.

TEACHER PROTECTION ACTS HELP DETER LITIGATION AND EMPOWER TEACHERS TO ENFORCE DISCIPLINARY POLICIES

Many believe that one of the most important purposes of teacher protection acts are the value they have in deterring potential plaintiffs from suing school boards and an array of educators. For instance, if potential plaintiffs think that it will be more difficult to prevail in claims against school boards, then they are less likely to invest in bringing litigation.

In addition, many maintain that the deterrent effect of teacher protection acts plays an important role in empowering school officials to place expectations on students regarding appropriate conduct while imposing discipline without fear of being sued. Regardless of whether these acts actually produce a measurable deterrent effect in terms of discouraging plaintiffs from bringing litigation, there is little doubt that they have drawn considerable public attention to the challenges school officials face in administering discipline to students. Moreover, there can be little doubt that these acts have prompted politicians and school leaders alike to notify their constituencies about the protections that are afforded to educational officials in these statutes. Many school boards have even published policies notifying their communities that educational officials may be immune from litigation arising out of the administration of discipline. The effect of adopting and publishing such policies communicates not only the commitment of school boards to the vigorous enforcement of their disciplinary policies, but also it communicates resounding support for the role that school staff have to play in enforcing those policies.

TEACHER PROTECTION ACTS REMIND SCHOOL OFFICIALS OF THE IMPORTANCE OF DISTRICT POLICIES AND CONSISTENT ENFORCEMENT

When school boards adopt and publish policies in response to teacher protection acts, it is common for such policies to set out the specific circumstances that must exist to trigger immunity for school officials. These circumstances typically require school officials to act in good faith and to comply with state and federal law as well as school policies and procedures. As a result, teacher protection acts, the argument of the counterpoint essay aside, and the policies that communicate them play an important role in emphasizing the importance of developing workable policies and in applying them consistently to ensure that schools remain safe and orderly learning environments.

COUNTERPOINT: Janet R. Decker
University of Cincinnati

U nlike a criminal wrong, a tort is a civil wrong that occurs when an individual is injured as a result of the unreasonable conduct of another. For example, a tort that might occur in a school setting could include a student who suffered a head injury caused by a faulty light fixture that fell from the classroom ceiling. If the injured student's teacher failed to act like a reasonable teacher and ensure that the dangerous fixture was repaired, then the teacher could be found liable and a court could award the student monetary damages. As the point essay notes, there seems to be a growing sentiment that an increase in lawsuits is hindering teachers' abilities to educate students.

Regardless of the concerns of teachers, state and federal teacher protection acts that shield educators from tort suits are unnecessary for four main reasons. First, teachers should not fear tort actions because they rarely lose when faced with this type of litigation and convincing evidence does not exist to suggest that they are finding it difficult to teach because of suits. Second, teacher protection acts, in many cases, do not shield educators from litigation expenses; liability insurance usually provided by unions serves this purpose. Third, once educated about the legal principles of negligence, teachers understand that it is difficult for plaintiffs to prove that educators are liable. Fourth, the current teacher protection acts are politically charged, narrowly construed, and ultimately unnecessary.

FEAR OF LITIGATION IMPEDING TEACHERS' ABILITIES TO EDUCATE IS UNSUBSTANTIATED

The overarching reason that the teacher protection acts exist is fear. However, teachers' fear of education-related suits is primarily an unfounded concern. Although it may be true that the United States has become a more litigious society, education suits are typically directed toward school boards and *not* toward teachers. Further, as long as teachers act reasonably, the legal principles of negligence already shield them from the threat of losing their cases. In fact, in the majority of cases in which teachers are sued, they prevail. In the small minority of cases where the teachers lose, it is typically as a result of an egregious wrong such as those who have sexual relationships with their students. In those rare instances when teachers lose, they *should* be responsible for their criminal and/ or unreasonable behavior. Further, the current teacher protection acts only provide educators with a limited qualified immunity after they have already been sued but fail to protect teachers from being sued in the first place. In fact, nothing can protect teachers from being sued; plaintiffs often are permitted to bring frivolous suits to court. Despite teacher protection acts, in many cases, defendants still must pay expensive legal fees to defend their innocence. As such, these federal and state laws offer a false sense of protection because they are not protecting teachers against legal expenses. Instead, since liability insurance offers financial protection, teacher protection acts are ultimately unnecessary.

Very little empirical evidence exists to show that teachers are finding it difficult to perform their jobs effectively as a result of litigation. The few articles that have been written about the negative repercussions of litigation against teachers have been criticized for their small and biased sample and multiple other methodological flaws. To the contrary, one could argue that of the millions of U.S. teachers, only a very small percentage end up in court as defendants. Additionally, an argument can be made to blame the media for sensationalizing the few cases that do occur.

In a review by Suzanne E. Eckes and Janet R. Decker in *The Yearbook of Education Law* for 2009 and 2010, every published tort case filed against teachers that was published by *West* was reviewed in Chapter 6. In both 2009 and 2010, the authors concluded that even when the defense of immunity was not used, plaintiffs lost more than 70% of their cases. In other words, the majority of plaintiffs who sued teachers have been unsuccessful in recent years. The supposed concern about teachers losing litigation is anecdotal and likely based on concerns that may be furthered by teacher unions and liability insurance companies. These two organizations provide financial assistance when teachers are sued. Many teachers state that a primary reason they joined unions was to have their legal fees covered just in case they should find themselves sued at some point in their careers, which seems to be a valid reason. Still, it is possible that the concern over litigation has been overemphasized not only by unions and private insurance companies but also by the media. Indeed, even some union leaders have criticized private insurance companies for playing on the fear of teachers to convince them to purchase insurance that is not needed.

LIABILITY INSURANCE CAN PROVIDE TEACHERS WITH LITIGATION FUNDING

Joining a union or obtaining liability insurance seems to be a better way to protect oneself as opposed to teacher protection acts. These federal and state laws do little to alleviate the potential for litigation because they are narrowly construed. For example, in some states (e.g., Indiana), the teacher protection laws cover teachers only when they are engaged in disciplining a student. Thus, a teacher would not be covered under Indiana's law if a student was injured after falling off the monkey bars and sued the teacher for negligent supervision. To be certain, some teacher protection laws are not very wide in scope. As a result, these laws provide a false sense of security to those who fail to understand that, as noted, even with teacher protection acts, educators are not shielded from being sued. Anyone can file suit, and regardless of whether the litigation is frivolous, teachers who are sued must defend themselves. The state and federal teacher protection acts do *not* prohibit litigation-happy plaintiffs from filing suits.

At the same time, the defendant teachers must endure the stress of defending themselves regardless of whether protections acts assist them in their defenses. The purpose of the acts is to protect teachers, but regardless of whether educators are ultimately victorious, these laws do *not* (in most cases) protect them from enduring the financial and emotional repercussions of, for example, negligence litigation.

The focus, then, should be on teacher liability insurance to cover legal fees in the case of lawsuits. Still, teachers should be aware that their school boards usually protect, or indemnify, teachers if they are sued. Typically, if teachers are named as defendants, so are their school boards. Of course, an exception to this would be cases that do not involve tort claims, such as employment suits where the controversies were between teachers and supervisors. Yet, the teacher protection acts do not address these types of suits.

ONCE EDUCATED ABOUT TORTS, TEACHERS UNDERSTAND THEY ARE LIKELY TO PREVAIL IN LAWSUITS

In addition to having their potential legal fees covered, teachers should be educated about the trends in negligence lawsuits involving teachers. Studies show that many teachers are confused, unaware, and intimidated by the law. However, once educated about torts, teachers would likely conclude that plaintiffs are rarely victorious when suing teachers for negligence. To prevail, claimants must prove all four elements of negligence by a preponderance of the evidence *and* have cases that are not excused by one of the defenses to negligence. Therefore, it is not an easy feat for plaintiffs to prevail in negligence cases against teachers and their school boards.

State laws, typically via common or case law rather than statutes, in every jurisdiction dictate the four elements that plaintiffs must prove to prevail: The teacher had a *duty* to the injured party; the teacher *breached his/her duty;* the party was *injured;* and the injury was *caused* by the teacher's breach of duty. To illustrate, if an elementary student who fell off a swing at recess and broke his arm sued a teacher, then the child, through his parents and attorney, first would have to prove that the teacher owed him or her a duty of care. In this situation, it is likely that a duty could be proven because in elementary school playground situations, teachers usually owe students a duty of adequate supervision. Thus, the first of the four elements could be proven.

Second, the student would have to prove that the teacher breached his or her duty. If the teacher was acting like a reasonable educator observing the children and preventing foreseeable harm from occurring, then the student would not be able to prove this element of negligence. Because the plaintiff could not prove one of the four elements of negligence, the teacher would already prevail in the suit. However, for the sake of illustration, if the student was able to show that the teacher breached his or her duty, then the student would still need to prove the third element of negligence that he or she was injured. In the current example, proving the arm is broken would not be difficult.

The fourth element of causation, though, is typically the hardest element for plaintiffs to prove. To prove this element, the student must demonstrate that the breach of the teacher's duty was the reason why he or she was injured. In other words, a breach of duty may be shown if the teacher was not properly supervising and his or her failure to supervise caused the student to be injured. Rare situations can be envisioned in which children engage in unsafe behavior such as swinging too high or jumping off the swings and the dangerous behavior ceases after a teacher's reprimand. In this way, it is possible that a teacher's supervision could prevent student injuries. On the other hand, it is more convincing that a teacher simply watching children swinging would not prevent many injuries. Therefore, in the latter situation, the student once again would be unable to prove an element and the teacher would prevail.

For the sake of discussion, imagine the student was able to prove all four elements of negligence. If this were to occur, the teacher would still have an opportunity to present a variety of defenses that could exonerate him or her from liability. For example, the teacher could claim procedural defects such as the plaintiff's failure to provide proper notice to defendants that they are being sued. The teacher could also seek to assert the defenses of contributory negligence or comparative negligence and possibly assumption of risk. Contributory negligence is a defense in which if the plaintiff is found at fault for any percentage of the injury, the defendant is freed from all culpability. The defense of comparative negligence states that if the plaintiff and/or one or more defendants are at fault for the plaintiff's injury, then they all share the responsibility of the damages in proportion to their level of responsibility. Depending on where a case was litigated, a teacher would be able to claim one or the other of these defenses of contributory and comparative negligence, but not both. Assumption of risk allows the defendant to claim that because the plaintiff was aware of the risk, the defendant should not be held liable for the injury.

The defense that aligns most closely with the teacher protection acts is governmental immunity. School boards can rely on the defense of governmental immunity if it is provided by the state law in the jurisdiction within which they reside. Although states often have limitations pertaining to how it is applied, the general defense is that because school boards are state entities, they are protected from being liable in litigation. The purpose behind governmental immunity is that the government should not be allowed to be sued because if taxpayers sue the government, it is not in society's best interest. If plaintiffs sue the government, which represents taxpayers, it would be similar to suing themselves. Thus, simply because teachers are employed by the government, they may already be protected against liability. In addition to having to prove all four elements of negligence, a plaintiff must rebut the defenses. In sum, even though a student may be able to prove that the teacher was negligent, the teacher often prevails after presenting a defense.

EXISTING TEACHER PROTECTION ACTS ARE UNNECESSARY

State and federal statutory protections that are already in place are controversial, and many regard them as unnecessary because they fail to offer much true protection. For instance, as discussed earlier, these laws do not prevent teachers from being sued. In many instances, even with the teacher protection acts in place, innocent teachers must pay expensive legal fees and endure the emotional stress to defend themselves in litigation.

Additionally, teacher protection acts are politically charged. The current federal teacher protection act is the Paul D. Coverdell Teacher Protection Act of 2001 ("Coverdell Act"). Its history can be traced back to the presidential election of 2000, which occurred a year after the tragedy at the Columbine, Colorado, high school. During this time, teachers were nervous about school safety and desired legal protection when disciplining students. As part of his political platform, George W. Bush campaigned for tort reform of all types. As a result, he promised that he would support a federal teacher protection act. In a presidential debate, Bush stated, "I support a teacher liability act at the federal level. It says if a teacher or principal upholds reasonable standards of classroom discipline they can't be sued. They can't be sued." Yet, as mentioned, teacher protection acts have limited authority to protect teachers from all lawsuits related to negligence. Thus, it is not surprising that the Coverdell Act, a federal law that limits the extent of liability for which teachers (and other school employees) can be held responsible, is rarely relied on by school personnel. The Coverdell Act was passed soon after Bush became president and is part of the No Child Left Behind Act.

The purpose of the Coverdell Act is to provide school professionals "the tools they need to undertake reasonable actions to maintain order, discipline, and an appropriate educational environment" (§ 6732). The Coverdell Act states that "no teacher shall be liable for harm caused by an act or omission" if carried out "in the scope of the teacher's employment" (§ 6736(a)(1)) and "not caused by willful or criminal misconduct, gross negligence, reckless misconduct, or a conscious, flagrant indifference to the rights or safety of the individual harmed by the teacher" (§ 6736(a)(4)). Thus, the act limits the liability for teachers who are trying to "control, discipline, expel, or suspend a student or maintain order or control in the classroom or school" (§ 6736(a)(4)). The act also provides for limits on punitive damages awards (§ 6736(c)).

As much protection as it seeks to offer, though, the Coverdell Act does not necessarily provide additional protection to teachers above what general negligence statutes already offer them. First, the Coverdell Act is not necessary to protect teachers from negligence suits. It is replete with exceptions. For example, under Section 6736(b), the exceptions are twice as long as the protections outlined. To illustrate, Section 6736(b)(1) requires school boards adhere to "risk management procedures, including mandatory training of teachers." Therefore, teachers whose schools have not followed this guideline are not protected by the law. Second, the Coverdell Act does not protect teachers who are not acting within their scope as teachers or who are engaged in criminal behavior. Further, teacher protection laws are unnecessary because states already allowed indemnification for teachers who acted reasonably while within their scope of their employment. These exceptions mirror the reasons why school boards would not protect teachers who are sued. Yet, similar to the protections of the Coverdell Act, boards do protect or indemnify teachers by providing legal support for cases that do not fall into these exceptions.

These types of limitations have motivated some critics to state that the Coverdell Act merely provides an "illusion of a solution" and is in fact only symbolic of protecting teachers. Additionally, organizations such as the Association of Trial Lawyers of America have criticized the act for providing "little or no justification for such a sweeping exercise of federal control." Currently few state teacher protection acts have been enacted, although organizations such as the American Tort Reform Association have been lobbying to have these measures passed. Again, however, similar to the Coverdell Act, these state statutes are ultimately unnecessary.

CONCLUSION

In sum, the arguments of the point essay notwithstanding, supporting teacher protection acts is unwise policy. These laws are motivated by an unsubstantiated fear that has not been empirically shown to have a negative impact on the ability of teachers to teach effectively. In the rare cases where teachers are sued, they typically prevail and need assistance in paying for legal fees more than they need qualified immunity. Moreover, state laws often provide school boards with the defense of qualified immunity; plus, the current law that is in place in every state makes it very difficult for plaintiffs to prevail when suing teachers for negligence.

The Coverdell Act is a politically motivated federal act that is narrowly construed and ultimately unnecessary because it provides a false sense of protection. Teachers already have protection through state law and often garnish legal support from unions or private liability insurance. Thus, contrary to the point essay's argument, teacher protection acts are not needed.

FURTHER READINGS AND RESOURCES

Common Good. (2004). *Evaluating attitudes toward the threat of legal challenges in public schools.* Rochester, NY: Harris Interactive.

Eckes, S. E., & Decker, J. R. (2009). Tort law and public schools. In C. Russo (Ed.), *The yearbook of education law* (pp. 152–171). Dayton, OH: Education Law Association.

Eckes, S. E., & Decker, J. R. (2010). Tort law and public schools. In C. Russo (Ed.), *The yearbook of education law* (pp. 143–162). Dayton, OH: Education Law Association.

General Accounting Office. (2009). Seclusions and restraints: Selected cases of death and abuse at public and private schools and treatment centers, GAO-09-719T. Retrieved February 27, 2011, from http://www.gao.gov/new.items/d09719t.pdf (Collection and summary of cases, many of which include claims for negligence, in which students have been injured in seclusion rooms or while being restrained at school.)

Insurance Journal. (2009, August 18). Indiana Attorney General: New law protects teachers from lawsuits. Retrieved May 15, 2010, from http://www.insurancejournal.com/news/midwest/2009/08/18/103096.htm

Maher, P., Price, K., & Zirkel, P. A. (2010). Governmental and official immunity for school districts and their employees: Alive and well? *Kansas Journal of Law and Public Policy, 19,* 234–238.

Miller, A. (2003). *Violence in U.S. public schools: 2000 school survey on crime and safety, NCES 2004–314 REVISED.* U.S. Department of Education, National Center for Education Statistics. Washington, DC: U.S. Government Printing Office. Retrieved February 27, 2011, from http://nces.ed.gov/pubs2004/2004314.pdf

NEA-NM. (n.d.). *Teacher Protection Act.* Retrieved May 13, 2010, from http://www.nea-nm.org/ESEA/TPA.html

Portner, J. (2000). Fearful teachers buy insurance against liability. *Education Week, 19*(29), 1–2.

Public Agenda. (2004). *Teaching interrupted: Do discipline policies in today's schools foster the common good?* Retrieved February 27, 2011, from http://commongood.org/assets/attachments/22.pdf

Robers, S., Zhang, J., & Truman, J. (2010). *Indicators of school crime and safety: 2010.* NCES 2011-002/NCJ 230812. Washington, DC: National Center for Education Statistics, U.S. Department of Education and Bureau of Justice Statistics, Office of Justice Programs, U.S. Department of Justice. Retrieved February 26, 2011, from http://nces.ed.gov/pubs2011/2011002.pdf

Robison, D. (2009, May 22). School officials question need for teacher lawsuit shield. *Indiana Public Media.* Retrieved May 13, 2010, from http://indianapublicmedia.org/news/school-officials-question-need-for-teacher-lawsuit-shield

Thomas, S. B., Cambron-McCabe, N. H., & McCarthy, M. M. (2009). *Public school law: Teachers' and students' rights.* Boston: Allyn & Bacon.

Zirkel, P. A. (2003). The Coverdell Teacher Protection Act: Immunization or illusion? *West's Education Law Reporter, 179,* 547–558.

Zirkel, P. A. (2006). Paralyzing fear? Avoiding distorted assessments of the effect of law on education. *Journal of Law & Education, 35*, 461–496.

Zirkel, P. A. (2011). Empirical trends in teacher tort liability for student fights. *Journal of Law & Education, 40*, 151–169.

COURT CASES AND STATUTES

Indiana's Teacher Protection Act, Pub. L. 121–2009; Ind. Code § 4-6-2-1.5.

Individuals with Disabilities Education Act, 20 U.S.C. §§ 1412 (a)(24), 1418 (d)(1)(A)(B).

No Child Left Behind Act, 20 U.S.C. §§ 6301–7941 (2006).

Paul D. Coverdell Teacher Protection Act of 2001, 20 U.S.C. §§ 6731 *et seq.* (2010).

12

In loco parentis: should teachers take the place of parents in all school disciplinary matters?

POINT: Dana N. Thompson Dorsey, *University of North Carolina at Chapel Hill*

COUNTERPOINT: Allison A. Howland, *Indiana University–Purdue University Columbus*

OVERVIEW

Relying on the concept of in loco parentis, literally "in the place of the parent," school boards typically base their disciplinary actions and policies on the common-law presumption that parents voluntarily submit their children to the authority of teachers and other educators. The doctrine first appears in the writings of Sir William Blackstone, an English commentator, in his four-volume treatise, *Commentaries on the Laws of England* (1765).

Blackstone explained that parents have a duty to provide maintenance, protection, and an education for their young, specifying that they can act reasonably to keep their children in order. In the part of his work most relevant to education, Blackstone specified that

> [a parent] may also delegate part of his parental authority, during his life, to the tutor or schoolmaster of his child; who is then in loco parentis, and has such a portion of the power of the parent committed to his charge, viz. that of restraint and correction, as may be necessary to answer the purposes for which he is employed. (1 Blackstone, 431, cited at *Vernonia School District 47J v. Acton*, 1995, p. 655; *Morse v. Frederick*, 2002, p. 413)

As American jurisprudence evolved, "Chancellor James Kent noted the acceptance of the doctrine as part of American law in the early 19th century" (*Morse v. Frederick,* 2002, p. 413). In loco parentis was apparently first cited as justification for discipline in the United States in a case from Vermont where a teacher punished a student for speaking out of turn to him while both were away from school (*Lander v. Seaver,* 1859). Almost 20 years later, the Supreme Court of Wisconsin applied in loco parentis to permit a principal/head teacher to discipline misbehaving students (*State ex rel. Burpee v. Burton,* 1878). Moreover,

> [a] review of the case law shows that in loco parentis allowed schools to regulate student speech as well. Courts routinely preserved the rights of teachers to punish speech that the school or teacher thought was contrary to the interests of the school and its educational goals. (*Morse v. Frederick,* 2002, p. 413)

In the wake of a case from higher education that signaled the demise of in loco parentis on state-funded campuses (*Dixon v. Alabama State Board of Education,* 1961), judges and lawmakers began to take a new look at the doctrine. Even so, courts allowed educators to use reasonable force to discipline students for an array of infractions including corporal punishment, even if parents did not agree with the actions of school officials (*Baker v. Owen,* 1975a, 1975b).

Although the judiciary continued to defer to state lawmakers in allowing corporal punishment, following the lead of *Dixon,* the U.S. Supreme Court provided greater protection in two key cases to students who exercised their rights to free speech (in *Tinker v. Des Moines Independent Community School District,* 1969) and those who faced disciplinary suspensions (in *Goss v. Lopez,* 1975). However, it has since become clear that *Tinker* and *Goss* arguably represented the high-water mark of student rights in the face of the in loco parentis authority of public school officials. In fact, since the mid-1980s, the Court more often than not upheld the rights of educators to discipline students by, for example, permitting searches of their property (*New Jersey v. T.L.O.,* 1985) but not strip searches of their persons (*Safford Unified School District #1 v. Redding,* 2009) while limiting their rights to speech (*Morse v. Frederick,* 2002).

As debate rages on over whether it is appropriate for school officials to assert common-law authority to discipline students by acting in loco parentis, the two debates in this chapter take divergent viewpoints on this timely topic. In the point essay, Dana N. Thompson Dorsey (University of North Carolina at Chapel Hill) takes the position that educators should, in fact, have the authority to act as parents when children come to school. In so doing, she reviews cases wherein the Supreme Court has more often than not deferred to the authority of school officials to make reasonable disciplinary rules, recognizing that insofar as there typically are limited numbers of adults in schools and large numbers of students, adults must have the authority to act as they see fit when dealing with misbehaving children. Thompson Dorsey added that having effective disciplinary positions in place, allowing educators to act in loco parentis, is the best way to ensure that schools are safe places where students can learn.

Allison A. Howland (Indiana University–Purdue University Columbus), on the other hand, disagrees. She notes the problems that the doctrine of in loco parentis has created in some cases. Specifically, she suggests that when matters of discipline are left completely to school officials, there have been issues involving the overrepresentation of poor and minority students in school disciplinary matters. Thus, Howland contends that the doctrine should be expanded to include parents, the community, and educators in deciding school disciplinary matters. She maintains that as important as it is for educators to create safe and orderly learning environments, school leaders "should expand the concept of in loco parentis to include authentic partnerships with, not in place of, parents" since most forms of school discipline focus on punishment and the criminalization of student (mis)behavior. The point essay and counterpoint essay demonstrate the many complexities involving this issue.

As you read these essays, ask yourself two questions. First, in light of compulsory attendance laws and the Supreme Court's deference to the rights of students and parents, is the common-law concept of in loco parentis a viable concept? Put another way, this question asks about the continuing viability of the presumed voluntary nature of in loco parentis, given that compulsory attendance laws and other school rules, including those with which parents and students may disagree, allow school officials to discipline those who fail to comply with their dictates. Thus, debate ensues over whether schools officials should discontinue their reliance on in loco parentis when disciplining students, instead of grounding their actions in state and federal statutes designed to help keep schools safe and orderly learning environments. Second, regardless of whether limits are common law or statutory, how far should school officials be able to go in disciplining students?

Charles J. Russo
University of Dayton

POINT: Dana N. Thompson Dorsey
University of North Carolina at Chapel Hill

A major concern for parents, teachers, and educational administrators is the safety of children while they are in school or participating in school-sanctioned activities. In an effort to maintain order and discipline in schools, particularly in light of tragedies such as the shootings in Columbine, Colorado, teachers and administrators have struggled to preserve a balance. On the one hand, school officials have the duty to educate students in safety while disciplining children who have been placed in their care when they do not obey lawful rules; such discipline is based on the common-law principle of in loco parentis, literally, in the place of the parent. On the other hand, educators must uphold the basic constitutional rights of students even when they are subjected to discipline for misbehavior. In this regard, a 2008 survey of school law attorneys and educators indicated that school disciplinary matters are the third most crucial legal issue confronting schools today after special education and student expression issues (Skiba, Eckes, & Brown, 2009/2010). With student discipline playing such a critical role in schools, teachers and administrators should have more flexibility in disciplining students along with some guidance on appropriate disciplinary options.

There are two primary goals of school discipline. The first aim is to ensure the safety of students and school personnel. The second goal is to create environments conducive to learning. Although the most common discipline problems in schools are noncriminal student behavior (Gaustad, 1992), Congress enacted the Gun-Free Schools Act in 1994 (hereinafter "the act") in response to the growing concern of increased violence and crime in schools. After Congress struck the act down as unconstitutional in 1995, it reauthorized the act as Section 4141 of the Elementary and Secondary Education Act of 1965 (ESEA), as amended by the No Child Left Behind Act of 2001 (NCLB). The act requires each state receiving federal funds under ESEA to have a law requiring students be expelled from school for at least 1 year if they bring weapons to schools (Gun-Free Schools Act, 2002). The act also mandates that special education students be expelled for gun possession and placed in alternative school settings (Gun-Free Schools Act, 2006). As a result, most states have implemented zero tolerance policies to comply with the mandates of the Gun-Free Schools Act, thereby adding a new dimension of complexity regarding discipline in schools and students' constitutional rights. According to the American Psychological Association Zero Tolerance Task Force (2008), the goal of an effective disciplinary system should be to ensure a safe school climate while avoiding policies and practices that lessen students' opportunity to learn and achieve.

BACKGROUND OF IN LOCO PARENTIS

As discussed in the overview, the common-law principle of in loco parentis originated in 18th-century England before migrating to the United States, where it remains a widespread standard in American schools today. As the judicial understanding of in loco parentis has evolved, a study of case law regarding student discipline and zero tolerance policies found that courts are disinclined to interfere with school disciplinary matters (Skiba et al., 2009/2010). As such, some courts have ruled that school disciplinary matters are better resolved by those who deal directly with students regularly. Under this perspective, in loco parentis gives teachers and school administrators the legal right to stand in place of parents when it comes to disciplining the students in their care. Based on the in loco parentis standard, educational officials and students share a mutual relationship in which teachers and administrators have the broad authority and discretion to exercise control over student behavior while addressing matters involving school safety and discipline. Of course, as noted in the counterpoint essay, because not all courts, parents, and perhaps educators agree with this point of view, litigation has ensued.

IN LOCO PARENTIS AND THE CONSTITUTIONAL RIGHTS OF STUDENTS

The Supreme Court has ruled in numerous cases that students' constitutional rights are based on what is appropriate for children in school. The Court has noted in some cases that insofar as the power of school boards, as exercised through educational officials, is custodial and tutelary, they may act in loco parentis to exercise their legal duty to protect, discipline, and enforce rules against conduct that would impede the educational environment (*Bethel School District v. Frasier,* 1986; *New Jersey v. T.L.O.,* 1985; *Tinker v. Des Moines Independent Community School District,* 1969; *Vernonia School District 47J v. Acton,* 1995).

In the 1969 free speech case of *Tinker v. Des Moines,* the Supreme Court acknowledged that students do not shed their constitutional rights at schoolhouse gates. At the same time, the Court has also recognized the need for school officials to have some autonomy and freedom in disciplining students without being punished for constitutional violations.

As part of this debate, a variety of Supreme Court justices, over a period of time, have warned against affording elementary and secondary students too many constitutional rights as plaintiffs challenged the disciplinary decisions of educational officials. Specifically, Justice Black, more than 40 years ago in a dissent in *Tinker*, and Justice Thomas' concurrence in another free speech case of *Morse v. Frederick* (2007) as well as his dissent in the strip search case of *Safford Unified School District #1 v. Redding* (2009), maintained that the Court should defer to the judgment of school officials and allow teachers to have the traditional authority to discipline and maintain order in their schools. The Court itself essentially adopted this position in *Ingraham v. Wright* (1977), discussed in the following paragraphs.

In *Ingraham*, the Supreme Court addressed whether the use of corporal punishment in public schools was cruel and unusual punishment in violation of the Eighth Amendment of the United States Constitution. At issue was a Florida public school board's authorized use of corporal punishment in the form of paddling where officials deemed such a measure as a less drastic means of disciplining disobedient students than suspensions or expulsions. The Court held that disciplinary corporal punishments in schools did not violate the cruel and unusual punishment clause of the Eighth Amendment or the Fourteenth Amendment's guarantee of procedural due process.

In its analysis, the Supreme Court focused on the use of corporal punishment as a disciplinary measure in American public schools, noting that although controversial and unpopular, it continued to be employed in districts across the country pursuant to the common law principle of in loco parentis which allows educators to impose reasonable, not excessive force to discipline children. The Court mentioned, of course, that punishment that is excessive or goes beyond what is necessary for the proper education and discipline of children may result in criminal and civil charges against school boards and individual educators. Still, the Court expressed its doubt that such abuses would occur in public schools given their openness coupled with supervision from local communities as officials provide safeguards against cruel, unusual, and/ or excessive punishment. In other words, the *Ingraham* Court endorsed in loco parentis as an appropriate standard for disciplining students so that school officials may maintain the proper control and education of the children in its care.

Post-*Ingraham*, it is important to note that there has been a decrease in the use of corporal punishment in schools since the 1980s and 1990s. In fact, as discussed in the debates on this topic in another chapter of this volume, only approximately 20 states have laws allowing corporal punishment in schools. Yet, the number of out-of-school suspensions and expulsions has more than doubled since the 1970s and reached 3.1 million during the 1990s (Skiba et al., 2009/2010). Moreover, educational research has revealed that a strong predictor of student achievement is active academic engagement (Skiba et al., 2009/2010).

Although school attendance is essential for academic engagement and student achievement to occur, such goals are difficult to accomplish if out-of-school suspension and expulsion are the disciplinary practices of choice in today's schools. As noted previously, effective disciplinary systems involve policies maximizing students' opportunity to learn, not minimizing their chances to do so. Accordingly, allowing in loco parentis as a disciplinary standard in schools provides educators with flexibility in disciplining students and may significantly decrease the number of out-of-school suspensions and expulsions perhaps resulting in improved academic achievement among students.

At the same time, the use of in loco parentis in school disciplinary matters does not eliminate or reduce students' due process rights. The Supreme Court explained in *Goss v. Lopez* (1975) and reiterated in *Ingraham* that "events calling for discipline are frequent occurrences and sometimes require immediate, effective action" (*Goss v. Lopez,* 1975, p. 739). Instead, in loco parentis allows teachers and administrators to take immediate, effective actions to discipline students but still requires procedural due process such as notice and opportunity to be heard if students are threatened with long-term suspensions or expulsions (*Goss v. Lopez,* 1975). As such, the in loco parentis standard in school disciplinary matters does not violate the constitutional rights of students.

RECOMMENDATIONS FOR IMPLEMENTING IN LOCO PARENTIS IN SCHOOLS

In loco parentis and its implementation in school systems can be significant because it allows educators to fulfill their duty to society by providing the appropriate edification and rearing of children. The duty of school officials is to preserve safe climates, to encourage productive and positive learning environments, to teach students the personal and interpersonal skills they will need to be successful in school and society, and to reduce the likelihood of disruption (American Psychological Association Zero Tolerance Task Force, 2008).

The basic duty of school officials is similar to the duties and responsibilities parents have to their children. For instance, parents should take preventive measures to keep their children safe and to promote safe environments such as plugging electrical outlets and adding locks to cabinets with poisonous chemicals. Parents also should use various forms of reasonable discipline with children, such as timeouts, spankings, or taking away certain privileges, to teach the difference between right and wrong and to help produce responsible citizens in society. These duties can be duplicated through an in loco parentis standard for disciplining students.

School leaders—from boards as a whole to administrators, teachers, and staff—can develop schoolwide discipline plans that may include preventive interventions such as screening and early intervention for problem students. The preventive intervention may include crisis teams composed of school resource officers, school psychologists, counselors, social workers, other mental health professionals, and parents, who will prepare a plan for handling disciplinary events (Martinez, 2009). Additionally, preventive interventions may provide anger management and antibullying training for all students. Discipline plans may also allow students to earn points for good behavior that may be used to acquire more school privileges or lose points for bad behavior. Poor student behavior that results in losing points may additionally lead to different levels of discipline depending on the severity of the student's misbehavior. For example, the different levels of student discipline may include losing privileges to participate in extracurricular activities, having to take time out by remaining in a cooling-off room, participating in community service within or outside of a school, being assigned to in-school suspension, and/ or participating in mandatory counseling sessions with a school psychologist or social worker (American Psychological Association Zero Tolerance Task Force, 2008; Martinez, 2009).

None of these disciplinary options involves suspension or expulsion, which means the students are not being deprived of an opportunity to learn. Similar to parental responsibilities for rearing and disciplining children, these school disciplinary options also consider preventive measures and a variety of reasonable disciplinary measures to promote a safe environment and to help produce responsible citizens in society who know the difference between right and wrong. These disciplinary options also may be applied to both mainstream and special education students without violating students' constitutional rights or an opportunity to receive a free and appropriate public education.

CONCLUSION

Teachers, administrators, and other educational staff share the duty to maintain order and discipline in the schools. Disciplinary policies should promote safe school climates without threatening students' opportunity to learn. The centuries-old common-law principle of in loco parentis delegates the duty of parents to provide maintenance, protection, and an education to their children while acting reasonably to keep their children in order and obedient, to teachers and administrators.

The concerns of the counterpoint essay notwithstanding, in loco parentis should be implemented in all school disciplinary matters because school personnel are in just as good a position to decide how to deal with children in their care as the children's parents. The previously referenced recommendations are reasonable, do not constitute excessive forms of discipline, and allow teachers, in particular as the usual first line of contact with students, to exercise the proper control over children while providing the opportunity for all students to learn.

The Supreme Court has offered its opinion in a variety of cases that because the power of school officials is custodial and tutelary, it may act in loco parentis to exercise its duty to protect, discipline, and enforce rules against conduct that would impede the educational environment. Accordingly, in loco parentis is the appropriate standard to follow in all school disciplinary matters.

COUNTERPOINT: Allison A. Howland
Indiana University–Purdue University Columbus

P olicymakers, school administrators, teachers, and parents agree regarding the duty of school officials to establish and maintain safe and disciplined learning environments that are free from chaos and disruption often under the common-law doctrine of in loco parentis. However, controversy has arisen over school discipline policies enacted nationwide to achieve these aims. Despite clear evidence that crimes of any sort in schools have steadily declined since 1990, disciplinary tactics focusing on punishment and criminalization rather than educational goals are prevalent in today's schools. In this regard, law school professor Deborah Archer explains that children are now far more likely to be arrested at their schools than they were a generation ago. Moreover, the number of student suspensions from school each year has jumped from 1.7 in 1974 to 3.1 million in 2002, and suspension and expulsion rates continue to increase. In 2006, the most recent year for which data are available, 1 in every 14 students was suspended at least once during the school year. These findings suggest that perhaps school officials acting "in place of parent" are not taking the most appropriate approach in school disciplinary matters.

Notably, less than 1% of all violent incidents involving adolescents occur in schools or on school grounds. Indeed, the American Bar Association reports that youth are three times more likely to be struck by lightning than to die violently at school. Still, school officials continue to implement strict policies resulting in suspensions, expulsions, and even arrests, irrespective of legitimate explanation. This phenomenon is sustained seemingly in response to public fear of the unthinkable fueled by extended media coverage of isolated events of school violence. The American Psychological Association Task Force on Zero Tolerance contends that relying on suspension and expulsion as disciplinary measures will negatively affect some students' opportunity to learn. Thus, communities, schools, and families must *share* the responsibility of in loco parentis for creating safe and positive school environments, while reducing the implementation and use of disciplinary policies that prevent student access to education and learning. As a result, the concept of in loco parentis should be approached in a much more nuanced way than allowing educators to act in place of the parent. Instead, educators should be acting *with* the parent and community to share the responsibility for disciplinary matters.

IN LOCO PARENTIS IN PUBLIC SCHOOLS

In loco parentis is a legal doctrine that describes a relationship similar to that of a parent to a child. It historically referred to an *individual* who assumes parental status and responsibilities for another individual, usually a youth, outside of formal adoption. By far the most common use of in loco parentis relates to teachers and students. An English common-law concept, American colonists derived it from the English ideal that schools have an ethical and moral responsibility, as well as an educational responsibility, for students.

Ultimately, the strict underlying premise of in loco parentis in public schools continues to be maintained by the Supreme Court, which has limited students' rights based on what it deems appropriate for school-aged youth. In *Ingraham v. Wright* (1977), the Court held that the disciplinary paddling of public school students was not a cruel and unusual punishment prohibited by the Eighth Amendment.

The courts traditionally provide public school students less protection with regard to their First and Fourth Amendment rights. Citing the duty of school officials to safeguard students, in 1995 the Supreme Court first permitted school officials to conduct random urinalysis of student athletes without prior suspicion in *Vernonia School District 47J v. Acton* (1995). This ruling accompanied congressional enactment of the Gun-Free Schools Act (GFSA) in 1994, requiring schools to institute a zero tolerance policy enforcing a minimum of a 1-year expulsion for students who bring a firearm on school grounds or forfeit federal funds provided by the Elementary and Secondary Education Act. Yet, the Supreme Court struck down the initial version of the GFSA in 1995 on the ground of federal overreaching (Russo, 1995).

Congress subsequently amended the language of the GFSA from *firearm* to *weapon,* which broadened interpretation of what could be construed as a

weapon. By the 1996–1997 school year, most schools had instituted zero tolerance policies that far exceeded violations mandated by GFSA; 94% of schools
targeted firearms and other weapons, 88% targeted alcohol, and 79% targeted
fights. Drugs were added to the policy in 1997 and by 1999, many schools
identified swearing, truancy, insubordination, disrespect, and dress code violations as infractions targeted by zero tolerance policies.

Policies and laws of this nature complicate the application of in loco parentis, which in Blackstone's original view in 1765 is limited to discipline solely for
education purposes by a teacher with unique knowledge of the student and the
misconduct involved. The concept of delegation of authority as granted by
parents to teachers has evolved into delegation by the state to meet the mandates of policies requiring application of predetermined consequences regardless of student needs, judged seriousness of the behavior, or situational context.
Given this conceptual shift of delegation of authority from parent to state, in
loco parentis cannot and should not extend to all disciplinary matters.

BALANCING IN LOCO PARENTIS AND
STUDENTS' CONSTITUTIONAL RIGHTS

Public school officials have the responsibility to provide for the protection and
safety of students and staff. Under the doctrine of in loco parentis, officials
have duties comparable with parents and families when they assume control of
students. These duties can be in direct conflict with another of their duties, to
advance the education of all students, an entitlement to each student under the
due process clause as recognized in *Goss v. Lopez* (1975). This conflict becomes
increasingly complicated given the constitutional rights of offending students
coupled with their need for an education and the obligation of school officials
to provide safe environments for nonoffending students.

In loco parentis has been used to uphold rules that are reasonably related to
the general purposes of creating a safe and supportive environment. Examples
include censoring lewd public speech and conducting student searches for
educational purposes when officials have reasonable suspicion. At the same
time, the courts agree that in loco parentis does not provide school officials
with immunity for violations of the First Amendment and Fourth Amendment
rights of students. In contrast, many studies highlight the misuse and abuse of
suspensions and expulsions, and the crippling of student and parent due process rights when in loco parentis is applied in the zero tolerance climate of our
nation's schools.

However, in its only full consideration of the constitutionality of corporal
punishment, the Supreme Court in *Ingraham v. Wright* (1977) did not definitely

determine the status of the doctrine of in loco parentis. In previous court rulings, in loco parentis was used as a broad, but not unlimited, defense in criminal and civil suits for assault and battery. Under this doctrine, teachers could be liable only if they inflicted permanent injury or acted with legal malice. Implicit in one court's opinion is Blackstone's notion of a direct relationship between a teacher and the student being punished, which supports the concept of delegation of authority to the teacher by the child's parents.

Previously, another court ruled that a school administrator was not covered by the doctrine (*Prendergrast v. Masterson*, 1917). The *Prendergrast* decision supported the notion of a close and direct relationship between the person administering correction and the student being corrected. Specifically, the court found that a superintendent was not permitted to use corporal punishment against a student. The court reasoned that only a teacher was permitted to use this form of punishment because a teacher had a more frequent and close relationship with students than a superintendent. Although courts in some states clung to the permanent injury/legal malice rule, most cited these arguments as no longer applicable to public schooling insofar as parents are required to send their children to schools under compulsory attendance laws and could no longer personally select the teachers. This meant the idea of parents delegating authority to teachers merely by sending their children to school no longer made sense.

In *Ingraham v Wright* (1977), the Supreme Court rejected challenges to corporal punishment based on the Eighth and Fourteenth Amendments, relying in part on the principle that teachers may use reasonable force when disciplining students. Even though there was no explicit reference to in loco parentis, the Court addressed the relationship between teacher and student originally described by Blackstone and qualified its evolution as follows:

> Although the early cases viewed the authority of the teacher as deriving from the parents, the concept of parental delegation has been replaced by the view ... that the state itself may impose such corporal punishment as is reasonably necessary for the proper education of the child and for maintenance of group discipline. (p. 662)

In the aftermath of *Ingraham*, teaching remains the only profession in which it is still lawful to punish a client physically. Moreover, schools are the only public institution in the United States that are legally allowed to administer corporal punishment. Although, clearly, persons who are in prisons and other institutions are not always safe from physical abuse, residents of these settings have due process rights that are denied school children. Even though

Ingraham held that corporal punishment in schools was not a violation of due process, its application in schools does not require any kind of formal paper trail, nor does it require that the offense was a violation of a specific local, state, or even school statute. To be legally protected from corporal punishment, a child must be in the criminal justice system to have equal protection under law.

Even though the use of corporal punishment under in loco parentis has declined during the past 20 years, the practice is still widespread, with about 20 states still permitting its use in public schools. It is applied more often to children in the primary and intermediate grades who are male, from a minority background, and poor. A recent report from the Human Rights Watch and the American Civil Liberties Union found that students with disabilities also get a disproportionate share of this treatment.

Some researchers note that the use of suspension and expulsion rates for students has grown while the use of corporal punishment across states has declined (Skiba et al., 2009/2010). Their article discusses the overrepresentation of minority students in suspension and expulsion. Both the Human Rights Watch and the work of Skiba et al. suggest that when educators take the place of parents in disciplining students through the use of suspension, expulsion, or corporal punishment, they must ensure that school disciplinary measures are practiced fairly.

NEW APPLICATIONS FOR IN LOCO PARENTIS

The Supreme Court described the application of the doctrine of in loco parentis in the context of *Goss v. Lopez* (1975), a case involving a situation that required immediate disciplinary action. Despite the need for immediate action in this case, it was not clear whether school officials were mindful of all the issues surrounding the students' behavior. When applied in combination with the zero tolerance policies present in most schools today, this doctrine currently employs little or no consideration of the student's intentions, unique needs, or any mitigating circumstances surrounding the misbehavior. This has evolved from the Blackstone's original intent and early applications that states,

> The teacher the law has in mind ... is one who for the time being is *in loco parentis* to the pupil; who, by reason of his frequent and close association with the pupil, has an opportunity to know about the traits which distinguish him from other pupils; and who, therefore, can reasonably be expected to more intelligently judge the pupil's conduct than he otherwise could, and more justly measure the punishment he deserves, if any. (Book I, Chapter 16)

As with the type of teacher referenced above, research supports the effectiveness of teachers who balance adolescent needs for enforcement of rules and monitoring with responsiveness to their individuality. Described as *authoritative* disciplinarians, despite individual variations in how they implement discipline procedures, an emerging body of evidence demonstrates that teachers who offer high structure and support are effective in eliciting student cooperation, engagement, and high levels of achievement. Moreover, Gregory and Weinstein (2008) illustrated greater acceptance of the authority of teachers among African American students when they perceived their teacher as caring and as maintaining high academic standards. Another study found that the combination of teacher structure and support predicted increased high school achievement for students experiencing the negative effects of poverty. A shift in policy to embrace the original student–teacher relational tenets of in loco parentis for today's teachers could help mitigate the negative effects caused by unilateral application of authoritarian discipline that emphasizes high structure and control with an absence of individual support and understanding characterized by zero tolerance policies.

Currently in American courts, the concept of in loco parentis has educators assuming parents' rights and responsibilities toward their children rather than parents delegating their authority to teachers. Additionally this doctrine has expanded to include questions of search and seizure and reasonable rules the school can set for students concerning such issues as whether they can eat lunch off-campus or how long they can wear their hair. In a related but broader sense, in loco parentis refers to educators' beliefs and practices that they, rather than parents, are responsible for providing students with an academic and social-emotional education. This represents a deficit assumption that working-class and low socioeconomic families cannot contribute to the educational outcomes of their children in meaningful and positive ways. Specifically, sometimes the doctrine of in loco parentis enforces negative stereotypes about poor families not being able to parent their own children. Such an approach also seemingly assumes that teachers can compensate for what they perceive as parental deficits. In this context, teachers characterize in loco parentis as having high expectations for students, but limited or low expectations for families.

Multiple studies confirm the link between parent involvement and academic achievement as well as social-emotional development. Perhaps of greater significance is that a recent meta-analysis of studies conducted by William H. Jeynes (2005) who examined the relationship between parent involvement and academic outcomes. This study confirmed that the relationship between parent involvement and academic outcomes holds true for students across race, gender, socioeconomic status, and academic ability of students. Additionally, its positive effects were not only statistically significant for overall academic ability, but also for GPA, standardized tests, and behavioral outcomes. This suggests that perhaps educators cannot, or should not, act in loco parentis for parents in all circumstances.

CONCLUSION

An entirely different and highly effective dynamic occurs in contexts when educators and parents trust and respect one another and form authentic partnerships. Teacher education research describes schools where expectations for relationships between parents and teachers guide all school events and parent conferences. Instead of traditional roles, as fundraisers or room moms, parents were involved as members of a community and educational collaborators that, with educators, take action to address the issues facing schools, students, and their families. In light of the current pressures to reduce achievement gaps and improve behavioral outcomes, public school officials should expand the concept of in loco parentis to include authentic partnerships with, not in place of, parents, particularly when it comes to disciplining students who misbehave.

FURTHER READINGS AND RESOURCES

American Psychological Association Zero Tolerance Task Force. (2008). Are zero tolerance policies effective in the schools? An evidentiary review and recommendations. *American Psychologist, 63*(9), 852–862.

Archer, D. (2009). Challenging the school-to-prison pipeline. *New York Law School Law Review, 54,* 867–875.

Blackstone, W. (1765). *Commentaries on the laws of England 441.* Book 1, Chapter 16.

Gaustad, J. (1992). School discipline (Eric Clearinghouse on Educational Management). *Eric Digest, 78.* Retrieved from http://www.ericdigests.org/1992-1/school.htm

Gregory, A., & Weinstein, R. S. (2008). The discipline gap and African Americans. Defiance or cooperation in the high school classroom. *Journal of School Psychology, 46,* 455–475.

Jeynes, W. H. (2005). A meta-analysis of the relation of parental involvement to urban elementary school student academic achievement. *Urban Education, 40*(3), 237–269.

Martinez, S. (2009). A system gone berserk: How are zero-tolerance policies really affecting schools? *Preventing School Failure, 53*(3), 153–157.

Russo, C. J. (1995). *United States v. Lopez* and the demise of the Gun-Free School Zones Act: Legislative over-reaching or judicial nit-picking? *Education Law Reporter, 99*(1), 11–23.

Skiba, R. J., Eckes, S. E., & Brown, K. (2009/2010). African American disproportionality in school discipline: The divide between best evidence and legal remedy. *New York Law School Law Review, 54,* 1071–1112.

U.S. Department of Education. (2010, September). *Report on the implementation of the gun-free schools act in the states and outlying area: School years 2005–06 and 2006–07.* Retrieved June 20, 2011, from http://www2.ed.gov/about/reports/annual/gfsa/gfsarp100610.pdf

COURT CASES AND STATUTES

Baker v. Owen, 395 F. Supp. 294 (M.D.N.C. 1975a), *aff'd,* 423 U.S. 907 (1975b).

Bethel School District No. 403 v. Fraser, 478 U.S. 675 (1986).

Dixon v. Alabama State Board of Education, 294 F.2d 150 (5th Cir. 1961), cert. denied, 368 U.S. 930 (1961).

Goss v. Lopez, 419 U.S. 565 (1975).

Gun-Free Schools Act, 20 U.S.C. § 7151 (2006).

Gun-Free Schools Act of 1994, 20 U.S.C. § 8921 (2000) (repealed 2002).

Ingraham v. Wright, 430 U.S. 651 (1977).

Lander v. Seaver, 32 Vt. 114 (Vt. 1859).

Morse v. Frederick, 551 U.S. 393 (2007).

Morse v. Frederick, 551 U.S. 393, 413 (2002), Thomas, J., concurring.

New Jersey v. T.L.O., 469 U.S. 325 (1985).

No Child Left Behind Act, 20 U.S.C.A. §§ 6301 *et seq.* (2010).

Prendergast v. Masterson, 196 S. W. 246, 247 (Tex. Civ. App. 1917).

Safford Unified School District #1 v. Redding, 129 S. Ct. 2633 (2009).

State ex rel. Burpee v. Burton, 45 Wis. 150 (Wis. 1878).

State v. Prendergrass, 19 N. C. 365, 367 Am. Dec. 416, 417 (1837).

Tinker v. Des Moines Independent Community School District, 393 U.S. 503 (1969).

Vernonia School District 47J v. Acton, 515 U.S. 646 (1995); *on remand,* 66 F.3d 217 (9th Cir. 1995).

Wisconsin v. Yoder 406 U.S. 205 (1972).

13

Are existing controls sufficient to prevent the overuse and abuse of seclusion and physical restraint in the discipline of students with disabilities?

POINT: Allison S. Fetter-Harrott, *Franklin College*

COUNTERPOINT: Michelle Gough McKeown, *Indiana Department of Education*

OVERVIEW

Special educators often use time-outs, whereby students are placed in secluded rooms or sections of classrooms, as part of overall behavior modification programs. Generally, time-outs are looked on as minor disciplinary sanctions that do not trigger the due process safeguards outlined in the 2004 reauthorization of the Individuals with Disabilities Education Act (IDEA) as long as they are temporary and for specified, minimal amounts of time. For example, the Tenth Circuit held that time-outs normally do not constitute changes in placements under the IDEA (*Hayes v. Unified School District No. 377*, 1989). For the most part, when educators use such methods, they are outlined in students' individualized education programs (IEPs) or are part of behavior intervention plans (BIPs). Even so, it is necessary for educators to be careful that students in time-outs are properly supervised and that time-outs are implemented consistently with the terms specified in IEPs or BIPs.

Unfortunately, from time to time school administrators and special educators must use physical restraints on students who are unruly. Although the IDEA does not directly address the application of physical restraints, their use is often governed by state law or regulations. Again, prudent school officials contemplating the necessity of using physical restraints should specify the situations in which they may be used in students' IEPs or BIPs. Further, anyone who is to administer physical restraints must be properly trained in their use to minimize the chance of injury to both students and restrainers. Properly trained educators are more likely to use only the minimum amount of restraint required to control students, thereby minimizing the risk of inflicting injury in the process. In one such case involving the use of physical restraint, a federal trial court in Virginia dismissed a claim, in part, because it was satisfied that a teacher and a classroom aide restrained a child in accordance with the terms of his IEP (*Brown v. Ramsey,* 2000). However, in contrast, a federal trial court in New York allowed a suit to proceed when it saw evidence that the force a teacher used to restrain a child was disproportionate to the need presented (*Dockery v. Barnett,* 2001).

It must be noted that although the use of physical restraints is legal, educators should use them only when necessary to protect students and staff from danger. In fact, it would be irresponsible for educators to fail to use restraints in the face of danger, thus allowing injuries to occur. In one such situation, a federal trial court from Texas ruled that educators acted responsibly by wrapping an out-of-control student in a blanket for safety reasons (*Doe v. S & S Consolidated Independent School District,* 2001). In another case, the federal trial court in Connecticut decided that school personnel who implemented restraints in response to a student's misbehavior exercised reasonable professional judgment while acting in accord with accepted professional standards (*M.H. by Mr. and Mrs. H. v. Bristol Board of Education,* 2002).

It is thus clear that educators can use time-outs and other forms of seclusion as well as physical restraints when needed. Still, this does not give educators the right to use such techniques whenever students are disruptive. Time-outs are often an effective means of helping a child regain self-control, and their use can forestall implementation of more restrictive disciplinary measures. Physical restraints, on the other hand, must be used only when absolutely necessary. The essence of this debate centers on whether existing policies, laws, and legal remedies are sufficient to make sure that these techniques are not used excessively. Both of the authors in this chapter cite a report by the Government

Accountability Office (GAO) detailing numerous instances where educators misused seclusion and restraint techniques, in many instances causing serious injuries to and even the death of students.

In the point essay Allison S. Fetter-Harrott (Franklin College), while acknowledging that there are circumstances when time-outs and restraints are necessary, notes that the GAO reports may indicate that these methods are being overused. Yet, Fetter-Harrott cautions that these reports should not be read as an indictment of all public schools and further emphasizes that the courts can respond in situations where children are harmed from the inappropriate use of seclusion and restraints. Although claims are often brought after the fact, the threat of litigation can act as a deterrent for abuse. These protective mechanisms, Fetter-Harrott argues, provide a sufficient deterrent to the overuse and abuse of seclusion and physical restraint. Even so, Fetter-Harrott advocates for better training of educators along with the implementation of policies designed to promote better behavior management techniques.

Citing the same GAO reports of instances of inappropriate use of seclusion and physical restraints, Michelle Gough McKeown (Indiana Department of Education) maintains that although some claims of misuse of these techniques may not be actionable in court, their use is not necessarily consistent with best practices in the field. She argues that schools need to do more because existing policies and legal remedies do not do enough to protect children from overzealous educators. Gough McKeown concludes that schools must be vigilant and should take steps to minimize the times when personnel are too quick to resort to such techniques.

Fetter-Harrott and Gough McKeown both make specific recommendations for policy and procedures that, if implemented, would help school administrators ensure that disciplinary tools are not misused or abused. Fetter-Harrott stresses the need for using positive behavioral interventions, establishing policies, investing in training, and monitoring use of seclusion and restraints. Gough McKeown offers practical suggestions in the areas of planning, training, communication, and monitoring. Implementing the suggestions of both authors would help ensure that seclusion and restraint are not overused and, thus, should help avoid liability.

Both authors agree that seclusion and physical restraint must be used when appropriate. Given that any degree of overuse, misuse, or abuse of these techniques is troublesome, both authors present a viable list of recommendations that school officials can use to better protect students from physical and emotional harm from educators who may be too quick to use seclusion or physical restraint or who may use the techniques inappropriately.

As you read these essays, ask yourself two questions. First, consider when seclusion and physical restraint are absolutely necessary and when other methods may be more effective. Second, if seclusion and physical restraints are used often, it begs the question of whether students are being educated effectively. Stated another way, if a child's behavior continuously requires use of such techniques, and progress toward better behavior is not being made, is that student receiving an appropriate education?

Allan G. Osborne, Jr.
Snug Harbor Community School (Retired Principal),
Quincy, Massachusetts

POINT: Allison S. Fetter-Harrott
Franklin College

When children are injured or otherwise harmed by school officials, it is often traumatic for all involved. Such events also pose a threat to the individuals involved, to the relationship between students and their families and school officials, and to the trust and cohesion of school communities overall. Perhaps because the prospect of children being harmed at school is so very troubling, some may in fact overestimate the extent to which such instances occur. Yet, in considering whether public school officials are indeed too quick to seclude or restrain students, this point essay takes the position that one must acknowledge that there are circumstances in which such methods are necessary. It is important not to confuse the troubling nature of the issue with a high incidence of misconduct.

The overuse or abuse of methods of seclusion or restraint, especially against students with disabilities is, no doubt, a weighty matter. However, numerous policies and legal remedies exist to prevent or prohibit such misconduct. Still, to engage in an authentic assessment of the challenges of ensuring safe and appropriate behavior management for students in public schools, one must avoid casting overly broad accusations, using anecdotal evidence to indict an entire profession, or pointing fingers without cause at those who most want to see students succeed. Instead, one must focus on how to ensure proper support and training for school personnel, especially in preventing and addressing stressful and highly challenging student behaviors, rather than focusing on whether these techniques are overused or abused. Abuses can occur and can never be completely prevented; however, existing policies, state laws, and legal mechanisms are in place to address adequately the overuse or abuse of seclusion and restraint.

CIRCUMSTANCES WHEN TIME-OUT OR RESTRAINT METHODS ARE APPROPRIATE

In some narrow circumstances, it is necessary or appropriate for school personnel to use methods of restraint or time-out. Most authorities accept that appropriate restraint methods may be used to prevent students from harming themselves or others. For example, a federal trial court in California rejected parents' challenge of the use of restraints by trained school personnel to stop a third-grade student from jumping dangerously across wet tabletops in a school cafeteria (*Alex G. v. Board of Trustees of Davis Joint Unified School District*,

2005). Further, a federal trial court in Florida noted that a teacher's restraint of a middle school student, with a history of running away, outside at a bus stop to prevent him from fleeing acted for safety purposes and was not excessive (*G.C. v. School Board of Seminole County,* 2009).

Likewise, time-outs or other methods of separating children from classrooms may be necessary to de-escalate or otherwise manage challenging student behaviors. The Third Circuit ruled that the use of time-out was not inappropriate under the law for a high school student who displayed a history of kicking and screaming, striking out at other students, spitting at or grabbing staff, and sitting on the floor of the school and refusing to move (*Melissa v. School District,* 2006). Additionally, the Tenth Circuit found that school officials' use of a time-out room was constitutionally reasonable in managing the behavior of a young child who sometimes threatened other students, cursed in class, and punched or kicked teachers (*Couture v. Board of Education of Albuquerque Public Schools,* 2008). Accordingly, one must view reports of the use of restraints or time-out methods mindful that there are circumstances in which these methods are necessary or appropriate.

POSSIBLE OVERESTIMATION OF THE USE OF RESTRAINTS AND SECLUSION IN PUBLIC SCHOOLS

Many who complain of excessive use of restraint and seclusion methods in schools point to the well-researched and thoughtful 2009 report from the Government Accountability Office (GAO) to the U.S. House of Representatives. Although the GAO's report highlighted a list of anecdotal accounts of egregiously inappropriate, dangerous, and even cruel instances in private and public schools, the report itself should not be read as an indictment of all public schools.

As the GAO's report makes plain, there is no central information authority recording the incidence of misuse of seclusion or restraint in public schools. The GAO conducted an extensive investigation into the use of restraints or seclusion in schools and could not identify any central repository or monitoring agency that collects evidence regarding the use or misuse of such methods on a national scale. The GAO identified only a handful of states that record statistics on the use of restraints or seclusion in schools.

The GAO's troubling report stated that the agency identified hundreds of allegations of misuse of restraints and seclusion over the 20-year period from 1990 to 2009, but the report admitted that there was not sufficient evidence from which the agency could determine whether the use or abuse of such methods was "widespread" (GAO, 2009, p. 5). Reports simply identifying the number of instances of restraint or seclusion do not provide context sufficient to determine whether such use is excessive. For example, the GAO reported that in the 2007–2008 school year, Texas records reflected that 18,741 instances of restraint of 4,202 students were reported in public schools (p. 7). Although these numbers may seem large, they represent a small percentage of the total number of students. At the same time, during the same school year, the State of Texas (2010) educated over 4.6 million students in its more than 8,000 public schools. Although any mistreatment of school children is unacceptable, the comparison of these figures demonstrates that the extent to which educators use methods of restraint—and therefore, the extent to which they are employing such methods in an abusive manner—may in some circumstances be overstated.

Additionally, the GAO report acknowledged that its investigation uncovered complaints but did not (and could not, given current information and storing systems) have a clear method of treating allegations of wrongdoing differently from confirmed instances of misconduct. The distinction between the two is significant, the GAO report noted. This report and others like it, then, should be read with healthy attention to the difference.

The GAO's report also detailed abuses that occurred in both private and public schools, further obscuring the landscape of such occurrences in public schools alone. Generally speaking, private schools are far less regulated and far less subject to scrutiny by the public or governmental authorities. Accordingly, inclusion of statistics regarding the use of methods of seclusion and restraint in private schools to some extent obfuscates research regarding the use and abuse of such methods in *public* schools.

There are also instances in which the use of time-out or restraints is appropriate. Neither counting the number of times such methods were used nor counting the number of complaints regarding the use of such methods adequately answers the question as to whether schools are too quick to restrain or seclude children. Although all should be concerned about the effects of inappropriate methods of behavior management, including and especially abusive restraint or seclusion, one must be cautious not to cast aspersions on schools for statistics that include appropriate uses such as restraints employed when necessary to prevent children from hurting themselves or others, for instance. Doing otherwise unhelpfully demonizes school professionals with distracting irrelevancies.

EXISTING MECHANISMS FOR PROTECTING THE RIGHTS OF CHILDREN WITH DISABILITIES

Numerous mechanisms and legal authorities prohibit the inappropriate restraint or seclusion of students in U.S. public schools. The U.S. Constitution prohibits school officials from imposing unreasonable restraints or seclusion on students. Children and parents all over the country have challenged successfully such inappropriate methods of behavior management under varying constitutional theories.

The Fourth Amendment to the Federal Constitution forbids the government, including public school officials, from subjecting persons to unreasonable involuntary search or seizure. In many cases, plaintiffs have alleged that the use of restraints or excessive time-out or other seclusion violates their Fourth Amendment rights. In such cases, courts must consider whether the measures taken are constitutionally reasonable. In this area of the law, courts commonly look to standards in the fields of medicine, psychology, and education for guidance on the reasonableness of the actions of school employees. Courts have not looked favorably on school officials in instances where those employing restraints, for example, have done so completely out of sync with acceptable practice in the field, such as cases in which school professionals were alleged to have used such methods for solely punitive reasons or used prone restraint methods, those that restrict breathing.

Some have challenged the use of methods of seclusion or restraint in schools under the Due Process Clause of the Fourteenth Amendment. The U.S. Supreme Court has held that government conduct toward individuals that is so invasive or egregious that it "shocks the conscience" is unconstitutional (*Rochin v. California*, 1952, p. 172). In evaluating whether teachers or other school officials violated the Fourteenth Amendment by imposing wrongly a method of seclusion or restraint, courts consider

- the extent to which the methods used comply with acceptable standards in the field;

- whether the circumstances at issue indicated a need for the application of force;

- the relationship between the apparent need for force and the amount of force used;

- the extent of any injury, if any; and

- whether the complained-of force was imposed in a good faith effort to address a challenge or whether it was based on a punitive or sadistic interest in causing harm.

For example, a federal trial court in Pennsylvania addressed a claim where parents alleged that a teacher violated their son's Fourteenth Amendment rights by confining him to chairs using bungee cords, failing to remove the child from chairs that overturned, and even hitting him. Applying the factors above, the court found that these allegations, if true, shocked the conscience and established a viable claim for violation of the student's Fourteenth Amendment rights (*Vicky M. v. Northeastern Education Intermediate Unit 19*, 2009). Likewise, the Fourth Circuit found that unnecessary and extended confinement of a student to a wheelchair could amount to conscience-shocking behavior running afoul of a student's Fourteenth Amendment rights (*H.H. v. Moffett*, 2009).

Insofar as the Eighth Amendment prohibits government imposition of cruel and unusual punishment, some have questioned whether the inappropriate use of restraints or seclusion amounts to such a violation in theory. In practice, though, despite some creative theories advanced by litigants, courts have been hesitant to find the use of restraint or seclusion violates this provision of the Constitution. Most often, courts cite the U.S. Supreme Court's 1977 decision in *Ingraham v. Wright*, which held generally that the imposition of what was then somewhat common corporal punishment did not violate the Eighth Amendment. Given the relatively high standards required to prove a violation of the Eighth Amendment, there may be instances in which challenged conduct does not rise to the level of "cruel and unusual" punishment but is nonetheless constitutionally unreasonable under either the Fourth or Fourteenth Amendments.

The weight of these constitutional mandates is not trivial. Federal statutes provide children and/or their parents a cause of action for constitutionally inappropriate use of methods of seclusion or restraint in public school. Accordingly, parents and/or students may obtain injunctive relief, for example, in the form of court orders prohibiting school officials from taking similar actions in the future; money damages against individuals; or, in rarer circumstances, local education agencies accountable for unconstitutional treatment.

Additionally, a variety of institutional supports and authorities are designed uniquely to protect the rights of students with disabilities. For example, the Individuals with Disabilities Education Act (IDEA) specifically requires school boards to educate each eligible student with a disability (or disabilities) in the least restrictive environment to the maximum extent appropriate for each child. The IDEA also requires school boards to employ behavior management techniques appropriate to the specific needs of each child with a disability. This requirement necessarily implicates issues surrounding the use of methods of seclusion or restraint. Extended or otherwise inappropriate relegation of a student to highly restrictive time-outs, for example, may violate a student's right to education in the least restrictive environment under IDEA.

Another federal law, Section 504 of the Rehabilitation Act of 1973, likewise prohibits discriminatory treatment of students because of their disabilities. Accordingly, seclusion, restraint, or time-out, if, for example, imposed on a student in a discriminatory manner, may amount to violations of the law as well. Moreover, although procedures vary somewhat from state to state, students have panoplies of avenues for seeking redress for alleged violations.

In addition to federal mandates, there may be a wide range of state laws, including tort statutes, state special education provisions, common law causes of action, licensure revocation procedures, or even criminal statutes, which provide students for redress for inappropriate seclusion or restraint.

This brief survey demonstrates the broad array of existing authorities at various levels of government protecting the rights of students with disabilities to be free from harmful restraint or seclusion. These authorities not only provide retrospective redress, but they act protectively to deter violations as well.

FURTHER ADMINISTRATIVE AND LEGISLATIVE PROTECTIONS

Perhaps spurred by the GAO's report, in July 2009, U.S. Secretary of Education Arne Duncan issued a letter to state education authorities expressing concern regarding the use of restraints and seclusion in U.S. public schools and calling on state education officers promptly to review their state regulations or to draft such regulations on the use of such methods. Following Duncan's letter, numerous states revised or supplemented such regulations, and others issued guidance letters or drafted provisions establishing more uniform standards for the use of such methods in schools. Moreover, in March 2010, the U.S. House of Representatives passed what is presently known as the "Keep America's Students Safe Act" (KASSA). The bill was referred to the Senate and then referred to committee. Both KASSA and its state-level analogs address broad principles and guidelines for the appropriate use of restraints and time-out methods, requirements regarding documentation and recordkeeping regarding instances in which such methods have been employed, and various other related considerations.

Although it is unclear at the time that this essay heads to press whether KASSA or some other federal statutory iteration will be passed (it appears no action was taken on the bill in committee, and it was not reintroduced in 2011), it is clear that in addition to the existing mechanisms protecting students with disabilities from harmful seclusion or restraint, additional measures are on the horizon.

COMMON GROUND

There may be significantly more common ground on the matter than some might think. Although some school professionals and advocates may not believe that the problem of overuse of restraint and seclusion in schools is as prevalent as often reported or feared, many, if not the vast majority, take very seriously the dangers posed by even one instance of such inappropriate discipline. However, to paint broadly public school professionals as menacing or eager to employ restraint techniques is overly simplistic and misleading. In fact, given the very practical challenges of a career in public school teaching and administration and the fact that these professions are staffed largely by individuals motivated intrinsically to educate children and youth, a more realistic appraisal indicates that public school professionals must balance a host of competing factors and considerations in managing student behaviors. Moreover, educators must do so, often, by making split-second decisions in high stress situations implicating important interests in student safety and the maintenance of an appropriate learning environment for all students.

Many school professionals, like student advocates, are exceedingly concerned about the topic. Many are also desperately reaching out to government officials and experts for information on how to prevent and address severe and dangerous student behaviors in a more student-centered and appropriate manner. Relatively few teacher or administrator preparation programs require highly practical courses on behavior management, and even fewer require or even offer courses that address the kinds of nuts and bolts issues implicated by the use of restraints and methods of seclusion in schools. Again, this does not condone inappropriate use of restraint or seclusion methods. Still, recognition of the very practical challenges school professionals face in managing student behavior informs the discussion of how best to prevent or respond to misuse or abuse of these methods. Accordingly, programs and policies designed at providing schools guidance on appropriate behavior management methods are most useful.

RECOMMENDATIONS FOR SCHOOL PROFESSIONALS

Insofar as the public is casting greater scrutiny on the use of methods of restraint and time-out in public schools—whether fairly or unfairly—and given that many public school professionals are themselves interested in obtaining guidance on the use of such methods, it is prudent to consider some appropriate practices and concepts relating to this issue.

- From Secretary Duncan's letter to draft provisions of KASSA, numerous authorities are encouraging teachers and other school leaders to learn about and to use schoolwide positive behavioral interventions and supports designed to teach and to manage behavior at various levels.

- School officials should develop policies on the use of restraints and seclusion in behavior management of all students and should consult relevant leaders in the field to inform the features of such policies.

- Educational leaders should invest in properly training relevant individuals in when and how to employ methods of restraint or time-out techniques.

- School officials should develop a usable and efficient system of documentation for tracking, monitoring, and evaluating the use of methods of time-out, seclusion, or restraint. These systems should account for timely communication with parents regarding such interventions or regarding any failure to provide appropriate services.

- Educational leaders must consider safety, security, practicality, and local building codes when establishing or designing rooms for use as time-out or other behavior-related spaces. For example, various authorities require schools to maintain time-out space where a student is either face to face or constantly visible to school authorities at all times and prohibit the use of locked time-out areas or time-out areas that are not sufficiently large to comfortably accommodate two people.

Clearly, although the use of force can present concerns, there are times when educators must apply physical restraint to children in order to protect the safety and well-being of those in their care.

COUNTERPOINT: Michelle Gough McKeown
Indiana Department of Education

The use of restraints and seclusion in schools has recently become the subject of a great deal of public attention. Along with the myriad of reports by advocacy and interest groups as well as by the Government Accountability Office (GAO, 2009) detailing tragic instances contributing to the awareness, parents have litigated claims alleging that the improper use of such measures violated the rights of the children under the Individuals with Disabilities Education Act (IDEA), Section 504 of the Rehabilitation Act of 1973, and an array of federal constitutional provisions and state laws.

The GAO report described numerous instances where school professionals misused seclusion and restraint techniques, including occurrences resulting in serious injuries to and deaths of students. Following the GAO report, Secretary of Education Arne Duncan sent a letter to school officials throughout the nation referencing it and encouraging states, including Alabama, Colorado, Indiana, Minnesota, South Carolina, and others to develop guidelines about their use of seclusion and restraint techniques (U.S. Department of Education, 2010).

On the litigation side, in 2008, a school board in Iowa was ordered to pay more than $50,000 to parents of a child alleged to have been inappropriately placed in a time-out room for long periods (National School Boards Association [NSBA], 2008). In contrast, a multitude of legal actions have been dismissed at the summary judgment stage, meaning that they dealt primarily with procedural concerns rather than with the merits of the claims, but which include descriptions of the misuse of such methods that caused students mental, physical, and emotional injury and regression. Another important consideration is that psychologists disagree over the use of restraint and seclusion for students, particularly those with disabilities.

At the same time, even critics of the use of seclusion and restraint techniques agree that in some circumstances the use of aversive techniques is appropriate and even necessary to protect the safety of the particular child, the teacher, and other students. Some courts have described it as a duty when safety is at issue. Accordingly, a simple bright-line rule to outlaw seclusion and restraint techniques is inappropriate, leaving educators in the murky territory of having school personnel administer techniques that are circumstance-dependent, requiring individual judgment. Still, such discretion by teachers and school administrators is not, and should not be, unlimited. Legislative acts, judicial precedent, and best practices all provide guiding principles for when the use of restraints and seclusion are acceptable or necessary in schools. It is in response to reports that school personnel have all too often acted outside the scope of these guiding principles that we must answer the question of whether these existing controls are sufficient to prevent the overuse and abuse of seclusion and restraint in the negative.

LEGAL FRAMEWORK

Under legal analyses, when school officials are too quick to restrain and seclude misbehaving children with disabilities, their parents may have actionable claims. Parents may draw on multiple sources of law when alleging that educators violated the rights of their children.

In the federal sphere, the Fourth and Fourteenth Amendments of the U.S. Constitution as well as the IDEA and Section 504 have formed the basis of successful suits by parents for the use of restraint and seclusion in schools. Additionally, some states, including Rhode Island, Washington, and Texas, have enacted laws addressing restraint, seclusion, and time-outs by schools. Additionally, Congress is currently in the process of considering the Keeping America's Students Safe Act ("KASSA"), which was passed by the U.S. House of Representatives in March 2010 and is now under review in the U.S. Senate.

Constitutional Claims

Substantive due process and procedural due process both fall under the Fourteenth Amendment. Educators may violate the substantive due process rights of students if they act arbitrarily or in conscience-shocking manners when they impinge on the fundamental rights of students. Claims for excessive corporal punishment are analyzed as to whether they violate substantive due process. To violate substantive due process, the actions of public school educators must be unjustifiable by a government purpose. Procedural due process, on the other hand, is about notice and opportunity to be heard. Here, courts consider whether students (and perhaps their parents) should have received notice and a hearing before being deprived of their rights in response to their having misbehaved.

Inappropriate use of seclusion and restraint methods may also lead to allegations that school personnel violated students' right to be free from unreasonable seizure as protected by the Fourth Amendment. The use of seclusion and restraint techniques, by definition, constitutes a seizure for Fourth Amendment purposes. Whether school personnel violate this constitutionally protected right of the students in their care is a fact-sensitive inquiry as to the reasonableness of the methods in light of the total circumstances leading to such use. Courts ordinarily agree that the actions of school officials are reasonable unless their behavior represented a significant departure from accepted professional standards.

Legislation

When seclusion and restraint methods are applied inappropriately, parents may assert that their use violated the rights of their children to a free appropriate public education under the IDEA. However, before parents may assert civil claims under the IDEA for what may be construed as educational strategies, the legislation itself requires them to engage in what is described as "exhausting administrative remedies" under its due process provisions. More specifically, exhausting administrative remedies includes participating in impartial due process hearings with the school boards responsible for providing the students' education. When courts consider claims under the IDEA involving seclusion, they usually examine whether the actions of school personnel served a legitimate educational purpose. Finally, and as mentioned, the U.S. Senate is now reviewing KASSA. If KASSA is passed, new federal regulations will apply to schools regarding the use of restraints and seclusion.

Although 42 U.S.C. § 1983 provides a mechanism for litigating federal claims only, some jurisdictions have enacted laws regulating state-law based claims against schools. A Georgia statute, for example, provides that state actors are subject to private suits only if they fail to perform their ministerial (or mandatory) functions or if they act with actual malice or with intent to cause injury. State laws may also enable parents to file claims such as assault and battery. Some states have laws specifically addressing the use of seclusion and restraint methods in schools, including Washington and Rhode Island. However, a 2009 survey by the National Disability Rights Network indicated that nearly half of states do not have such laws in place. The trend in new state laws and the current consideration of KASSA highlights the increased attention and scrutiny being paid to the use of seclusion and restraint in schools.

Policy Considerations

The previous section addressed the broad legal contours for the use of restraints and seclusion in schools. Still policy considerations and best practices that are used in schools are not the standards by which civil actions are adjudicated. In other words, actionable legal claims do not capture all of the circumstances in which schools have been "too quick" to restrain and seclude and do not squarely speak to the broader evaluative-normative question. Hence, what is legally permissible is not always what is approvable as a normative matter. Best practice dictates additional considerations.

Indeed, judicial opinions in cases involving alleged inappropriate use of seclusion and restraint methods have often indicated that although actions by a school actor may not have been actionable, they may represent significant deviations from best practices. For example, the Eleventh Circuit upheld a grant of summary judgment for defendant school officials but included the following comment indicating its disapproval of a teacher's use of seclusion and restraint:

> Although the circumstances that give rise to T.W.'s claim are truly unfortunate, the Due Process Clause imposes liability only in "extraordinary circumstances." We disapprove of [the teacher's] alleged actions in no uncertain terms, and we are sympathetic to the harm that T.W. and his classmates suffered. . . . Nevertheless, we cannot say that the exercises of corporal punishment and force in this appeal are so brutal, demeaning and harmful as literally to shock the conscience of the court. (*T.W. v. School Board*, 2010, p. 602, internal citations omitted)

The Eighth Circuit's 2010 ruling in *C.N. v. Willmar Public Schools* provides another example. Here, a student who was diagnosed as developmentally delayed with a speech and language component was subjected to alleged misuse of seclusion and restraint methods from kindergarten through third grade. Testing additionally revealed that the child had attention and hyperactivity problems. Yet, the child's individual educational plan (IEP) did include seclusion and restrain methods for specific behaviors. However, as her behavior problems continued, the child was evaluated again by an outside evaluator who eventually specifically recommended against seclusion methods and objected to the use of restraints. Despite the recommendations by the outside evaluator and other modifications, the child's IEP continued to include these aversive techniques. During the child's third grade year, the special education teacher to whom she was assigned allegedly improperly and excessively used the techniques including requiring her to sit at a "thinking desk" for a set period and threatening to use restraint and seclusion techniques as consequences if she failed to do so. These allegations were combined with other behaviors such as refusing to let the student go to the bathroom and causing an accident, hair pulling, and general demeaning and belittling treatment. The teacher was ultimately reported by a paraprofessional for maltreatment related to the child.

The Eighth Circuit affirmed a grant of summary judgment in favor of the defendants, noting the mother's failure to exhaust administrative remedies. The court added both that a Fourth Amendment seizure was not reasonable because the use of restraints was contained in her child's IEP and that the mother failed to set forth the required specific facts for the substantive due process claim. Still, the court commented that the teacher's use of the restraint and seclusion methods was "overzealous at times and not recommended by [the outside evaluator] (p. 633)."

Another illustration of a court dismissing claims while suggesting that the school personnel failed to act within best practices is *Payne v. Peninsula School District* (2010). The mother of a child with autism alleged that officials locked her son in a 5 × 6 unventilated room, the window of which the teacher covered.

The use of the room led the student to urinate and defecate on himself repeatedly. Educators allowed the use of the room to continue to remain in the child's IEP despite his mother's continued expression of concern, which led her to claim that the misuse of these methods caused her son to regress mentally and emotionally. Although the mother requested the administrative measure of mediation, it failed to resolve all of her concerns. Unfortunately, since the mother did not request the due process hearing required under IDEA following mediation, a divided Ninth Circuit affirmed a dismissal in favor of the defendants because the mother failed to exhaust administrative remedies even in expressing its disapproval of the actions of educators.

Judicial indications of discomfort with the behaviors of educators who applied restraints are significant. These judicial opinions show that educators may resort to the use of restraint and seclusion techniques too quickly and/or inappropriately even if their doing so has not violated the legally enforceable rights of students and their parents. Thus, although school personnel have at times been too quick to use seclusion and restraint methods and by doing so have caused students to suffer physical, mental, or emotional harm, the courts concede that there may be no means of recompense for the students or parents. This is additionally problematic when parents must expend additional resources to address these injuries.

A special policy concern is the number of abuses reported that involve students with disabilities. Even though the aim of both the IDEA and Section 504 is to provide legal rights and protections for students with disabilities, these children are disproportionately represented in the reports of misuse of restraint and seclusion.

The fact that students with disabilities are disproportionately the subject of the misuse of restraints is problematic not only because vulnerable children are potentially mistreated but also because their conditions threaten to hamper the ability of their parents to know about such misuse or gather evidence for legal actions. In *C.N.*, the court noted that it was

> not unsympathetic to C.N.'s arguments that her ability to provide additional factual allegations has been hampered by her communicative problems and the fact she has not been provided complete access to the District's records . . . C.N.'s vague allegations fall far short of [the Supreme Court's] standard. (p. 635)

LIMITATIONS OF LEGAL AND POLICY CONSTRAINTS

When analyzing the various legal claims that may arise from the use of seclusion and restraint techniques, courts consider the reasonableness of the use of the methods as well as whether they served educational purposes. Additionally, courts address the applicable procedural requirements involved in the filing of claims. It should also be highlighted that when students have IEPs, courts consider whether they include aversive treatments. If IEPs cover aversive treatments, courts are unlikely to find their use as violating students' rights as long as school personnel used the aversives in a manner consistent with the terms of the IEPs. However, some states have enacted laws regulating the school's use of restraint and seclusion.

At the same time, laws and regulations have not always ensured that best practices are followed and that students' interests are fully protected. Despite the presence of legislation at the federal and state levels, misuse of restraining techniques continues to occur even though the resulting injuries may not be compensable. Since existing policies and legal remedies have not sufficiently controlled the overuse and abuse of seclusion and restraint, school officials must be vigilant to take additional steps to minimize the occasions where personnel are too quick to resort to the use of aversive techniques.

RECOMMENDATIONS

With legal and policy considerations in mind, the following represents considerations that school officials should undertake to minimize and hopefully eliminate the potential for personnel to be too quick in the administration of restraints or seclusion to students. Officials should implement these recommendations in schoolwide approaches of developing awareness and vigilance of best practices.

Planning

IEPs: Courts have been unlikely to find that school officials violated students' rights when restraint or seclusion techniques are addressed in IEPs. To this end, school personnel should think broadly and include potentially necessary aversive techniques when developing IEPs in the event that they are needed. However, it is worth keeping in mind that the current version of the proposed KASSA prohibits this approach as it forbids the listing of seclusion and restraint methods in IEPs.

Emergency/Crisis Plan: Although school officials should think broadly in the design of IEPs by addressing aversive techniques, the potential exists that situations may arise in which students without IEPs may require the use of restraint or seclusion. Officials should consult with appropriate mental health professionals in the creation of universal plans.

Consultations With Attorneys: Educators should consult with their attorneys about the legal considerations of using restraints, seclusion, and isolation time-outs.

Consultations With Mental Health Professionals: School officials should consult with mental health professionals to determine how best to meet with student needs.

Training

School officials should make efforts to ensure that faculty and staff receive appropriate training including interventions that include hopefully reducing the occasions where student behavior escalates to require restraint or seclusion, appropriate techniques for using restraint and seclusion methods, CPR, first aid, and emphasis on the inherent risks of the techniques, appropriate occasions, and technical implementation and procedures, as well as reporting and notification requirements. If KASSA is passed, those who implement such techniques will have to be certified by a state-approved crisis training program. Additionally, Child Abuse Reporting Statutes should be included in the training discussion to highlight school personnel's awareness of potential violations.

Communication

Notifying Parents: In the event that restraint or seclusion techniques must be used, school personnel should inform the parents expeditiously. Some professionals recommend requiring that communication occur within an absolute 24-hour deadline (*Today's School Psychologist*, 2010). The current version of KASSA requires the immediate notification of parents.

Documenting: Officials should adopt procedures by which the use of restraints or seclusion is documented and maintained. These records can become a form of communication themselves through monitoring by school personnel as well as through parents' access to the records. Courts have examined whether school officials have documented the measures they have taken when evaluating whether educators have violated applicable laws.

Monitoring

Under the IDEA, educators must review IEPs annually at a minimum. Beyond this, boards should develop their own reporting requirements to self-monitor the use of restraint and seclusion in their schools. For example, each school should have a designated administrator or other officials who are responsible for monitoring and overseeing data compiled through documentation requirements; this person should also take appropriate action when data on the use of aversive techniques indicate it has exceeded its predetermined minimal amount.

CONCLUSION

Planning, training, communicating, and monitoring are not isolated steps to ensuring that restraints and seclusion are not implemented inappropriately. Each category and its steps should inform the others successively. Designing IEPs and emergency plans with breadth and foresight can enable administrators and appropriate specialists to determine the content of the training. Through training, personnel learn the best practices for restraint and seclusion. Further, through communicating, data are provided to indicate the types of occasions aversive techniques are used and accompanying details.

Rather than developing checklists, educators need to have continual cycles in place in which each step in each of the categories feeds the next. When school officials apply these considerations as a continual process, there should be fewer occasions where restraints and seclusion are inappropriately administered to students. Moreover, although incorporating these steps will require resources, improving practices will help fulfill the aims of providing nurturing environments to all students. As a consequence, the investment of such resources promises the pay-off of reducing the resources lost when school officials must address the legal battles, damage to their reputation in the community, as well as the internal morale issues that surface when educators misuse restraints and seclusion techniques to the detriment of students with disabilities.

FURTHER READINGS AND RESOURCES

Don't wait for seclusion, restraint legislation to improve policy. (2010, June). *Today's School Psychologist, 13*(11).

Lonestar, Texas Education Agency. (2010). *Texas education reports*. Retrieved from http://loving1.tea.state.tx.us/lonestar/Menu_state.aspx

National Disability Rights Network. (2009, January). *School is not supposed to hurt: Investigative report on abusive restraint and seclusion in schools*. Retrieved June 20, 2011, from http://www.napas.org/images/Documents/Resources/Publications/Reports/SR-Report2009.pdf

National School Boards Association. (2008). *Iowa families sue district over use of time-out rooms*. Retrieved May 11, 2011, from http://www.nsba.org/SecondaryMenu/COSA/Search/AllCOSAdocuments/TimeoutRooms.aspx

U.S. Department of Education. (2010). *Information as reported to the regional comprehensive centers and gathered from other sources.* Retrieved from http://www2.ed.gov/policy/seclusion/summary-by-state.pdf

U.S. Government Accountability Office. (2009, May 19). *Seclusions and restraints, selected cases of abuse at public and private schools and treatment centers,* GAO-09-719T. Retrieved June 20, 2011, from http://www.gao.gov/new.items/d09719t.pdf

COURT CASES AND STATUTES

Alex G. v. Board of Trustees of Davis Joint Unified School District, 387 F. Supp. 2d 1119 (E.D. Cal. 2005).

Brown v. Ramsey, 121 F. Supp.2d 911 (E.D. Va. 2000).

C.N. v. Willmar Public School Independent School District No. 347, 591 F.3d 624 (8th Cir. 2010).

Couture v. Board of Education of Albuquerque Public Schools, 535 F.3d 1243 (10th Cir. 2008).

Dockery v. Barnett, 167 F. Supp.2d 597 (S.D.N.Y. 2001).

Doe v. S & S Consolidated Independent School District, 149 F. Supp.2d 274 (E.D. Tex. 2001).

G.C. v. School Board of Seminole County, 639 F. Supp. 2d 1295 (M.D. Fla. 2009).

Hayes v. Unified School District No. 377, 877 F.2d 809 (10th Cir. 1989).

H.H. v. Moffett, 335 Fed. Appx. 306 (4th Cir. 2009).

Individuals with Disabilities Education Act (IDEA), 20 U.S.C. §§ 1400 *et seq.*

Ingraham v. Wright, 430 U.S. 651 (1977).

Melissa v. School District, 183 Fed. Appx. 184 (3d Cir. 2006).

M.H. by Mr. and Mrs. H. v. Bristol Board of Education, 2002 WL 33802431 (D. Conn. 2002).

Payne v. Peninsula School District, 598 F.3d 1123 (9th Cir. 2010).

Rehabilitation Act, Pub. L. 93-112, H. R. 8070 (1973).

Rochin v. California, 342 U.S. 165 (1952).

T.W. v. School Board, 610 F.3d 588 (11th Cir. 2010).

Vicky M. v. Northeastern Education Intermediate Unit 19, 689 F. Supp. 2d 721 (M.D. Pa. 2009).

14

Are positive behavioral interventions effective at reducing misbehavior in students with behavioral disorders?

POINT: Theresa A. Ochoa, *Indiana University*

COUNTERPOINT: Diana Rogers-Adkinson, *University of Wisconsin–Whitewater*

OVERVIEW

The term *positive behavior support* (PBS) was first formally defined in academic literature in 1990 (Crimmins & Farrell, 2006). Since then, notions concerning PBS or positive behavioral interventions and supports (PBIS) have evolved in ways that have profoundly impacted educational policy and school operations (Brown & Michaels, 2006). PBIS was included in the reauthorization of the Individuals with Disabilities Education Act (IDEA) in 1997 and is based on the principles of applied behavior analysis. The PBIS approach focuses on a preventative school discipline model where behavioral supports are integrated throughout the school to address both social and academic behavior. When managing student behavior using PBIS, educators develop plans to address behavior both inside and outside the classroom. As such, PBIS should be viewed as a multifaceted support system for students in which educators work with families and others to address an individual student's needs. Generally, PBIS is thought of as having three key components:

1. PBIS uses various strategies to examine persistent problem behaviors in a range of educational, social, and physical environments;

2. PBIS seeks to modify these environments as needed to produce positive behavioral results; and

3. PBIS attempts to provide students with explicit instruction on appropriate behaviors.

Insofar as a number of the early studies conducted on the effectiveness of PBIS strategies provided convincing endorsements of the support system, the approach was largely adopted in the 1997 reauthorization of IDEA (Crimmins & Farrell, 2006).

Experts agree that the best intervention for students with emotional and behavioral disorders (EBDs) is prevention. Research shows that the earliest possible interventions are needed to halt the destructive progression that EBDs can take throughout the elementary and secondary school years of children (Webster-Stratton & Reid, 2004). One model for prevention using a three-tiered approach that initially focuses on all students in schools but that becomes more selective and intensive as additional services are needed is the PBIS model.

There is much enthusiasm over the use of PBIS for students with EBDs because improving the culture of schools and the behaviors of all children in classrooms can also bring stability and predictability to the learning environment for students with EBDs. In addition, Lucille Eber, Teri Lewis-Palmer, and Debra Pacchiano (2002) posited that teachers and administrators feel less overwhelmed when the general behavior of schools improve, thus giving them more time and energy to commit toward implementing effective interventions for students with EBDs. In this regard, the point essay posits that "empirical evidence continues to mount attesting to the effectiveness of PBIS to help school officials reduce misconduct exhibited by students with behavior disorders."

In general school populations, the PBIS model has been shown to reduce office referrals, expulsions, suspensions, and detentions; improve standardized test scores; and reduce the number of playground incidents (see Lechtenberger, Mullins, & Greenwood, 2008). Despite the overwhelming enthusiasm for the PBIS model and its highly touted use for students who receive special education services for EBDs, though, little data actually prove that the PBIS model is effectively reaching students with EBDs. This is in part because at the third tier of interventions, where most students with EBDs would receive services, each intervention is tailored precisely to the individual needs of children. With highly individualized interventions such as these, it is nearly impossible to group children together so that they can be grouped together in order to be studied to determine the effectiveness of PBIS as a whole. The counterpoint essay suggests that there is a lack of data demonstrating the impact of PBIS on students. To this end, the counterpoint essay asserts: "What is missing in the literature is an understanding of what happens to students over time in PBIS environments. Research is needed to evaluate whether these students have better learning outcomes and become better citizens of their communities over time."

Although there are some questions as to the reliability of the research base supporting individualized PBIS strategies, many scholars in the field still agree that individualized PBIS interventions provide the best approach when attempting to modify the behavior of students with intense or chronic behavior problems (Bambara & Lohrmann, 2006). The early research on individualized PBIS has been criticized for being grounded in restrictive settings using clinicians rather than practitioners, and less research has been conducted on what it takes to achieve positive student outcomes in schools lacking access to clinicians (Snell, 2006). Although Daniel Crimmins and Anne F. Farrell (2006) recognized that more research needs to be conducted on the use of individualized PBIS to clear up issues of reliability and validity in the literature, they still argue that the use of individualized PBIS is critical to the success of students with the most intense behavioral problems.

In this chapter, Theresa A. Ochoa (Indiana University) argues in the point essay that PBIS reduces misconduct rates in students with EBDs, citing its effectiveness for creating safer learning environments. She contends that in addition to reducing misbehavior, PBIS also promotes adaptive behaviors. In the counterpoint essay, Diana Rogers-Adkinson (University of Wisconsin–Whitewater) responds by highlighting some of the limitations and criticisms involved in using the PBIS model. She cautions that some of the outcome data are difficult to interpret, that several of the current studies on PBIS include a variety of limitations, and that the cost of implementing this model is often difficult for school boards.

Suzanne E. Eckes
Sarah B. Burke
Indiana University

POINT: Theresa A. Ochoa
Indiana University

E vidence garnered from years of research shows that positive behavioral interventions and supports (PBIS) reduce misconduct in students with behavior disorders. Empirical studies indicate that the positive behavior support approach to discipline is an effective method that school officials can use not only to reduce misbehavior but also to promote adaptive behavior from all students in general and from students with behavior disorders in particular. According to its advocates, the PBIS model is a proactive and positive method by which educational officials explicitly tell students the rules they are expected to follow while teaching them ways of behaving to keep them out of trouble.

The PBIS model is a shift away from punitive and reactive disciplinary measures that have largely proven ineffective in curbing crime, violence, and student misbehavior in schools. This essay provides an overview of both the foundations of PBIS and the components of PBIS programs, pointing out the research that shows its effectiveness for creating safer learning environments in schools. Unlike the views expressed in the counterpoint essay, this point essay focuses on the strengths of PBIS.

FOUNDATION OF PBIS

Two years after the 1997 reauthorization of the Individuals with Disabilities Education Act, the federal law safeguarding the rights of students with disabilities, George Sugai and Robert H. Horner (1999) proposed a systems approach to discipline and crime prevention in schools in which they radically shifted away from punitive responses to misbehavior and emphasized a positive and preventative approach. However, despite its relative novelty to schools, the PBIS model is a derivative of applied behavior analysis (ABA), a discipline that has had a well-established conceptual, methodological, and technological foundation since the 1960s. Like ABA, PBIS strives to understand the nature of behavioral problems by examining antecedents and manipulating consequences that will motivate individuals to exhibit appropriate behavior by providing meaningful and positive reinforcements. The PBIS model for student discipline follows a three-tiered approach.

PRIMARY INTERVENTIONS: SCHOOLWIDE SUPPORTS

The first level of PBIS, known as primary interventions, is a universal tier in which behavioral expectations are explicitly communicated to all stakeholders including students, faculty, and staff in schools. Schoolwide PBIS is a noncurricular universal prevention strategy that aims to alter school environments by creating improved systems and procedures promoting positive behavioral changes in staff and students. The key elements of any schoolwide or classwide PBIS system include selecting a small set of behaviors to focus on, typically between three or five; teaching and reinforcing appropriate behavior; establishing consistent procedures to follow when misbehavior occurs; and developing an objective data-based system to monitor progress toward the school's behavioral goals, which is capable of being adjusted as needed.

To start, a group of individuals, usually five to eight, in a school is selected to identify the behaviors that are of concern to the school. Individuals selected can include teachers and administrators. For example, the school may identify behaviors such as smoking, truancy, and showing disrespect toward others. Once the problem behaviors are designated, teams recast the problem behaviors in positive terms reflecting the behavioral goals they want to achieve. Thus, for example, truancy is redefined as the goal of regular attendance. Although this difference in language is subtle, it is critical because the focus of the PBIS model is on framing behavior and behavioral interventions in a positive manner. The idea is to increase the likelihood of "catching" students engaging in the appropriate behavior and reinforcing it, rather than inadvertently reinforcing maladaptive behavior by continuing to focus attention solely on inappropriate behavior.

Once behavioral problems have been identified and behavioral targets, or replacement behaviors, have been developed, the next step in a schoolwide PBIS program is to communicate behavioral expectations to students. Kelly L. Morrissey, Hank Bohanon, and Pamela Fenning (2010) implemented a schoolwide PBIS plan, finding that the most effective way of communicating behavioral goals to students was in a schoolwide assembly where all students and faculty received information and instruction simultaneously instead of hearing it in staggered form and in smaller groups across several months.

In communicating behavioral expectations, the critical element is ensuring that students are given examples of both unwanted behavior and adaptive positive behavior, so that students will be more likely to know what behavior they are expected to emit and which to avoid. For teachers, it is important to communicate all the procedures for responding to appropriate behavior because it will take concerted efforts and retraining to encourage teachers to attend to and reinforce positive rather than inappropriate behavior. In addition, consistency is also more likely when communication takes place with teachers as a group. Monitoring progress toward behavioral goals is also an important component of schoolwide PBIS programs.

With respect to the previous example of attendance as a schoolwide behavioral target, PBIS programs require the collection of data to determine whether the intervention program is having the desired effect. If the school team who designed the intervention plan used daily attendance in each class as the way of monitoring attendance and data show that attendance is improving across classes, then they can conclude that the attendance intervention is effective and can continue on the same path. However, if the data obtained reveal that truancy continues or increased, then the team should reevaluate and adjust the intervention until the desired outcome is achieved. In general, schoolwide PBIS programs are expected to address the behavioral concerns of most of the student population. Most advocates of PBIS agree that up to 80% of students in any school will respond favorably to any well-implemented universal prevention PBIS program.

SECONDARY INTERVENTIONS: TARGETED SMALL-GROUP SUPPORTS

Central to any PBIS approach is the understanding that schoolwide interventions will not be effective for all students. Conceptually, PBIS programs expect that approximately 15% to 20% of the student body population in any given school will require more targeted attention to reach behavioral expectations set by the school's PBIS team. Therefore, the second tier in a PBIS program is known as secondary interventions. Secondary-level interventions are designed for at-risk students who need more intensive and small group behavioral instruction beyond what was available at the primary intervention level.

To be sure, students who are unresponsive to universal prevention receive additional, more intense, and targeted interventions and supports. In the continuum of behavioral supports, Tier 2 interventions are implemented in small groups for students who are at risk for school failure. Secondary targeted interventions may include teaching skills such as self-regulation and conflict resolution to students who have acquisition, fluency, or performance deficits. Check-in/check-out (CICO) systems, First Step to Success, peer mentors, and homework clubs are examples of specific secondary interventions designed to provide efficient behavior support for students at risk of more intense problem behavior. The CICO system uses behavioral report cards to increase structure and feedback to students who exhibit persistent problematic classroom behavior.

CICO Systems

Behavioral report cards provide students with structures and prompts during school days, adult written feedback through the day, visual reminders of personal goals for the day, data collection, and communication between adults at school and home. Anne W. Todd, Amy L. Campbell, Gwen G. Meyer, and Robert H. Horner (2008) implemented the CICO approach with four elementary school-age boys whose teachers and school administrator agreed that they exhibited repetitive disruptive classroom behavior resulting in referrals to the office. At the end of the 10-week program consisting of a morning check-in with a trained staff member who evaluated the home reports and provided the students with new report cards as well as verbal encouragement, the disruptive behavior of all four students decreased significantly. The daily report cards contained the three rules students were expected to follow and areas where teachers rated the level of achievement and compliance with each rule. Students carried their report cards and presented them to specified teachers at 3 times during the day, and the teachers indicated points earned for a total of 9 possible points during a day. At the end of a day, students met with the same staff member to check out. Check-out consisted of reviewing performance, totaling up points, and deciding how to spend reward points. The students' daily report cards were summarized and taken home to share with their parents, who were expected to sign and give them back to their children to return to their teachers in school the next day.

First Step to Success

The Oregon First Step to Success Program is another example of a secondary-level intervention that has proven to reduce the disruptive behavior of at-risk students. The intervention includes three elements: screening and early detection procedures that provide four different options for use by adopters; a school intervention component that teaches an adaptive behavior pattern to facilitate successful adjustment to the normal demands of schooling; and a parent training component called HomeBase that teaches parents how to develop their child's school success skills such as cooperation, sharing, completion of school work, or accepting limits set by schools.

To evaluate the program's effectiveness, Hill M. Walker, Annemieke Golly, Janae Zolna McLane, and Madeleine Kimmich (2005) conducted a replication study scaled up to include a total of 181 children from schools within 11 of Oregon's 36 counties. The program took place over a period of 18 months and included behavioral training coaches who recruited students, teachers, and parents to participate. Children selected to participate in the study had to exhibit significant externalizing social-behavioral adjustment problems. Problems may include chronic noncompliance, severe tantrums, oppositional defiant behavior, aggression toward others, and frequent conflicts in playground or classroom settings with peers. At the conclusion of the 18-month program, pre-post change scores for the First Step group were statistically more positive than the scores for the control group. In sum, students in the First Step program showed less aggression and maladaptive behavior and increased their adaptive behavior and academically engaged time on school tasks compared with students who did not take part in the Tier 2 (secondary) intervention. Despite the strength of secondary-level interventions, the PBIS framework notes that a small percentage of students will be nonresponsive to first- or second-level interventions and will need tertiary interventions.

TERTIARY INTERVENTIONS: INDIVIDUALIZED BEHAVIORAL SUPPORTS

Under the PBIS framework, Tier 3 interventions, also referred to as tertiary interventions, are reserved for students who are already immersed in antisocial behavior and have been resistant to any lower level supports. It is estimated that 5% to 7% of students will need tertiary interventions to minimize the detrimental impact of their behavioral challenges. Students who require tertiary interventions are likely to have behavioral disorders. Tertiary interventions are intensive and administered at the individual student level. Functional behavioral assessments (FBAs) and mental health supports such as wraparound community services are examples of Tier 3 interventions. FBAs help educators determine the variables that sustain inappropriate behavior and cue the student to engage in adaptive behavior. The main goal of FBAs is to understand the function that maladaptive behavior serves in the lives of students in order to replace it with adaptive socially acceptable alternative behavioral responses.

Lee Kern, Patricia Gallagher, Kristin Starosta, Wesley Hickman, and Michael George (2006) conducted a 3-year study to investigate the long-term effects of FBA-based interventions on a student diagnosed with attention-deficit hyperactivity disorder, Down syndrome, and oppositional defiant disorder who also engaged in chronic aggression. His teachers had implemented other lower level interventions with limited success. Following PBIS Tier 3 intervention guidelines, a support team was formed consisting of his grandmother, one certified teacher and three teachers in training, the technical assistance program coach, and the program director. The technical assistance program coach completed a review of available data by reviewing school records and gathered information from the teaching staff using a questionnaire about the student's behavioral and educational strengths and weaknesses. After information was gathered, hypotheses were developed and tested in an attempt to determine the variables (or circumstances) that maintained inappropriate behavior. Once variables were confirmed to maintain behavior, an intervention was developed to reduce the student's aggression and teach him socially appropriate behavior.

In this case, the team developed a plan to teach the student to use a communication book to tell teaching staff about his needs and wants or when he needed a break from tasks. The team tailored school work to the student's level from easiest to more difficult and put rewards in place for successful accomplishment. The intervention was phased in during the first year so as not to overwhelm the student or staff. The team made adjustments to the intervention plan in the second year, and new teaching staff was trained to administer the intervention plan. Team members made additional changes to the student's intervention in year three to account for deterioration of student behavior and inconsistency in following the student's individualized education program goals and interventions. Training of new teaching staff also took place during year three. In their analysis, the researchers found that tertiary intervention succeeded in reducing behavioral problems (aggression) by teaching the target student to communicate his needs. In response to the functional assessment, which found that the student engaged in aggression to avoid difficult and unwanted tasks and to gain attention from staff members, the intervention taught him how to request a break and obtain attention from desirable teaching staff in a socially appropriate and an age-appropriate manner.

CONCLUSION

In sum, empirical evidence continues to mount attesting to the effectiveness of PBIS to help school officials reduce misconduct exhibited by students with behavior disorders. The three-tiered approach to discipline within the PBIS framework offers schools an opportunity to improve the learning climate of schools for all students by reducing misconduct and increasing appropriate behavior. The universal level interventions in Tier 1 prevent many school infractions from occurring by making sure that all students are aware of school rules and behavioral expectations and by focusing on reinforcing positive behavior when it occurs. Small-group, targeted interventions at Tier 2 provide focused instruction design to support students who need additional and direct instruction that allow students at risk for behavioral problems to learn and implement appropriate social skills. Finally, tertiary interventions at the third and final tier reduce the likelihood that students with behavioral disorders will engage in extreme misconduct through sustained, intensive, and extensive behavioral supports that encompass the instructional, social, and mental health realms of the lives of students.

COUNTERPOINT: Diana Rogers-Adkinson
University of Wisconsin–Whitewater

A s clearly articulated in the point essay, there are numerous strengths to the positive behavior intervention and support (PBIS) model that can be used to help discipline misbehaving students as a means of maintaining safe learning environments in schools. The widespread use of the PBIS model also illustrates that it resonates with school personnel. Yet, it is important to explore some of the limitations and criticisms of the PBIS model. Among the difficulties with the PBIS model are issues related to treatment fidelity, reliability of office discipline referrals as a measure of school improvement, cost factors, and methodological limitations of the research regarding this approach.

TREATMENT FIDELITY

Treatment fidelity related to PBIS refers to the consistency with which interventions are applied by multiple staff members in similar, preferably identical, manners. Treatment fidelity under the PBIS model is linked to the concept of reliability. In other words, this is an intervention that is applied consistently in similar situations over time. In educational research, the minimally acceptable standard for reliability is considered to be 80%. This means that in 8 out of 10 experiences, interventions were delivered in a consistent manner regardless of who administered them. Unfortunately, fidelity of treatment is difficult to create during large-scale interventions such as PBIS and is one reported concern regarding the PBIS intervention process at all three levels such as Tier 1 or Tier 2.

Proponents of the PBIS model state that as a result of staff training, all children will experience schoolwide positive behavior supports to provide a sense of constancy of expectations and consequences in educational environments. Unfortunately, since this definition of consistency is loose, it results in concerns regarding the fidelity of the interventions cited in most of the PBIS studies. Limited literature has attempted to address treatment fidelity to date, but those works that have explored fidelity are typically on a small scale such as with one grade level in a school building.

PBIS trainers have attempted to increase the rate of treatment fidelity in classrooms and schools through a training model that includes integration of performance feedback by means of direct observation and immediate feedback to the staff providing the intervention. The extent to which trainers are able to observe and provide feedback varies greatly by school district, often as a result of the cost of personnel needed to provide extensive staff feedback on a more frequent basis.

Immediacy of feedback is also critical but difficult to achieve on a large scale in most school districts. Specifically, classwide Tier 1 interventions are most open to variability in the consistency implementation across classrooms or buildings because of the volume of personnel involved in the intervention process. Variability also occurs across grade levels based on the varying developmental needs of students. This fluctuation of implementation then has the potential to cloud the impact data since the interventions used in Grade 1 may not resemble the developmentally appropriate interventions that are applied in Grade 5. At the same time, Tier 2 and 3 interventions have the potential to have a higher rate of treatment fidelity as a result of the lower numbers of children and staff involved in the process; yet research continues to indicate limitations in consistent implementation of small-group interventions at the Tier 2 level and with behavior intervention plans for children with Tier 3 interventions.

OFFICE REFERRAL DATA

Office discipline referrals (ODRs) are a discipline technique that educators use to signal to students that their behavior has reached a level of concern warranting the reporting of their actions to school administrative teams. This involves the completion of a form of some type that students may be given to take with them to school offices for disciplinary conferences with appropriate staff. In other cases, reports may be submitted electronically to the disciplinary administrators. ODRs consist of a check sheet to indicate the type of infraction, such as disrupting a classroom or insubordination, and blanks to fill in the demographic information, including the names of the student and staff members, witnesses to the conduct, date, time, and setting data. Finally, there is usually space for open-ended input should teachers wish to clarify situations.

The ODR became a measure of choice in PBIS as it was less cumbersome and more immediate than data such as individualized behavior rating scales or implementation of screening systems like Hill Walker's Systematic Screening for Behavior Disorders. ODRs as an indicator of school improvement have numerous flaws. The first concern is reliability insofar as ODRs are teacher self-reports of their perception of situations, with teachers deciding when ODRs are necessary. Discipline referrals also tend to vary based on teacher tolerance for behavior or their perceived belief that the ODRs will correct future misbehavior by the students in question. Latency of form completion is another concern since delays in completion of forms may negatively impact the accuracy of the reported data.

Second, limitations occur when ODRs are used to determine the intensity of behaviors across a school setting or as a measure of school improvement. Kent McIntosh, Amy L. Campbell, Deborah R. Carter, and Bruno D. Zumbo (2009) have illustrated some key issues including the following:

- influence of training on the type of behaviors teachers believe should be sent to the office, with a reduction in the number of referrals but with no change in the conduct within that same classroom;

- perceived pressure from administration to reduce referrals in order to suggest impact of the PBIS intervention; and

- negative perceptions of teacher performance based on the number of ODRs completed.

Another concern regarding ODRs is the low rate of referrals for internalizing behaviors such as sullenness and appearing depressed, although such issues suggest a need for intervention within a PBIS model. Finally, it is important to note that cultural bias in the number of referrals has been suggested, with African American and Hispanic students receiving a greater proportion of ODRs in schools. School boards and educators must be keenly aware of how their demographics may skew or impact ODR data.

COST

The cost of long-term implementation of PBIS is significant. Financial outlays are primarily related to personnel, initial and ongoing training issues, and material costs. The most significant cost is the initial training of all staff. In launching PBIS, typically a schoolwide advisory board is formed. This team includes a paid outside consultant as well as numerous internal stakeholders who are typically redirected from previously assigned duties to meet and assess baseline needs before PBIS implementation. As a result, the duties of team members may be reassigned, or substitutes may be hired to cover instructional staff members. Personnel are also needed to facilitate the baseline data collection process.

The second phase, initial implementation of PBIS in a building or district, includes the cost of trainers, fidelity training during the academic year, continued team meetings, and ongoing data collection. Long-term training costs require structures for training new staff, monitoring of long-term fidelity across the setting, and ongoing PBIS team meetings to review data for office referrals. Other associated costs include materials and supplies. For example, a schoolwide, computer-based software system for recording information system is often recommended to improve the data collection process. Such a system costs school boards $250 to $300 per school annually. Student incentives such as rewards for good behavior tickets, schoolwide reward programs, and student assemblies are also required with the PBIS model at the Tier 1 level. Other materials include new social skills programs, a bullying curriculum, and/or anger management materials associated with Tier 2 or 3 PBIS interventions.

Bruce A. Blonigen and his colleagues (2008) have illustrated the costs of implementing the PBIS model from a cost/benefit perspective and suggest that first-year costs for a single school implementation of PBIS are more than $170,000. Large-district implementation in the initial year is more than a million-dollar investment. For large-scale implementation to occur, school boards must address the cost factor. If PBIS is a primary building/district goal, then the expense may prevent the use of resources that are specific to academic needs. Grants at the state and federal level have been the most frequent tool to foster implementation of PBIS. In states without such grants, little has occurred to foster implementation of PBIS statewide.

EVIDENCE-BASED PRACTICE

Beginning in the mid-2000s, the U.S. Department of Education placed increased emphasis on the use of "proven" methods or curriculum in schools. This process of determining what practices are evidence-based—that is, have a base of research behind them to demonstrate the effect of the practice— became required. Experimental and quasi-experimental studies are considered de rigueur in determining whether a practice can be considered an evidence-based practice (EBP). The five primary criteria that are used to evaluate whether practices meet the EBP criteria are illustrated in Table 14.1. Tyler L. Renshaw, K. Richard Young, Paul Caldarella, and Lynnette Christensen (2008) asserted that PBIS should be conceived as a framework that educators apply evidence-based practices within rather than an EBP itself. Their analysis of the five aspects of EBP asserts that the procedures implemented within PBIS do not meet EBP standards. Using Renshaw et al.'s model, PBIS fails as an EBP primarily as a result of the lack of comparative studies using replicable implementation of practice.

METHODOLOGICAL CRITICISMS

The final issue presented regarding the PBIS model relates to a type of methodological criticism often discussed in the research literature. First, little

Table 14.1

Criteria for Evidence-Based Practice

Criteria	Definition	Adequacy of PBIS	EBP
Procedures	Should be clearly replicable set of criteria for implementation	Process oriented with procedures defined by individual implementers utilizing the PBIS elements, context determines procedures in varied settings	No
Settings	Applied in clearly identified place	Schools	Yes
Implementers	Training and expertise of implementer clear and replicable in multiple settings	Varying school personnel	Possibly
Populations of interest	Practice must be applied in a consistent population	Students in schools	Yes
Expected outcomes	Aim of the intervention must be consistent and comparable	Variable goals or outcomes dependent on setting needs	No

Source: Renshaw, T. L., Young, K. R., Caldarella, P., & Christensen, L. (2008, November 18). *Can school-wide positive behavior support be an evidence-based practice?* Online submission paper presented at the Teacher Educators for Children with Behavioral Disorders Conference, Tempe, AZ.

control group research has been presented regarding the PBIS model. The Department of Education has illustrated a variety of research methods for educators that it views as providing clear evidence that interventions were the cause of the reactions such as learning outcomes that took place. This process is referred to as a control study. Some of the basic expectations in controlled research are that the participants were randomly assigned to groups, that some would not receive the treatment to allow a basis for comparison, and that treatment fidelity has occurred. Unfortunately, such studies are difficult to implement under the framework of schoolwide intervention processes. Small N (or number, referring to the fact that few participants are involved) studies with mild disability conditions are the most prevalent research to date.

Another common criticism is the lack of cohort model assessment data. Most of the PBIS literature uses academic year comparisons or whole school data to evaluate the impact of the process on school climate. What is missing in the literature is an understanding of what happens to students over time in PBIS environments.

Research is needed to evaluate whether these students have better learning outcomes and become better citizens of their communities over time, and whether there is improvement in school discipline and safety. Unfortunately, little work has explored the impact on student behavior of attending school in PBIS cultures over time or moving from PBIS to non-PBIS schools. There are also noted limitations regarding perception research. Perception studies explore how participants in the PBIS process feel the environment has changed as a result of implementation. However, there is a lack of student data regarding perceived changes in school climate. Some studies to date indicate students often report similar rates of problem behavior before and after PBIS implementation. Studies also suggest teachers are more likely than students to report perceptions of improved classroom climates. Furthermore, most studies use aggregate data of all teachers for teacher report data, thus failing to account for the more negative perception of classroom climate among younger, less experienced teachers.

CONCLUSION

Although there is considerable evidence that supports the implementation of the PBIS model, caution is warranted in interpreting ODR outcome data. In addition, cost is a critical factor to school boards. It is also important to note that since a majority of studies lack a control group design, such limitations must be considered when interpreting the impact of PBIS research. Finally, there is concern that the PBIS model does not meet the federal criteria for EBP. The practice should be considered a framework to facilitate effective implementation of identified EBPs in order to help educational officials discipline misbehaving students as they seek to maintain safe and orderly learning environments for all members of their school communities.

FURTHER READINGS AND RESOURCES

Bambara, L. M., & Lohrmann, S. (Eds.). (2006). Special edition: Severe disabilities and school wide positive behavior support. *Research & Practice for Persons with Severe Disabilities, 31*(1).

Blonigen, B. A., Harbaugh, W. T., Singell, L. D., Horner, R. H., Irvin, L. K., & Smolkowski, K. S. (2008). Application of economic analysis to school-wide positive behavior support. *Journal of Positive Behavior Interventions, 10*(1), 5–19.

Bradshaw, C. P., Koth, C. W., Bevans, K. B., Ialongo, N., & Leaf, P. J. (2008). The impact of school-wide positive behavioral interventions and supports (PBIS) on the organizational health of elementary schools. *School Psychology Quarterly, 23*(4), 462–473.

Brown, F., & Michaels, C. A. (2006). School-wide positive behavior support initiatives and students with severe disabilities: A time for reflection. *Research & Practice for Persons with Severe Disabilities, 31*(1), 57–61.

Crimmins, D., & Farrell, A. F. (2006). Individualized behavioral supports at 15 years: It's still lonely at the top. *Research & Practice for Persons with Severe Disabilities, 31*(1), 31–45.

Dunlap, G. (2006). The applied behavior analytic heritage of PBS: A dynamic model of research. *Journal of Positive Behavior Intervention, 8*(1), 58–60.

Eber, L., Lewis-Palmer, T., & Pacchiano, D. (2002). School-wide positive behavior systems: Improving school environments for all students including those with EBD. *Proceedings from the 14th Annual Conference Research Conference: A system of care for children's mental health: Expanding the research base*. Tampa, FL: Research and Training Center for Children's Mental Health.

George, H. P., & Kincaid, D. K. (2008). Building district level capacity for positive behavior support. *Journal of Positive Behavior Interventions, 10*(1), 20–32.

Kern, L., Gallagher, P., Starosta, K., Hickman, W., & George, M. (2006). Longitudinal outcomes of functional behavioral assessment-based intervention. *Journal of Positive Behavior Interventions, 8*(2), 67–78.

Lane, K. L., Wehby, J. H., Robertson, E. J., & Rogers, L. A. (2007). How do different types of students respond to schoolwide positive behavioral support programs? Characteristics and responsiveness of teacher-identified students. *Journal of Emotional and Behavioral Disorders, 15*(1), 3–20.

Lechtenberger, D., Mullins, F., & Greenwood, D. (2008). Achieving the promise. *Teaching Exceptional Children, 40*(4), 56–64.

McIntosh, K., Campbell, A. L., Carter, D. R., & Zumbo, B. D. (2009). Concurrent validity of office discipline referrals and cut points used in schoolwide positive behavior support. *Behavioral Disorders, 34*(2), 100–113. Retrieved from Academic Search Complete database.

Morrissey, K. L., Bohanon, H., & Fenning, P. (2010). Teaching and acknowledging expected behaviors in an urban high school. *Teaching Exceptional Children, 42*(5), 26–35.

Renshaw, T. L., Young, K. R., Caldarella, P., & Christensen, L. (2008, November 18). *Can school-wide positive behavior support be an evidence-based practice?* Online submission paper presented at the Teacher Educators for Children with Behavioral Disorders Conference, Tempe, AZ.

Snell, M. E. (2006). What's the verdict: Are students with severe disabilities included in school-wide positive behavior support? *Research & Practice for Persons with Severe Disabilities, 31*(1), 62–65.

Stewart, R. M., Benner, G. J., Martella, R. C., & Martella-Marchand, N. E. (2007). Three-tier models of reading and behavior: A research review. *Journal of Positive Behavior Interventions, 9*(4), 239–253.

Sugai, G., & Horner, R. H. (1999). Discipline and behavioral support: Practices, pitfalls, and promises. *Effective School Practices, 17*(4), 10–22.

Todd, A. W., Campbell, A. L., Meyer, G. G., & Horner, R. H. (2008). The effects of a targeted intervention to reduce problem behaviors: Elementary school implementation of check in-check out. *Journal of Positive Behavior Intervention, 10*(1), 46–55.

Walker, H. M., Golly, A., McLane, J. Z., & Kimmich, M. (2005). The Oregon First Step to Success replication initiative: Statewide results of an evaluation of the program's impact. *Journal of Emotional and Behavioral Disorders, 13*(2), 163–172.

Webster-Stratton, C., & Reid, J. M. (2004). Strengthening social and emotional competence in young children—The foundation for early school readiness and success: Incredible Years classroom social skills and problem-solving curriculum. *Infants and Young Children, 17,* 96–113.

Court Cases and Statutes

Individuals with Disabilities Education Act (IDEA), 20 U.S.C. §§ 1400 *et seq.*

15

Should teachers have more training in the identification and treatment of maladaptive internalizing behaviors?

POINT: Theresa A. Ochoa, *Indiana University*

COUNTERPOINT: Potheini Vaiouli, *Indiana University*

OVERVIEW

There is debate within the education community over the role of teachers in the identification, diagnosis, and treatment of students with internalizing disorders. Internalizing disorders, such as depression and anxiety, often go undetected in the school-age population because their symptoms can be masked by more observable acting-out behaviors that impact issues of discipline and safety. Sometimes, symptoms are overlooked because students simply appear quiet or reserved. However, this problem is unlikely to go away. A staggering number of students—one study, for example, cites as many as 20% to 25%—will struggle with depression before their 18th birthdays (Lewinsohn, Hops, Roberts, Seeley, & Andrews, 1993). Therefore, it is not surprising that advocates suggested that schools are the logical place for screening and treatment of students with internalizing disorders (Shirk & Jungbluth, 2008). Tensions within this debate revolve around whether teachers would specifically be involved in such efforts and what their role would look like. The authors of the point and counterpoint essays examine two different sides of the debate concerning the role of classroom teachers in working with students with internalizing disorders.

Despite their lack of mental health training, some believe that teachers are well suited to be involved in all aspects of a child's school day—including the identification, diagnosis, and treatment of mental health conditions (Moor et al., 2000). Teachers spend more time with students than either school psychologists or outside mental health therapists. They already have an established rapport with their students. In addition, teachers have an immediate comparison with other students in their classrooms and a good understanding of "normal" behavior during class time and in different circumstances such as tests, group work, and homework completion.

On the other hand, some suggest that delving into aspects of mental health in schools is outside the role and training of teachers. One study showed the difficulty in training teachers to spot the symptoms of their depressed students, despite specific training (Moor et al., 2007). Many believe that teachers are responsible primarily for the academic welfare of the children in their classes. Other aspects of the lives of children, these researchers maintain, should fall under the purview of psychologists, counselors, parents, and school administrators. In addition, it may not be in the best interest of children to receive treatments from individuals who lack appropriate professional preparation.

Indeed, teachers of students with learning disabilities are required to have specific knowledge about how to individualize instruction. As argued in this chapter, the level of attention a classroom teacher must give to students with internalized behavior is open to debate. If the classroom teacher needs to play a greater role in this area, professional development will be needed. As Theresa A. Ochoa (Indiana University) notes in her point essay:

> [T]he current professional preparation programs available to general and special educators do not focus on providing mental health training or credentials that would enable educators to respond independently to the needs of students diagnosed with anxiety or depression.

Despite the lack of training, Ochoa argues that it could be feasible to consider educators as possible service providers.

In the counterpoint essay, Potheini Vaiouli (Indiana University) argues that "it is important to recognize the limitations of educators in identifying and treating maladaptive internalizing disorders in students, and to take note of criticisms of increasing teachers' role in this area." She argues that both general educators and special educators must focus on academics while being responsive to any issues that arise as a result of maladaptive behavior. At the same time, teachers cannot be expected to be responsible for treating all maladaptive behaviors in class.

This chapter, then, includes debates discussing the arguments for and against teacher involvement in the identification, diagnosis, and treatment of internalizing disorders with an eye toward how these conditions can impact school discipline and safety. In her point essay, Ochoa argues that classroom teachers should be better trained in providing mental health services to respond to the needs of students diagnosed with anxiety or depression. She contends that the amount of time they spend with students makes teachers the most viable option for delivering mental health services to students (in coordination with other mental health professionals in schools). In the counterpoint essay, Vaiouli explains how students with maladaptive behaviors may not benefit from a teacher's intervention during instructional school time. She argues that teachers cannot be required to carry the load of treating the full range of internalizing maladaptive behaviors in their classrooms.

Suzanne E. Eckes
Indiana University

POINT: Theresa A. Ochoa
Indiana University

Anxiety and depression mood disorders are examples of internalizing behavioral problems that are increasingly diagnosed among school-age children and adolescents; however, teachers have limited awareness of their nature, symptoms, and their treatment. According to the *Diagnostic and Statistical Manual on Mental Disorders* (4th edition), it is estimated that the yearly prevalence rate for generalized anxiety among adults is approximately 3% and the lifetime prevalence rate is 5%. The lifetime risk for major depression disorder in the adult population varies from 10% to 25% for women and from 5% to 12% for men. Yet, since anxiety and depression are not limited to adults, their effect on children can impact issues involving discipline and safety in schools.

Anxiety and depression also affect children and adolescents. Anxiety is the most common type of emotional disorder affecting children. Approximately 20% to 30% of children and adolescents referred to clinics for behavioral disorders are referred for anxiety. Generalized anxiety disorder is a condition characterized by excessive anxiety and worry in which the individual finds it hard to control the worry. Other characteristics of anxiety important for teachers to know about include restlessness, fatigue, difficulties concentrating, irritability, and muscle tension. Symptoms of depression in children and adolescents include irritability, changes in eating habits and sleep patterns, psychomotor agitation, inactivity and feelings of fatigue, excessive feelings of guilt, hopelessness, indecisiveness, diminished ability to concentrate, suicidal ideation, and maladaptive information processing.

Clinical levels of anxiety, depression, mood disorders, if untreated, more often than not increase in severity or progress from a milder disorder to a more severe disorder (e.g., anxiety usually precedes depression). Worst of all, the failure to identify and treat maladaptive internalizing behavioral disorders can lead to tragic outcomes in school settings such as violent and even lethal acts against others or oneself. Sometimes children as young as 5 years old who suffer from depression are obsessed with suicidal thoughts. Suicide is the third cause of death among children and youth ages 10 to 24. Given the overlap between these two internalizing disorders and the overlap of symptoms with normal (or at least nonclinical) anxiety and unhappiness, it is critical that teachers have accurate information about internalizing disorders and be actively involved in their treatment because data from the National Survey on Drug Use and Health (Office of Applied Studies, Substance Abuse and Mental

Health Services Administration, 2005) show that approximately 900,000 youth ages 12 to 17 considered suicide during the most recent episode of major depression. Of those considering suicide, 712,000 actually attempted to end their lives. In fact, approximately 30,000 individuals in the United States die annually because of suicide, and 4,000 of those suicides are children and youth. The typical high school classroom will have three students who have attempted suicide. It is estimated that 1 in 100 to 200 youth suicide attempts results in death. The position in this point essay, then, is that teachers should have more training in the identification and treatment of internalizing disorders in order to be proactively responsive to the academic challenges of children and adolescents with mental health needs and to help maintain schools as safer learning environments for all.

A MULTITIERED APPROACH TO THE IDENTIFICATION AND TREATMENT OF INTERNALIZING DISORDERS

The response to intervention (RTI) model currently used by many schools across the country to identify and respond to academic or externalizing behavioral needs of students in schools is also useful in conceptualizing how teachers might respond to students who exhibit maladaptive internalizing disorders. Such a multitiered approach to maladaptive behavior is an effective way of providing gradual and timely interventions with students. In the case of anxiety, a general education teacher who is aware of the symptoms of the disorder would be able to identify the early signs of anxiety observed in the general education classroom and report them to a designated mental health professional such as a school psychologist or mental health counselor.

In the midst of this debate, Howard S. Adelman and Linda Taylor (2000) acknowledged that teachers are not mental health or social services providers, but they noted too that teachers often ask for assistance in facilitating their students' social and emotional development. In other words, teachers seem to understand that emotional imbalances such as anxiety and depression are barriers to learning. Clearly the main focus of teachers should be attending to the academic development of their students. Even so, it is highly improbable that learning can take place when students are anxious to the point of being unable to perform academic tasks because they are preoccupied with an internalized fear. At the first tier of the RTI model, teachers could consult with a school mental health professional at the first signs of an internalizing disorder. If anxiety persists and the general education teacher remains concerned, a higher level of mental health support might be provided for a student suffering from a maladaptive internalizing disorder by eliciting help from other professionals.

The second tier of intervention in the RTI model consists of providing students in need with more intense intervention in a small group. For students who present internalizing disorders, special educators might be appropriately prepared to deliver small group mental health interventions. To be sure, special education teachers (special educators) would not diagnose anxiety or depression, but they could assist general educators (e.g., teachers in the general education classroom) in coordinating and delivering interventions to small groups of students under the direction of a school psychologist. John W. Maag and Susan M. Swearer (2005) pointed out that intervention techniques for depression, such as social skills training, self-management training, and cognitive behavioral approaches to the treatment of depression, are likely to be intervention techniques used by special educators to address a variety of problematic behaviors in students. An advantage of using special educators as resources in addressing internalizing behaviors is that students suffering from anxiety can receive mental health support without having to wait until their problems have escalated to more severe levels or progressed to depression that can impact their in-school behavior. In other words, special educators can collaborate effectively under the RTI model to reduce the symptomatology of internalizing disorders like anxiety so as to minimize the likelihood that it will develop into a more severe disorder like depression.

The third tier of the RTI model is typically reserved for students who need the most intense and individualized treatment. Interventions to treat severe levels of anxiety and depression are typically provided outside of school settings, in clinical environments. In addition, severe (or clinical) levels of anxiety or depression may require pharmacological treatment that can be prescribed only by medically trained professionals such as primary care physicians or psychiatrists. Students who do not respond to initial forms of interventions provided at Tier 1 or 2 within an RTI model should be referred promptly to a mental health professional. Stated more clearly and assertively, under no circumstances are school personnel to assume the role of a medically trained professional to diagnose or treat anxiety or depression with medication nor are they to prevent the treatment of these disorders using medication. Nonetheless, even at this third and final tier of the RTI model, school personnel such as school psychologists or school counselors can and should play an important role in the treatment of maladaptive internalizing disorders.

According to Maag and Swearer (2005), school psychologists are trained as assessment specialists and thus can collaborate with medically trained professionals who treat children and adolescents outside of schools. Moreover, the preparation that school psychologists and counselors possess can be coupled with medication to increase the efficacy of such treatments. In this way, the RTI model can serve as a way of preventing anxiety from developing into depression or other more severe psychological disorders; it can also serve to provide early intervention by using special educators to deliver small-group cognitive behavioral interventions, and finally it can serve as a way to reduce the risk of depression leading to suicide by forging stronger ties among all professionals—in school and clinical settings—as they identify, diagnose, and treat children and adolescents with internalizing disorders.

RTI AND IDEA

The RTI model for the identification and treatment of internalizing disorders has, until now, been offered as a conceptual suggestion. In other words, it has not been until recently that RTI has been put into practice in many school districts. Currently schools are under federal obligation to identify, assess, and treat students who need specialized help. Under the Individuals with Disabilities Education Act (IDEA), children and adolescents who present with internalizing maladaptive behavioral challenges are entitled to special education services in schools under the category of emotional disturbance (ED). The IDEA defines an ED as

> (i) A condition exhibiting one or more of the following characteristics over a long period of time and to a marked degree, which adversely affects educational performance:
>
> > (A) An inability to learn which cannot be explained by intellectual, sensory, or health factors;
> >
> > (B) An inability to build or maintain satisfactory interpersonal relationships with peers and teachers;
> >
> > (C) Inappropriate types of behavior or feelings under normal circumstances;
> >
> > (D) a general pervasive mood of unhappiness or depression; or
> >
> > (E) A tendency to develop physical symptoms or fears associated with personal or school problems.
>
> (ii) Emotional disturbance includes schizophrenia but does not apply to children who are socially maladjusted, unless it is determined that they have an emotional disturbance. 34 C.F.R. § 300.8(c)(4)(i)

The first part of the definition explicitly names depression as a disorder to be identified and treated under the umbrella category of ED. Anxiety, although not mentioned by name in the definition, can be identified and treated under the criteria of inappropriate types of behavior or feelings that negatively impact educational performance. Insofar as the IDEA covers internalizing disorders, school officials must, at the very least, identify students between the ages of 3 and 21 who are experiencing academic troubles while providing them with an individualized educational program addressing their needs regardless of whether the needs are related to academic or mental health.

BENEFITS OF TEACHER INVOLVEMENT IN IDENTIFYING INTERNALIZING DISORDERS

Aside from policy mandates requiring educators to identify and treat students with internalizing disorders, there are at least three additional reasons why educators should play a significant role in the treatment of anxiety and depression. First, teachers spend significantly more time with students than other school professionals like school psychologists or special educators. Indeed, general education teachers may spend more time with children and adolescents than anyone other than parents. Given that students spend the hours between 8 in the morning until 3 in the afternoon in school, teachers have 6 hours during the school week with students that constitute a large amount of concentrated time in which teachers have an opportunity to witness and attend to behavior that might not be detected by others. For example, even when special educators or school psychologists are formally observing students whose behavior is in question, they are likely to spend at most 1 or 2 hours at a time observing the children.

Second, teachers are better situated to notice changes in student behavior. For example, teachers, by virtue of time spent with students and the nature of their relationship to their pupils, are more likely to notice that a student is exhibiting anxious behavior triggered by academic demands made by the teacher. Furthermore, teachers will be in a better position than school psychologists or medical professionals to distinguish normal from aberrant student behavior. In other words, teachers who see students on a regular basis can determine, perhaps with more accuracy and expediency, what constitutes normal behavior for particular children. In the current system of identification, diagnosis and treatment of anxiety and depression, for example, do not typically occur until the symptoms have reached a clinical level, usually after several months. Clearly, if the goal is to identify and treat early symptoms of internalizing maladaptive behaviors before they reach clinical or dangerous levels that can impact school safety, then early identification and intervention are preferable.

Third, perhaps the most compelling reason why teachers should play a significant role in the identification and treatment of internalizing disorders is the fact that they alone are the best equipped to make the determination that an internalizing disorder is negatively impacting academic performance. Academic demands are imposed only by teachers on students. Thus, teachers alone are in the position to ascertain in the early stages that a student's academic performance is faltering. To be sure, although school psychologists can administer assessments at the tertiary level and can formally diagnose children and adolescents with anxiety or depression, the current system does not allow for early detection and treatment of these disorders.

CONCLUSION

In sum, the current professional preparation programs available to general and special educators do not focus on providing mental health training or credentials that would enable educators to respond independently to the needs of students diagnosed with anxiety or depression. Nonetheless, research has shown that it is feasible to consider educators as potential service providers in the identification of internalizing maladaptive disorders in school settings (Hallfors et al., 2006; Maag & Swearer, 2005).

Insofar as teachers spend so much time with students, a viable option for delivering mental health services to students in a timely fashion is the involvement of teachers acting in collaboration with other mental health professionals in schools, such as school psychologists and counselors. Indeed, teachers should be better trained to identify and treat internalizing disorders if school officials are to prevent catastrophic outcomes both for individual students and for safety and discipline in the school as a whole.

COUNTERPOINT: Potheini Vaiouli
Indiana University

A s stated in the point essay, there are compelling arguments for increasing the role teachers play in identifying and treating internalizing behavior problems in students that can influence school discipline and safety. Certainly, teachers can be important assets in identifying students with internalizing maladaptive behaviors. The amount of time educators spend with students at school is greater than the amount of time students spend in structured environments outside their home. Also, teachers have a strong sense of normative behavior that can guide their judgment of students with maladaptive internalizing behaviors. Further, teachers have carried out interventions such as positive behavioral support and cognitive behavior that have focused on helping students with maladaptive internalizing behaviors, and such interventions have proven to be successful.

At the same time, it is important to recognize the limitations of educators in identifying and treating maladaptive internalizing disorders in students, and to take note of criticisms of increasing teachers' role in this area. First, the primary responsibility of teachers at schools—regardless of whether they are general or special educators—is to teach academics and respond to the educational challenges facing students with internalizing disorders. In addition, the complexity of the symptoms of maladaptive internalizing behaviors and the intense emotional issues related to these disorders are not always evident in the academic profile of the children with mental health needs. Interventions by teachers typically focus mainly on students' academic growth and are therefore limited to preventive instructional strategies. The position taken in this counterpoint essay is that teachers should not be expected to bear the burden of treating the full range of internalizing maladaptive behaviors in their classrooms. Specifically, teachers should not be expected to play a greater role in the identification and treatment of maladaptive internalizing behaviors.

TIMELY INTERVENTION FOR STUDENTS WITH MALADAPTIVE INTERNALIZING DISORDERS
Impact of Internalizing Disorders on Academic Performance

Teachers and other educational personnel rely on standardized tests and various examinations to evaluate the performance and academic progress of their students. Another related responsibility, according to the Individuals with Disabilities Education Act (IDEA), is to identify factors that might impede the students' academic progress and work through them to the extent possible. Educators design interventions in the classroom to help their students acquire new skills and become familiar with content knowledge. When students experience negative thoughts that are often associated with depression or display somatic symptoms such as becoming physically ill from anxiety, their ability to participate in classroom activities may be impeded. When educators determine that there is a specific link between the state of anxiety experienced by the students and the inability of the students to perform academic tasks, they must respond to the students' needs to support the learning and academic growth of children because this is the primary responsibility of teachers.

According to IDEA, students who are identified with maladaptive internalizing disorders and meet the criteria for treatment interventions present a group of symptoms that coexist, and their intensity may have adverse consequences on behavior, interpersonal relationships, and academic achievement. For intervention to be mandated under IDEA provisions, the identification and treatment of maladaptive internalizing behaviors must be closely related to the students' academic growth and their achievements. Educators are asked to assess the educational performance of the students and decide whether a link exists between the inability to learn and the emotional instability experienced by the students. The level of academic performance guides the decisions that the educators make, placing in a secondary level the intensity of the symptoms or the negative outcomes in the social and emotional life of the students who experience internalizing disorders.

Internalizing maladaptive behaviors may not be readily identifiable by teachers. Students with maladaptive internalizing behaviors may display a variety of symptoms that range from anxiety, depression, or social phobia, to feelings of inadequacy and to worthlessness. It is not unusual for the students to experience extreme panic, lose interest in school activities, and suffer from sleep disturbances and/or abrupt changes in their appetite. Surely, those symptoms may affect the students' ability to cope, but the way in which they impact academic performance or school work may not be evident to or discernable by teachers. Symptoms of anxiety, depression, or social phobia may be present in students for some time before they affect their academic progress in a negative way. The students' level of academic competency may not vary significantly from that of their peers whereas they might struggle in their social and emotional lives. Thus, although teachers may have the best intentions, it is not clear that the students' school performance will provide educators with enough red flags to allow them to act proactively and in a timely manner to the emotional needs of students with internalizing disorders. Thus, relying more heavily on teachers to identify maladaptive behaviors may not be helpful in ensuring that students experiencing these disorders get a timely response.

Another barrier to the identification and intervention efforts from teachers is that when students suffer from anxiety and depression and show these symptoms, they are less likely to attend school and are therefore less likely to benefit from any intervention a teacher may be able to administer. As the point essay maintains, students with untreated maladaptive internalizing disorders are at higher risk of dropping out of school, of abusing substances and/or alcohol, of being bullied, or of attempting suicide. Nonetheless, one cannot help but notice that those symptoms come at a late time in the trajectory of the disorders, after the negative behaviors have been established and the students are experiencing the effects in their everyday lives, often in ways that can be disruptive in school environments. Intense, timely interventions are needed to support the students with maladaptive internalizing behaviors at this point, but at the time these behavioral manifestations are evident to the untrained educators' eye, it may be too late for action in the classroom.

Limitations of the Response to Intervention Model

Teachers can follow various procedures to support students at risk with internalizing maladaptive behaviors. According to the response to intervention model (RTI), educators should follow the system of primary, secondary, and tertiary level of intervention—a system based implicitly on a cause-and-effect behavioral link. In the first level of the universal screening, the educators' role is limited to monitoring closely the students at risk. They can apply various educational strategies to rule out the possibility of immaturity or that of personal traits affecting the student's behavior. Still, in the case of internalized behaviors, the students are not exhibiting disruptive behaviors; typically, they are reserved, and they seem uninterested and disengaged from their peers and/or with teachers when they are in the classroom. At the same time, their academic progress may seem adequate or at least not atypical enough to demand the attention of educators. Hence, these students are unlikely to qualify for early intervention approaches during the time they are in school. As long as teachers are expected to provide evidence that maladaptive internalized disorders are resulting in deficits in students' academic performance, a large number of students with these behaviors are likely to remain unidentified and underserved. Thus, while teachers are rightfully expected to identify the impact of disorders on academic performance, it would be a disservice to students if teachers were the main people to identify their disorders. This approach would be consistent with IDEA, which implies but does not state that the primary responsibility of educators is to teach the students knowledge and skills that will enable them to meet grade-level academic expectations. Symptoms such as anxiety, unhappiness, or mood disorders are of concern for teachers when there is evidence that the state of emotional imbalance is interfering with students' academic performance.

It is clear that learning cannot take place when students are struggling with feelings of anxiety, phobia, or inadequacy, but at the same time, even when teachers are highly trained to develop and implement treatment plans for students with maladaptive internalizing behaviors, universal screening is still a limited tool in offering appropriate and timely services to the students (because this screening is too general and often does not identify the disorder). Although the first tier of RTI requires educators to monitor those students carefully who seem to be at risk, it may be too difficult to identify these students in the first place. Educators are obligated to choose their actions based on the academic profile of their students—not their emotional growth. The services that the students can get are primarily defined by the level of the students' responsiveness to academic tasks; however, it is clear that the students mostly struggle in the emotional and social areas.

The second tier of intervention in the RTI model allows for small-group interventions when educators remain concerned about the students' academic and emotional growth because the symptoms of internalizing disorders persist. Special educators collaborate with the general educator to implement steps and techniques that can ameliorate the symptoms of anxiety, phobia, and/or depression so that the students can be more involved in the classroom routine and experience academic success. Again, these strategies can benefit students whose symptoms are related with their academic progress. Nonetheless, these intervention approaches may be less successful with the students whose academic performance is not affected by their limited academic abilities, but it is impeded by their emotional instability. Students with maladaptive internalizing behaviors usually complain about feeling sick, suffering from headaches, and/or experiencing intense dizziness or fatigue, all behaviors that do not allow children to remain in classrooms. Although structured group activities would offer an extra layer of support to the students and would help them face their phobias and their anxiety, the physical symptoms that they experience do not allow them to benefit fully from these strategies. Yet, at the same time, relying on teacher intervention may result in a lack of treatment for students. In summary, then, training teachers to take a more active role in diagnosis and treatment of internalizing disorders does not seem to provide the most efficient and effective way to ensure that students are treated in a proactive and timely way.

It is evident that the aforementioned processes associated with the RTI model can be useful and appropriate mainly on a preventive level. Realistically, they cannot meet the needs of students who exhibit prevalent, persistent, and recurring negative symptoms related to their maladaptive internalizing behaviors because educators can proceed in taking active steps to help their students only after they have waited long enough to rule out all other alternatives.

IMPACT OF INTERVENTIONS ON INSTRUCTIONAL TIME

Alarmingly, individualized support is available to students only at a late stage in the RTI process, when students have already exhibited an inability to cope with their feelings and are experiencing the negative consequences related to that in their interpersonal relationships and their academic performance. At this point, severe and intense individual interventions can be provided under the third tier of the RTI model.

Intense interventions typically include pharmacological treatment and are provided by mental health professionals outside of the school setting. For the implementation of the treatment, factors other than the students' academic performance along with their everyday experiences, environmental factors, family situations, or other routines need to be investigated as possible triggers of the students' maladaptive internalized disorders. The workload involved in such intervention plans can have a negative effect on the instructional time of the teachers. It can easily tip the scale of their responsibilities from academic issues to emotional and psychological ones, as educators have to spend instructional time for noninstructional purposes. Hence, the teachers' involvement in the treatment of maladaptive internalizing behaviors can prove to be contrary to the students' best academic interests. Specifically, interventions involving students with maladaptive disorder would take time away from classroom instruction.

There are also concerns regarding the types of interventions for which teachers are trained to administer in school settings. During instructional time, teachers can incorporate cognitive interventions and behavioral techniques such as modeling positive thinking, role playing, problem solving, and/or positive reinforcement for students who are withdrawn, anxious, or depressed. Nonetheless, cognitive and behavioral strategies address the students' needs only partially. The maladaptive internalizing behavioral patterns and responses associated in anxiety and depression are a result of not only environmental factors but also heredity and genetic factors. Thus, the school environment is only partially influential in changing maladaptive behavior. Well-designed instructional time can be important in alleviating the symptoms experienced by the students in the school context but the causes of the disorder still remain to be addressed. In other words, highly focused instructional time itself may help students with maladaptive behaviors. Accordingly, training teachers with the expectation that they will be more involved in intervention may have negative consequences for all students, including those with internalizing disorders, because such teacher involvement would decrease instructional time.

Considering the severity of the symptoms experienced by students with maladaptive internalizing behaviors, diagnosis and treatment should not be approached in a superficial way. Maladaptive internalizing behaviors are serious mental health disorders that can have life-threatening consequences for students and others. Despite the debate on medicating students, pharmacological interventions are the single most effective treatment for internalizing disorders, particularly depression. Cognitive behavior therapy (CBT) is also effective, but it is a time-intensive treatment modality, although it may be most effective when used in conjunction with medication. No matter how intensely they are trained, educators do not have the time needed to work collaboratively with out-of-school mental health practitioners, get proper supervision, and apply cognitive behavioral interventions to offer treatments for symptoms that result from psychiatric disorders. The current structure of the school day makes CBT unrealistic to implement in schools.

THE ROLE OF PROFESSIONALS

The current method of diagnosing and treating children with emotional disorders in schools involves a multidisciplinary child study team that includes various licensed specialists. Psychologists, psychiatrists, and social workers are usually consulted before a diagnosis is made. School counselors and psychologists are also involved even as teachers are asked to share their observations regarding students' behaviors. The final decision is made according to the observations and the expertise of all the professionals involved in the treatment plan. All the professionals included in the design of treatments need to have unique training and expertise to address not only the symptomatology but also the cause or causes of the disorders. High degrees of fidelity to the treatment protocol, special training for the implementation of the treatment, personal skills of the professionals, supervision, and continuing education of the staff affect how the intervention is delivered and consequently the students' progress and growth. Again, it is highly unlikely that educators can meet the intensity of such obligations or whether they can design them appropriately in the school context for students who present severe and persistent levels of anxiety, depression, or suicide ideation. Indeed, effective intervention requires more professional training than teachers can provide, even if they were given additional training.

Clearly, the team of professionals follows very specific mental health standards and procedures to decide on a diagnosis and on the appropriate treatment plan. Usually the treatment provides a combination of behavioral interventions along with pharmacological medication depending on the intensity of the symptoms displayed. During the delivery of a treatment, the child study team also monitors the students' behavior, conducts medical posttest exams, and monitors the follow-up plan for the student. Side effects and the efficacy of the treatment are considered and monitored to decide on indicated changes in the plan treatment, especially when medication has been prescribed. The fidelity of the treatment and issues related to the efficacy and effectiveness need to be considered in the case of educators delivering treatments in the school setting. Educators are not trained to provide mental health services, and they lack knowledge about psychopharmacology. Although educators can get the appropriate training to outweigh those concerns, the expertise of mental health professionals is highly recommended to address the complexity of the issues related to diagnosis and treatment of students who present internalizing disorders like anxiety and depression.

CONCLUSION

This counterpoint essay has highlighted several limitations educators face in identifying and treating maladaptive internalizing disorders in students. A model of identification and intervention such as the RTI may play a role in the treatment of students with maladaptive internalizing behaviors. However, one cannot help noticing that while such strategies serve the purposes of screening and may increase the possibility of early identification for students with these disorders, educators' interventions are mainly focused on the academic growth of the students. Such interventions are largely limited to preventive instructional strategies that deal mainly with the symptoms, not the causes, of the maladaptive internalizing behaviors that can emerge as disruptive behavior impacting school safety and discipline. It is highly unlikely that the students with major emotional problems, who are already exhibiting maladaptive behaviors, will benefit from the teachers' intervention during instructional school time. More important, if their health care is left in the teacher's hands, students miss the chance for appropriate, timely interventions related to the emotional struggles they are experiencing. Teachers can be important allies for the identification of students with internalizing maladaptive behavior but cannot carry the load of treating the full range of internalizing maladaptive behaviors in their classrooms. Furthermore, given the issues of instructional time and professionalism discussed earlier, both educators and students will be best served if teachers are not trained with the expectation of their carrying out broader mental health responsibilities.

FURTHER READINGS AND RESOURCES

Adelman, H. S., & Taylor, L. (1993). School-based mental health: Toward a comprehensive approach. *The Journal of Behavioral Health Services and Research, 20*(1), 32–45.

Adelman, H. S., & Taylor, L. (2000). Promoting mental health in schools in the midst of school reform. *Journal of School Health, 70*(5), 171–178.

Anderson, J., Houser, J., & Howland, A. (2010). The full purpose partnership model for promoting academic and socio-emotional success in schools. *School Community, 20*(1), 31.

Hallfors, D., Brodish, P. H., Khatapoush, S., Sanchez, V., Cho, H., & Steckler, A. (2006). Feasibility of screening adolescents for suicide risk in "real-world" high school settings. *American Journal of Public Health, 96*(2), 282.

Huntington, D. D., & Bender, W. N. (1993). Adolescents with learning disabilities at risk? Emotional well-being, depression, and suicide. *Journal of Learning Disabilities, 23*(6), 159–166.

Levitt, J., Saka, N., Hunter Romanelli, L., & Hoagwood, K. (2007). Early identification of mental health problems in schools: The status of instrumentation. *Journal of School Psychology, 45*(2), 163–191.

Lewinsohn, P. M., Hops, H., Roberts, R. E., Seeley, J. R., & Andrews, J. (1993). Adolescent psychopathology: Prevalence and incidence of depression and other DSM-III-R disorders in high school students. *Journal of Abnormal Psychology, 102*, 133–144.

Maag, J. W., & Swearer, S. M. (2005). Cognitive-behavioral interventions for depression: Review and implications for school personnel. *Behavioral Disorders, 30*(3), 259–276.

Moor, S., Maguire, A., McQueen, H., Wells, J., Elton, R., Wrate, R., et al. (2007). Improving the recognition of depression in adolescence: Can we teach the teachers? *Journal of Adolescence, 30*(1), 81–95.

Moor, S., Sharrock, G., Scott, J., McQueen, H., Wrate, R., Cowan, J., et al. (2000). Evaluation of a teaching package designed to improve teachers' recognition of depressed pupils—A pilot study. *Journal of Adolescence, 23*, 331–342.

Office of Applied Studies, Substance Abuse and Mental Health Services Administration. (2005). *The NSDUH report: Suicidal thoughts among youths aged 12 to 17 with major depressive episodes.* Retrieved from http://oas.samhsa.gov/2k5/youthDepression/youthDepression.cfm

Probst, B. (2008). Issues in portability of evidence-based treatment for adolescent depression. *Child and Adolescent Social Work Journal, 25*(2), 111–123.

Ruffolo, M., & Fischer, D. (2009). Using an evidence based CBT group intervention model for adolescents with depressive symptoms: Lessons learned from a school based adaptation. *Child & Family Social Work, 14*(2), 189–197.

Shirk, S. R., & Jungbluth, N. J. (2008). School-based mental health checkups: Ready for practical action? *Clinical Psychology: Science & Practice, 15*(3), 217–223.

Weems, C. F., & Stickle, T. R. (2005). Anxiety disorder in childhood: Casting a nomological net. *Clinical Child and Family Psychology Review, 8*(2), 107–134.

COURT CASES AND STATUTES

Code of Federal Regulations, 34 C.F.R. § 300.8(c)(4)(i).

Individuals with Disabilities Education Act (IDEA), 20 U.S.C. §§ 1400 *et seq.*

INDEX

Note: Bolded numbers refer to volume numbers in the Debating Issues in American Education series.